HOWARD THURMAN AND THE DISINHERITED

LIBRARY OF RELIGIOUS BIOGRAPHY

Mark A. Noll, Kathryn Gin Lum, and Heath W. Carter, series editors

Long overlooked by historians, religion has emerged in recent years as a key factor in understanding the past. From politics to popular culture, from social struggles to the rhythms of family life, religion shapes every story. Religious biographies open a window to the sometimes surprising influence of religion on the lives of influential people and the worlds they inhabited.

The Library of Religious Biography is a series that brings to life important figures in United States history and beyond. Grounded in careful research, these volumes link the lives of their subjects to the broader cultural contexts and religious issues that surrounded them. The authors are respected historians and recognized authorities in the historical period in which their subject lived and worked.

Marked by careful scholarship yet free of academic jargon, the books in this series are well-written narratives meant to be read and enjoyed as well as studied.

Titles include:

Abraham Lincoln: Redeemer President
by Allen C. Guelzo

A Christian and a Democrat: A Religious Biography of
Franklin D. Roosevelt
by James D. Bratt and John F. Woolverton

Harriet Beecher Stowe: A Spiritual Life
by Nancy Koester

For a complete list of published volumes, see the back of this volume.

Howard Thurman and the Disinherited

- A RELIGIOUS BIOGRAPHY -

Paul Harvey

WILLIAM B. EERDMANS PUBLISHING COMPANY
GRAND RAPIDS, MICHIGAN

Wm. B. Eerdmans Publishing Co.
4035 Park East Court SE, Grand Rapids, Michigan 49546
www.eerdmans.com

Published 2020
Printed in the United States of America

26 25 24 23 22 21 20   1 2 3 4 5 6 7

ISBN 978-0-8028-7677-5

Library of Congress Cataloging-in-Publication Data

Names: Harvey, Paul, 1961– author.
Title: Howard Thurman and the disinherited : a religious biography / Paul
    Harvey.
Description: Grand Rapids, Michigan : William B. Eerdmans Publishing Com-
    pany, 2020. | Series: Library of religious biography | Includes bibliographical
    references and index. | Summary: "A religiously focused biography of How-
    ard Thurman, one of the most significant progenitors of the Civil Rights
    movement"–Provided by publisher.
Identifiers: LCCN 2020017615 | ISBN 9780802876775 (hardcover)
Subjects: LCSH: Thurman, Howard, 1900-1981. | African American
    Baptists–Biography.
Classification: LCC BX6495.T53 H37 2020 | DDC 230/.044092 [B]–dc23
LC record available at https://lccn.loc.gov/2020017615

For Philip Goff,
Fellow Old Man and Partner-in-Crime

CONTENTS

ACKNOWLEDGMENTS

First and most important, thanks must go to the generation of scholars and archivists who have worked for many years with the Thurman papers, now at Boston University, and in the process produced five volumes of his papers along with two edited volumes of his sermons and other writings. These keepers of the Thurman flame have made possible this book and many others previously published and yet to come.

My thanks to Robert Sackett, my departmental colleague, for reading the manuscript and giving it a thorough edit; to friends and professional colleagues Randal Jelks and Stephen Prothero for offering early encouragement; to Stetson University, for providing me the opportunity to give a series of endowed lectures that served as a kind of first draft for my writing about Thurman; to Jason Sexton and the online magazine *Boom California*, for encouraging me to write on Thurman's years in San Francisco; and to numerous friends and colleagues in the field of African American religious history, who have taught me so much over the years.

And finally, thanks to David Bratt, Heath Carter, Mark Noll, and my former coauthor Kathryn Gin Lum for encouraging me in this project and seeing it through the process to be included in the Library of Religious Biography series at Eerdmans.

INTRODUCTION

The goal of life is God! The source of life is God! That out of which life comes is that into which life goes. He out of whom life comes is He into whom life goes. God is the goal of man's life, the end of all his seeking, the meaning of all his strivings.

—Howard Thurman, "Deep River"

As a boy growing up in a small black community situated by Daytona Beach, Florida, Howard Thurman loved nature. He learned from it lessons that shaped his life. And then he devoted that life to meditating on spiritual matters even while envisioning a world, as he put it, of "friendly men underneath a friendly sky." Thurman loved to sit near the ocean at night; it gave him a sense of "timelessness, of existing beyond the reach of the ebb and flow of circumstances." The periodic storms that lashed the coastline thrilled him: "Unafraid, I was held by the storm's embrace." His experience with the storms gave him, as he described it in his autobiography, an "overring immunity against most of the pain with which I would have to deal in the years ahead when the ocean was only a memory. The sense held: I felt rooted in life, in nature, in existence." But even in the midst of these storms that came in from the sea and stripped trees bare, the oak tree in his backyard held. "I needed the strength of that tree, and like it, I wanted to hold my ground." The young Thurman talked to the oak tree, and felt understood.

Thurman was growing up, too, in his local black Baptist church. He was educated in high school, college, and seminary in the Baptist tradition. Yet, even as a boy, he already had left that tradition. And as a boy, too, he experienced the sharp "psychic wounds" (as he called them) of American racism, and he spent his life channeling his religious experience toward combating the basic violence of hatred that stalked the lives of black Americans. The mystic and the movement philosopher, the poet and the preacher and prophet, the searing critic and the soothing soul—Thurman joined together in one soul qualities from diverse personalities, spirits, and intellects.

Howard Thurman (1899-1981) has interested me for a long time. In 2017, I began to consider writing his biography. There were parts of his life I didn't know very much about. I began by searching for other biographies. At that time, although two biographies of Thurman had been prepared during his life, no scholarly biography using the full range of his now publicly available papers existed. Since then, a lengthy and definitive biography of his life has been completed by a longtime editor with the Howard Washington Thurman Papers Project, Peter Eisenstadt: *Against the Hounds of Hell: A Life of Howard Thurman*. Readers interested in a magisterial, academically rigorous, and expertly produced academic biography of Thurman are well advised to begin with Eisenstadt's volume (expected out in 2021). Also, a biography of sorts can be compiled by reading the impeccably scholarly introductions to the five volumes of *The Papers of Howard Washington Thurman*, a project directed for several decades by the scholar Walter Fluker. In *Visions of a Better World*, Quinton Dixie and Peter Eisenstadt laid out the portions of his life most directly relevant to his trip to India and meeting with Gandhi in 1935-1936. More recently, one section of Gary Dorrien's *Breaking White Supremacy* provides a beautifully crafted introduction to his life and thought, set within the context of the long history of the black social gospel movement. (The reader may find full references for all these works in the bibliographic essay at the end of this book.) But with the exceptions of the forthcoming work by Eisenstadt and two documentary films (*The Psalm of Howard Thurman*, currently in production, and *Backs against the Wall: The Howard Thurman Story*, first aired on PBS in February 2019), it is remarkable how little attention the remarkable story of Thurman's life has garnered from scholars or from the general public. He hasn't yet made the starting team of African American all-stars of the twentieth century. But he should be on that squad.

Why are Thurman's life and career so little known, at least relatively speaking?

In certain quarters, of course, Thurman is a well-known figure, and the documentary film that premiered in 2019, *Backs against the Wall: The Howard Thurman Story*, covers his life well in a 55-minute film. But in general, Thurman certainly is not a household name. It's easy to see why: he was a mystic, an intellectual, a poet—much more than an activist. He was not on the front lines, or even in the rear, of the civil rights struggle. Thurman didn't appear before the cameras of national television, and he was best known by university students and an intellectual class. As Thurman explained himself, he never sought the limelight. He preferred to remain behind the scenes, a quiet force of intellect and faith.

This relatively short biography reflects on major portions of Thurman's life, and considers what made him so important, even though few outside the scholarly world have heard of him or know much about his life. Yet his relevance to our contemporary world is unmistakably clear.

Thurman was foremost a man of ideas. His theo-philosophical conceptions formed the basis for remaking not only the American South but also the very texture and contours of religious experience in America. Thurman's background was deeply immersed in the black Baptist tradition. He filtered these ideas through liberal social gospel Protestantism, Quaker introspection, nature mysticism, and a universalist cosmopolitanism. In the process, he shaped and transformed ideas about how to remake the country and the globe. The full implications of his intellectual pilgrimage are still being explored in various worlds of American religion. Thurman the man is not particularly well known; Thurman's ideas, though, have exercised a deep and wide influence, even among those who have never heard his name. In his own peculiar and unmistakable way, he put together diverse parts of the American religious tradition in a way unlike that of any other figure. He was, as one later-life friend and mentee put it, a teacher of teachers. And I would add, he was a seeker of seekers, a person always amplifying that which is God in us, but also deploying the God in us against the most basic forms of violence and inequality that shaped and distorted social life at home and abroad.

And the basic contradiction of his life, one he fully recognized and appreciated, was how much his poor and provincial background and training within one particular tradition, confined within the walls of the American racial system, gave him the power to speak to diverse audiences looking to find a way out of their own limitations. Thurman the black American from coastal Florida, who struggled his whole life with the demons of American racism, became Thurman the figure of an expansive vision of the potentialities of God within us. He was a spirit who taught people how to unlock their own spirits in their quest for God, and in pondering how to make those quests relevant to the struggle for a more just social and political world.

Two stories of major encounters in his life illustrate much of Thurman's philosophy and approach to human relations and religious teaching. One is Thurman's encounter with Mahatma Gandhi during his six-month sojourn in India, a story described later in this book and told as well, beautifully and completely, in Dixie and Eisenstadt's *Visions of a Better World*. The other is Thurman's most extended conversation, in person, with Martin Luther King, in 1958.

On September 20, 1958, a mentally disturbed African American woman named Izola Ware Curry came to a bookstore in Harlem, in uptown New York City. There, Martin Luther King Jr. was signing copies of his new book, *Stride toward Freedom: The Montgomery Story*. She took out a sharp-edged letter opener. Then she stabbed the twenty-nine-year-old minister, who had just vaulted to national prominence through his leadership of the Montgomery bus boycott. King barely survived. Doctors later told him that, if he had sneezed, he could have died. Of course, King later received a fatal gunshot wound in April 1968; Curry lived out her days in a mental institution, to the age of ninety-seven.

Resting in the hospital afterward, King received a visit from the African American minister, theologian, and mystic Howard Thurman. The two had met before. Thurman served from 1932 to 1944 as dean of the chapel at Howard University; then as minister of the Church for the Fellowship of All Peoples in San Francisco during 1944–1953; and then as dean of Marsh Chapel and professor in the School of Theology at Boston University from 1953 to 1965. King was a student at Boston University when Thurman first assumed his position there, and he heard the renowned minister deliver some addresses. King later remembered watching a World Series game together in a house with Thurman, who later commented with humorous irony that he was one of the few professors at Boston University to have exercised almost no influence on the young King. Indeed, Thurman was far from prophetic about the young King, once recommending another candidate over him for a particular ministerial post.

The two were never personally close. Thurman was the age of King's father, and indeed, was closely connected with King Sr. throughout his years at Morehouse College in Atlanta. But King was close, intellectually and spiritually, with Thurman. One legend has it that King carried around his own well-thumbed version of Thurman's best-known book, *Jesus and the Disinherited*, in his pocket during the long and epic struggle of the Montgomery bus boycott. Whether true in a literal sense, it certainly pointed to the ideas that formed the young civil rights leader. King quoted and paraphrased Thurman extensively in his sermons during the 1950s and 1960s. Drawing from Thurman, King understood Jesus as an emblem of the dispossessed—both to a group of Jewish followers in ancient Palestine and to African Americans under slavery and segregation. That was precisely why Jesus was so central to African American religious history.

By that time, Thurman had exercised an outsized intellectual and spiritual influence on the entire generation that became the leadership of the civil rights movement. Thurman's trip to India in 1935, where he met Mahatma Gandhi, was a key moment in the translation of the Indian nonviolent struggle for independence to the African American struggle for freedom. No wonder that, at the close of his meeting with Thurman, Gandhi told him (according to the account of the meeting published in India) that "it may be through the Negroes that the unadulterated message of nonviolence will be delivered to the world."

In that New York hospital, Thurman gave King the same advice he gave countless others over the decades: he should take the unexpected, if tragic, opportunity to step out of life briefly, meditate on his life and its purposes, and only then move forward. By doing so, he could recover in both body and soul. When told how long King had been given to recuperate, Thurman urged him to take an additional two weeks. Thurman wrote: "When he told me, I urged him to ask them to extend the period by an additional two weeks. This would give him time away from the immediate pressure of the movement to reassess himself in relation to the cause, to rest his body and mind with healing detachment, and to take a long look that only solitary brooding can provide. The movement had become more than an organization; it had become an organism with a life of its own to which he must relate in fresh and extraordinary ways or be swallowed up by it." King replied to Thurman that "I am following your advice on the question."

Later, after leaving the hospital, King took an unexpected respite from his public duties, one of the few times he did so in his adult life. And also during this time, nearly quoting Thurman via Gandhi, he said that "I am now convinced that if the Negro holds fast to the spirit of non-violence, our struggle and example will challenge and help redeem, not only America but the world." He then took the opportunity to travel in India in February and March of 1959. Before then, continuing their phone-tag-style correspondence (the two busy men could never find a date when both were free and one could preach at the other's house of worship), Thurman wrote to King of his pleasure in knowing that "plans are afoot in your own thinking for structuring your life in a way that will deepen its channel." He still hoped for an extended conversation with King, of some hours, to "talk about these matters that are of such paramount significance for the fulfillment of the tasks to which your hands are set." But they never had that opportunity. King was a whirlwind of activity, of course, but ironically the apostle of calm and serenity, Howard Thurman, was so in demand that he also could never squeeze such a meeting into his schedule.

As Walter Fluker, editor of the Howard Thurman Papers Project, has explained, Thurman the private mystic and Thurman the public activist found common ground in understanding that spirituality is necessarily linked to social transformation. Private spiritual cultivation could prepare the way for deeper public commitments for social change. King himself, according to one biographer, came to feel that the stabbing and enforced convalescence was "part of God's plan to prepare him for some larger work" in the struggle against southern segregation and American white supremacy. In previous years, some had tagged Thurman as the new Gandhi, the long-awaited messiah for a nonviolent movement in America. Thurman had no such pretensions; he knew he was no such thing. But he served as a mentor for the movement. This role fit his capacity for deep reflection and profound preaching that spread new spiritual understandings. King's stabbing was a bizarre and tragic event, but in some sense it gave him the period of reflection and inner cultivation needed for the chaotic days of the civil rights struggle that were to come. The prison cell in Birmingham, Alabama, where in mid-1963 King penned his classic "Letter from a Birmingham Jail," also accidentally but critically provided much the same spiritual retreat for reflections that helped transform America.

Thurman was a private man and an intellectual; he was not an activist, as King was, nor one to take up specific social and political causes to transform a country. But he mentored an entire generation, including King, who did just that. Thurman's lesson to King was that the cultivation of the self feeds and enriches the struggle for social justice. In a larger sense, the discipline of nonviolence required a spiritual commitment and discipline that came, for many, through self-examination, meditation, and prayer. Thurman transmitted that message to the larger civil rights movement. Thurman combined, in the words of historian Martin Marty, the "inner life, the life of passion, the life of fire, with the external life, the life of politics."

Nearly a decade later, in his last letter to Thurman prior to his assassination, King referred (obliquely but unmistakably) to this advice, expressing to Thurman his wish for a time of repose and meditation amidst the tumults of the later 1960s. And immediately after King's assassination, Thurman, then in retirement in San Francisco, delivered a memorable eulogy that beautifully captured the meaning of King's life. Thurman then went on to foster close personal relationships with young black ministers, politicians, activists, and scholars, the people who would carry King's legacy into the future.

Beyond the story of King, though, following the life of Thurman introduces us to a long history of religion and the civil rights movement, from the 1920s to the 1970s. And beyond that, it gives us a fuller picture of the interactions of twentieth-century black theologies with the worlds of liberal Protestantism, the social gospel, mysticism, interracial projects, and intraracial development in the major educational institutions of the black institutional world. Thurman's active and varied life thus put him in touch with, and gave him influence over, a diverse array of twentieth-century theologies, movements, and philosophies. Born and trained in the South, he left it behind but always returned to his southern background and training when reflecting on his life and its significance.

Howard Thurman was born during some of the ugliest years of Jim Crow and one of the worst possible times to be an African American in the post–Civil War United States. He lived to see the end of Jim Crow, and his career as a teacher, minister, theologian, writer, and mentor helped to bring about its demise. But his career extends beyond being a minister for civil rights, for he was a mystic, a cosmopolitan, a poet, and a seeker. His thoughts, ideas, mentorship, and teaching deeply influenced key figures of a civil rights generation, including everyone from Pauli Murray to James Farmer, Benjamin Mays, Martin Luther King Jr., Vincent Harding, and Jesse Jackson. If Mays was, in the words of his biographer Randal Jelks, the "schoolmaster of the movement," Thurman was its spiritual mentor. And his role in founding and leading one of the first self-consciously interracial churches in the United States, the Church for the Fellowship of All Peoples in San Francisco, gave him an institutional space in which to express his vision for the world. Thurman explored mysticism even as he provided guidance to a generation of students seeking a way to apply the religion of Jesus both to their own lives and to the problems of the world. He found his voice through poetry more than prose, but in the process he articulated a pluralism and cosmopolitanism that came to define the center-left of American Protestantism. He came from an isolated and provincial part of Florida but became a man of the world.

For all he meant to so many people, Howard Thurman is almost unknown to those outside the ken of religious history and civil rights history. Yet his life and thought illuminate many important developments and movements in twentieth-century American religion. In particular, he combined a mystic spirit and an activist heart for social justice. And he showed how those religious impulses could be combined in one person; how the head and the heart could work together in a person's soul and in transforming the world at large to better reflect that which is God in us.

1

"My People Need Me"
The Education of Howard Thurman

The fact that twenty-five years of my life were spent in Florida and in Georgia has left deep scars in my spirit and has rendered me terribly sensitive to the churning abyss separating white from black. Living outside of the region, I am aware of the national span of racial prejudice and the virus of segregation that undermines the vitality of American life. Nevertheless, a strange necessity has been laid upon me to devote my life to the central concern that transcends the walls that divide and would achieve in literal fact what is experienced as literal truth: human life is one and all men are members one of another. And this insight is spiritual and it is the hard core of religious.

—Howard Thurman, The Luminous Darkness

Born in 1899 in West Palm Beach, Florida, and growing up in a particular black neighborhood of Daytona Beach, Howard Thurman had a childhood full of what he would later describe as psychic scars. But his boyhood was also full of the wonders of nature along the Atlantic seaboard. Thurman lost the man he considered his father when he was seven. Later, he endured schoolyard taunts about his paternity, because his boyhood male role model was not his biological father. Howard never mentioned that publicly, perhaps because that psychic wound was too hard to accept. He was raised principally by his mother, Alice (Ambrose) Thurman, and his grandmother Nancy Ambrose. His mother, dear to him through his life, worked constantly to support the family. As Thurman recalled, she always carried with her a "deep inner sadness." She seemed unable ever to be spontaneously joyful.

Perhaps (it's impossible to know) she had some of the depression that later afflicted Thurman's younger sister, Madaline. Even if not, Alice Thurman had a rough go of it. She lost two husbands to early deaths and finally married a third who never would be close with her children. She also lost her firstborn child, Henrietta, Howard's older sister, who passed from an illness when Howard was in high school.

The kind of hardships Alice Thurman endured may be seen too in her own manner of passing. In the late 1940s, Thurman moved her to San Francisco to care for her during her declining days. When she was near death, Thurman admitted her to Stanford Hospital, but she refused to stay, saying of the "buckra" (white people) around her, "The first chance they get, you don't know what they will do to you. I'm scared to go to sleep at night, and you just have to take me out of this place." Alice's decades-long ungrammatical but loving correspondence with her son, and Howard's fiercely protective attitude toward his beloved mother, suggests the closeness of their relationship.

From his own account, his grandmother, in particular, fundamentally shaped his religious sentiments; she was his hero. His grandmother had been a slave, and later, when Thurman began writing his books on the spirituals, he had her words in mind. Nancy also was a midwife in Daytona, known generally by the community as "Lady Nancy," and remembered by Thurman as the "anchor person in our family." She came from a large plantation estate in South Carolina; her owner, John C. McGehee, had moved to Madison County, Florida, before the war, where the majority of the larger planters were from South Carolina. Growing up, Thurman made frequent pilgrimages to Madison County but remembered of his grandmother, "She granted to no one the rights of passage across her own remembered footsteps."

But there was one great exception. Nancy frequently repeated the story of the slave minister she remembered, who came once a year to preach to them. He would address the enslaved people, saying, "You are not niggers! You are not slaves! You are God's children!" Thurman recounted that story numerous times in his orations, sermons, and books, including the autobiography he prepared later in his life. It was one of his staple parables that he returned to time and again when he reflected on his life. Another of those stories was of the girl who lived with a family for whom Thurman's grandmother did laundry. Thurman worked raking leaves in their yard, and the girl tormented the boy by scattering the leaves. When Thurman told her to stop, she picked up a pin and jabbed him in the hand. "Oh Howard, that didn't hurt you! You can't feel!" she said. The grandmother's affirmation of worth, and the girl's negation of it, defined Thurman's experience growing up as a black boy in Daytona.

Thurman's mother, Alice, always a devout woman for whom Thurman cared deeply her entire life, married three times. The first, Saul, was the man Thurman assumed was his father, and Thurman revered him as a strongly built man who held opinions contrary to the general sentiments of the community. For one thing, he had some books by the famous agnostic Robert Ingersoll; for another, he conspicuously avoided going to church. Saul died in 1907; Alice then married Alex Evans, a skilled workman from Lake Helen, Florida, but he passed away in 1910. Thurman respected Evans as well. Finally in 1914, Alice married James Sams, and the two would be married for the next several decades. But Sams was someone for whom Thurman and his sister felt little affection, and in future years Thurman would write to Sams and lecture him, with uncharacteristically harsh words, about his mistreatment of his mother. Indeed, much later in his life, shortly before Alice's death, Thurman would instruct his mother on how to cash in an insurance policy that had matured, and how to do so in a way that James would not know about (Thurman always suspected that James schemed to take money away from his mother).

Socially awkward and physically gangly as a boy, Howard spent a difficult childhood communing more with nature than with other people. Nature "provided my rather lonely spirit with a sense of belonging that did not depend on human relationships," he later reflected. He particularly enjoyed the later hours, when he "could hear the night think and feel the night feel." One exception was with his sister Madaline, born in August of 1908, with whom he was close in his life. Madaline shared with Thurman a passion for music but also suffered from bouts of depression that sometimes were crippling. Thurman took care of her as a child, and then sometimes as an adult during her lowest moments; in exchange, when Thurman went to India, Madaline cared for Thurman's two young girls. But Madaline struggled with mental illness through her life, her artistic talents hampered by her bouts of crippling depression. Thurman also had an older sister, Henrietta, who passed away from an illness during Thurman's second year in high school in Jacksonville, Florida. Little wonder that, as Thurman later wrote, death surrounded him while growing up. The annual season of illnesses routinely struck down many in the community. With doctors helpless, impoverished black families could only place their loved ones' souls in the hands of God.

THURMAN'S EARLY RELIGIOUS LIFE AND EDUCATION

Thurman grew up in Mount Bethel Baptist Church, in Waycross, one of the black neighborhoods across the Halifax River from Daytona Beach and the tourist areas. Thurman learned to be wary of Baptist orthodoxy early on. When Saul Thurman died, a local Baptist minister initially had refused to give his father a proper burial. The pastor of their church initially refused to preach the eulogy. Thurman's grandmother, as he recounted it, pressed the deacons to allow a service in the church, but a visiting evangelist who gave the sermon used the occasion to make an object lesson of the fate of unsaved souls. "I listened with wonderment, then anger, and finally mounting rage," Thurman said, as his father was "preached into hell." He whispered to his grandmother, "He didn't know Papa, did he? Did he?"

Thurman's bitter experience with the funeral of the man he understood to be his father, his symbol of masculinity in his otherwise female-dominated world, had a long-lasting effect. Thurman would be in search of symbolic fathers, physical and spiritual, for years to come, but the conclusions of those relationships often were unsatisfactory. Also, the shocking events of his father's funeral set Thurman up for a love-hate relationship with religious experience and the institutional church. Thurman's own attempt to join his boyhood church furthered this early sentiment. At twelve, feeling that he had been converted, Thurman expressed an interest in joining the church. He told the deacons of Mount Bethel of his experience, but they initially refused to accept its validity.

In fact, it had long been a tradition in many black Baptist congregations to require repeated versions of the conversion story. Thurman's fellow Floridian Zora Neale Hurston, daughter of a Baptist minister in an all-black town in Florida, was a lifelong religious skeptic who knew intimately of the entirely ordinary lives of churchgoers in her hometown: "They plowed, chopped wood, went possum-hunting, washed clothes, raked up back yards and cooked collard greens like anybody else." Even with her doubts and questions, she enjoyed the oral artistry of the salvation narratives. She felt moved in churches "not by the spirit, but by action, more or less dramatic." Candidates for membership were pursued by "hellhounds" as they "ran for salvation" (perhaps the same "hellhounds" that dogged legendary bluesman Robert Johnson as he ran from the "blues falling down like hail"). They would dangle precariously over the fires of hell, call on Jesus, see a "little white man" on the other side calling them, and finally traverse to heaven. In publicly describing their spiritual journeys, they sometimes strayed from the scripted narrative expected of them, relying instead on extemporaneously created variations: "These visions are traditional. I knew them by heart as did the rest of the congregation. Some of them made up new details. Some of them would forget a part and improvise clumsily or fill up the gap with shouting. The audience knew, but everybody acted as if every word of it was new."

The twelve year-old Thurman was no religious anthropologist, however, but an awkward boy who sought community and acceptance. The deacons' initial rebuff brought grandmother Nancy back to the fray. "Maybe you do not understand his words, but shame on you if you do not know his heart," she told them. He joined the church. In his younger years he felt called to the ministry but resisted that call precisely because of his long-smoldering anger over the rejection he saw at Saul Thurman's funeral. He struggled with that sentiment for a long time, until finally feeling some release from his resentment when, years later, he encountered the man who had preached that funeral. But his quarrel with orthodox religious dogma continued through his days. The young Thurman was on his way to becoming a seeker, a path he followed the rest of his life.

Thurman's home community of Waycross was one of the three black neighborhoods of Daytona. It had about 1,800 black residents during his younger years (about half the growing city's population). The Daytona city directory of 1900 depicted a (relatively speaking) prosperous black community. Blacks worked in the citrus industry, for the railroad, and in other occupations a step above what was available for most rural black southerners. The presence of northern snowbirds helped, both in bringing money into the general area and in slightly lessening the degree of racial hostility and violence blacks experienced. "The tempering influence of these northern families made contact between the races less abrasive than it might have been otherwise," Thurman remembered. And in Thurman's case, it helped precisely because early on he developed white benefactors (including James Gamble, of the Proctor and Gamble company) who gave him modest ($5 a month) but indispensable early support in furthering his education.

Over time, however, as white southerners moved in, the town grew more visibly segregated. The influence of the northerners who had been prominent in the town's founding diminished, and the normal patterns of Jim Crow set in more or less around the time of Thurman's boyhood. He remembered how the movements of blacks were "carefully circumscribed," and that the worlds of whites and blacks were "separated by a wall of quiet hostility and overt suspicion." Most important for Thurman's later reflections was the complete absence of whites from his ethical field of vision. As he later described it, he did not regard whites "as involved in my religious reference. They were read out of the human race—they simply did not belong to it in the first place. Behavior toward them was amoral." Blacks and whites lived on opposite sides of a river, but they effectively dwelled on separate planets.

The Daytona area, then, was no paradise, nor an escape from the larger world of Jim Crow. And yet, there was evidence of black prosperity and black political activity. Thurman found it in the work and achievements of his lifelong friend Mary McLeod Bethune. In 1904, she founded what is now Bethune-Cookman College (originally called the Daytona Educational and Industrial Training School for Girls), a place that, together with the "inner strength and authority of Mrs. Bethune," gave younger blacks such as Thurman "a view of possibilities to be realized in some distant future." Thurman also looked up to role models such as Thornton L. Smith, a cousin who played baseball in the Negro Leagues and helped to stanch the tide of Ku Kluxism around Daytona in the 1920s. The physician for Thurman's family, John T. Stocking, also had white patrons, and Thurman remembered him as someone who resisted pressure to join the church. They were his "masculine ideals" as a young man.

Thurman later told the story of his grandmother's belief in the magic power of education. She had wanted, as a slave, to learn how to read; the daughter of the slave owner was going to help her, but the mother, upon discovering this, intervened, and Nancy Ambrose's hopes were dashed. But Nancy transmitted to the young Howard her belief in the power of education. Thurman managed to make it through seventh grade in Newton, one of the other black communities (aside from Waycross) where he grew up. It was the only school for young blacks in the area and extended only as far as seventh grade. The principal tutored Thurman through eighth grade individually, even as Thurman worked in a fish market to help support the family. Thurman received high marks throughout, setting his long pattern of being the valedictorian of virtually any educational institution he attended. Thurman graduated from eighth grade, the first black boy in Daytona to do so.

But there was no high school there for him. There were, in fact, only 492 black secondary school students in the state, just 3 percent of those eligible to go to high school; they attended two public and six private high schools. Thurman would have to go elsewhere to continue his education. One of the private high schools was in Jacksonville, a hundred miles north of Daytona. Thurman was desperately poor, and even the process of getting to Jacksonville on the train almost derailed his efforts. Thurman could not pay the passage for his small, ragged trunk of clothes and belongings, and, as he recounted in his autobiography, he sat in the station, crying. An unknown man asked him what was the matter. Upon learning it, he told Thurman, "If you're trying to get out of this damn town to get an education, the least I can do is to help you." He paid the trunk fare and disappeared, one of several instances of good fortune that Thurman understood as God's grace, his intervention in lives, the growing edge that produced fruit out of seemingly nothing. Thurman dedicated his autobiography to this unknown man, the "stranger in the railroad station in Daytona Beach who restored my broken dream sixty-five years ago."

Thurman attended Florida Baptist Academy from 1915 to 1919, again achieving stellar academic marks, working himself to a state of complete mental and physical exhaustion in school and in various odd jobs, and completing tough academic courses, including several years of Latin and some Greek. During his second year there his older sister, Henrietta, suddenly died. In his autobiography, Thurman claimed to have had some premonition of the tragedy, during which he received a telegram with the news of Henrietta's grave illness; he traveled immediately to Daytona, but she had passed before he arrived. Later, in 1958, he recounted a similar experience when he woke up obsessed with thoughts of needing to go visit Martin Luther King Jr., who, that day, as he soon learned, was stabbed and nearly killed.

Thurman's later mystical speculations on the powers of intuition, of foreknowledge and esoteric understandings of mysteries and inexplicable premonitions, had some roots in these early years. They may also have risen from African American folklore about "the veil." While dubious of it, Thurman grew up surrounded by the pervasive African American folklore of the "veil." This was the central image of W. E. B. Du Bois's *Souls of Black Folk*. The great black intellectual famously used the physical image of the "veil" of amniotic fluid over a baby's face (interpreted by African Americans as a sign of special wisdom or power given to that baby, but also a sign of trouble and grief), combining it with the veil worn by women to shield themselves, to speculate on the ways in which African Americans lived behind the veil. For Du Bois, it was a powerful image of being unable to see through clearly to the outside world, but also that the outside world could never see in, clearly, to the African American world. All was shrouded, veiled. And thus the world was darkened and made mysterious or even invisible.

Thurman's ears were pierced as a child, a common practice to "break" the veil and thus rid the child of the heavy burden of carrying it. "How deeply I was influenced by this 'superstition' I do not know," Thurman later wrote. "The veil" was not a central image in his writing, as it was for Du Bois. And yet, Thurman's lifelong project of creating real human relations between people, beyond the evils of separation and segregation, really involved breaking through the veil. Being able to see what was God in us, ridding ourselves of the spiritual obstacles that made such a vision impossible, and then transmitting that knowledge into movements to transform and redeem the social world—this was his lifelong vision. And it was one in the process of formation from the earliest years of his education both in school and in his lonely encounters with the forces of nature.

By his senior year, Thurman was known locally as the academic star, and he was proud of his excellent grades. His work ethic was unexcelled, both in school and in his long hours working at hard jobs to pay his rent and (barely) keep himself fed. At the same time, his drive for work always conflicted with his sensitive nature; he was prone to bouts of minidepression and suffered from physical symptoms of overwork. Much of his later focus on the words "sensitiveness" and "relaxation" surely stemmed from these years of ceaseless mental and physical exertion. His achievements were recognized, however, as he won a partial scholarship to attend Morehouse College in Atlanta; he could not have gone there otherwise. Further, in his senior year Thurman worked as something like the dean of students at Florida Baptist Academy, which had just moved to Saint Augustine, Florida, and become Florida Normal and Industrial Institute. Further, Thurman spent the summer of 1918, during the last months of World War I, at a student army-training-corps camp at Howard University, one of several places early in his life where he began to make connections to the wider black intellectual and social world. After the experience at Howard, he returned to finish high school. While giving his high school graduation speech, he collapsed, partly because of high blood pressure. He kept his demanding regimen of work in a hot bakery during the sweltering Jacksonville summer, saving the money necessary to attend Morehouse starting in the fall of 1919.

"DUD": THURMAN'S MOREHOUSE YEARS

Before making it to Atlanta, with the emotional but not financial support of his impoverished mother, Thurman had begun his correspondence with figures that would serve as mentors—most significantly, during his younger years, Mordecai Wyatt Johnson, who later served as president of Howard during its glory years as the capital of the intellectual world of black universities. Thurman began attending events such as YMCA student conferences while in high school, where he heard addresses delivered by Johnson and other black intellectual leaders. After hearing Johnson speak in 1917, he had wanted to introduce himself, but the shy high schooler just could not bring himself to do it. Finally in June 1918, he wrote directly to Johnson to introduce himself after hearing him at a YMCA student event in Kings Mountain, North Carolina. "Listen while I tell you my soul," he wrote in the second paragraph. He hungered to be heard, as yet far from fully mature but with a deep desire for service to the race. His participation in the YMCA and other student organizations and conferences furthered that desire.

Thurman told Johnson of the arduous path he had pursued. As the first black student in Daytona Beach to receive promotion (to move past eighth grade), he had told his mother of his desire to continue, and heard from her, "Son you may go but I cannot do anything for you financially, for I must care for your sisters." Thurman replied that he only wanted and expected her prayers. From there he recounted the rigors of his training at the Florida Baptist Academy of Jacksonville: surviving on one meal a day, walking two and a half miles to and from the school, dry cleaning clothes at twenty-five cents per suit, running a fish market, and working eleven-hour days on Saturday for fifty cents. And then scoring in the high nineties throughout his high school career and winning the scholarship medal. Now, he sought advice on how to proceed. It was 1918, the draft was on, and he was willing to serve his country, but at the same time he wanted to be a minister, and, as he put it, "I feel the needs of my people. I see their distressing condition, and have offered myself up on the altar as a living sacrifice." In considering how to respond to the war effort, he explained, "I am willing to fight for democracy, but my friend Rev. Johnson, my people need me." He pleaded with Johnson: "What would you advise me to do? Please take a personal interest in me and guide me and God will reward you." Thurman was often very discouraged, with so much work and so little help: "Sometimes I think nobody cares but thank God, Jesus does, mother does and I believe you do."

This was the voice of the young Thurman, knowing he had a mission but knowing almost nothing about how to pursue it. He would soon move away from the evangelical tone and YMCA idealism of the letter, and just a few years later would be a big man on campus at Morehouse.

Johnson responded sympathetically, urging Thurman to pursue his work carefully and thoroughly, avoiding any shortcuts. Between college and theological training, he should be able to complete a thorough course of training by the time he was twenty-six, he told Thurman. And essentially that is what Thurman did. Johnson also gave him advice that Thurman later adapted and transformed into one of his best-known axioms of wisdom: "Keep in close touch with your people, especially with those who need your service. Take every opportunity to encourage their growth and to serve them. School yourself to think over all that you learn, in relation to them and to their needs. Make yourself believe that the humblest, most ignorant and most backward of them is worthy of the best prepared thought and life that you can give." Later, Thurman frequently advised listeners, congregants, and readers to take people not necessarily where they were but where they ought to be, and then treat them as if they were already there. In effect, he was taking Johnson's advice and turning it into a deeper theological principle. Interestingly, in the same letter Johnson noted that he was sending Thurman a book on the history of the "people of Israel," noting that "you will find it to your advantage to cultivate the historical perspective that such books can give." It was one of Thurman's earliest exposures to modernism, or at least to higher historical criticism, in interpreting the Bible. This lesson stuck. From a fairly early age, Thurman rejected any literalist or textual interpretations and embraced the Bible as literature that taught metaphorical truths.

Another voice of the young Thurman was one of gratitude toward a high school teacher. He wrote to his English teacher Ethel Simons in June of 1919, just before entering Morehouse, recounting his return to Daytona and a visit to the doctor, who told him that he "owed a big bill to Dr. Sleep," and his health problems. Thurman adored Simons, and the letter has some hints of a teenage intellectual crush. Surely Thurman loved the attention that intellectually oriented adults lavished on him, the promising young student desperate to learn everything he could. Simons returned the favor with a lifelong interest in Thurman's career. Thurman kept writing to her during his first year at Morehouse, proudly informing her of his academic progress (outstripping some more advanced students, he noted) and thanking her again—"your life has at least blest me if none other." At the end of his first year, he wrote again to thank her for a card she had sent and noted that he was starting to serve as a substitute pastor for his home church in Daytona: "I am here holding this big job down as best I can under God." After detailing further academic successes—academic prizes, editorships of college literary magazines, and others—he concluded, "I am working, working, working. I preach real hard too. I must do my best even tho it is against my health."

Thurman's first year at Morehouse, which was founded just after the

Civil War, came under the presidency of the formidable personality and intellectual John Hope. Hope's earliest years coincided with the years of W. E. B. Du Bois. Both survived the harrowing Atlanta race riot of 1906. Hope later guided Morehouse generally in the direction of the kind of black liberal arts college valued by Du Bois, a place of academic accomplishment, rigorous expectations, and a demanding personal code of conduct that brooked little challenge. The idea was to be a "Morehouse man," an exemplar of intellectualism and respectability. And that was even the more demanded if one came from a poor family such as Thurman had. Hope called the students "young gentlemen," a label that stuck with Thurman for its affirmation of the essential manhood of the students. Hope's legendarily strict requirements for personal conduct meant that he was a distant father figure, respected rather than loved, but certainly Thurman respected him and did well with Hope's requirements that each student compose and deliver, without notes, his own oration each year. People would later say to Thurman (by his own recollection), "You're one of John Hope's men, aren't you?," a way of saying that Thurman's Morehouse training was "unmistakable." Thurman also fell under the sway of the dean of students, Samuel Archer, an avuncular figure whose personal warmth contrasted with the demanding front of John Hope. "Big Boy," they called him. "The men of the college honored and liked President Hope. They revered and loved Dean Archer," he later wrote. Together, the team of Hope and Archer "undergirded the will to manhood for generations of young black men, . . . which countered all the negatives beating in upon us from the hostile environment by which we were surrounded."

Equally important was a stress on service—service to the race, service to the community and church, and service to the world at large. The YMCA, Thurman's other major source of education, reinforced all these ideas and provided Thurman his earliest opportunities in speaking, leadership, and fraternizing with other leaders of the race as well as relationships with young white men. The YMCA functioned as one of the primary vehicles for carrying on the social gospel movement in the early twentieth century. It was a waystation for numerous southern liberals and radicals seeking to apply their Christian training to real-world social problems. The YMCA and YWCA also sponsored numerous speaking tours and international visits, and brought together people from widely varying backgrounds and gave them the opportunity to forge youthful cross-racial alliances. Thurman later rejected some of the strictures of the Victorian ethics and conduct required by the YMCA, but it was there that he was immersed in social gospel ideas. It was a limited yet indispensable training ground for his later work.

Relatively progressive though it was for its era, the YMCA was segregated, with black students participating through the "Colored Work Department." Eventually, the timidity of the YMCA leadership in challenging norms of segregation infuriated Thurman. But during the 1910s and 1920s, at least, the YMCA provided key forums for the development of African Americans in positions of religious, social, and political leadership. And it at least provided contact with younger whites who sometimes were willing to consider other possibilities for applying Christian ethics to southern life. Thurman started attending conferences in high school; it was at a YMCA conference that he saw Mordecai Wyatt Johnson and yearned to be mentored by him. There also Thurman made a lifelong friendship with Channing H. Tobias, a leader of the international YMCA.

At Morehouse two of Thurman's primary influences were Benjamin Mays (his psychology teacher there originally, who became his lifelong friend "Bennie") and the formidably cantankerous sociologist E. Franklin Frazier. The latter, in particular, seemed to take delight in puncturing Thurman's youthful YMCA-style Christian pretensions. Thurman remembered Frazier telling him in class, "I am the teacher and you are the student. From this day forward you are not to speak a word in this course, not even to answer 'present' when the roll is called. Understand?" But Frazier, in fact, respected Thurman's intellect and promise, giving him high marks and encouraging him toward further academic achievement. At the same time, Frazier's sarcasm and burlesque of biblical myths in the classroom clearly upset the young Thurman, not yet fully developed as a modernist, nor as a mature man who could recognize and appreciate a sense of wit and irony directed toward felling intellectual idols.

Thurman's life in Atlanta, during his years at Morehouse and later, left him depressed. Unlike the slightly more hopeful situation he had in Daytona, Atlanta was a place full of misery and destitution. As he remembered it later, he lived in Atlanta when Georgia was particularly infamous for its overt racism: "Lynchings, burnings, unspeakable cruelties were the fundamentals of existence for black people. Our physical lives were of little value. Any encounter with a white person was inherently dangerous and frequently fatal." Thurman's lifelong theological emphases on worth and dignity sprang in large part from these youthful and college-age experiences, when he saw firsthand what it meant to live in a society whose entire raison d'être was to demean and crush you.

Somewhat surprisingly, Thurman focused considerable study in economics, business, and sociology during his years at Morehouse. In particular, he was influenced by Lorimer Milton, who took to Thurman and tried to persuade him to enter business. Thurman had no interest in doing so, but perhaps the poverty and hardships of his earliest years led him to his intellectual, if not practical, interests in money. Thurman later frequently consulted with Milton on business and money matters, including in the founding of the Howard Thurman Educational Trust, originally designed to provide poor African American youngsters the means to attend college. Long before it was established, and probably during Thurman's college years, he proposed a Negro scholarship fund, funded from contributions by blacks, that could help black students receive college educations and then teach at black schools. His proposal in part reflected the influence of Milton and more generally the culture of black uplift and progress from that era.

And yet, Thurman was bitter at the lack of a program in philosophy. His true interests lay there, but the benefactors of black education (particularly white philanthropists who directed money through institutions controlled by Booker T. Washington and his disciples) had no interest in developing young black minds in the deepest craft of thinking. To do so would induce a questioning of the very system that produced well-educated black men who effectively could find no place in society. Thurman's later critique of black educational institutions, one based on an appreciative recognition of what he had received but a biting analysis of what deliberately was left lacking, drew directly from his Morehouse experience. Thurman was proud to be a Morehouse man, but he also understood what he had been denied.

Thurman excelled in nearly everything at Morehouse, and his fellow students recognized that by giving him monikers both warmly admiring and gently joshing. They called him "Dud." In the college yearbook of 1923, after his numerous prizes and awards were listed (Edgar Allen Poe Short Story Prize, Athenaeum Literary Prize, Chamberlain Scripture Reading Prize, president of the Atlanta Student Council, and so on), he was characterized as follows: "Slow in speech, large in stature, with long dangling arms, 'Dud' is a striking figure in any group. The personification of the Morehouse Ideal of a genuine Christian. His big heart and massive brain have been the repository of many student problems." As the "ideal of a minister," he had "won the confidence and respect of [the] entire school" and was considered "our most brilliant classmate." He also won the unofficial title of "most dignified" and "the busiest," owing to his schedule of "debating, teaching, preaching, editing the Annual, managing the 'Y' and office work." Another student named there was at best a "distant second." Thurman's classmate Clarence Gresham, who went on to a long career in the black Baptist ministry in Georgia, told Thurman in a personal letter from this time: "I really believe that my success in life depends on my relations with you, God and myself alone being excepted." Gresham was happy that their friendship had developed so well that "even the thought of a breach" was painful to him. Already developing as a personally mysterious but charismatic figure, Thurman had that effect on people.

His friend from those days stretching until the 1970s, Benjamin Mays taught psychology at Morehouse. Mays remembered the young student Thurman showing signs of possessing "more mysticism in his religion than the average person, so much so that I am inclined to think that he was considered queer by some of the students and professors. I believe he did not have the desire for constant city social contacts as most of the students had." Mays, Thurman later reflected, had been educated in the North but knew southern life well; "he knew what distortions segregation had produced in most of us. But he had also tasted the joy of real possibilities beyond the Southern way of life, and when he spoke to us about such things we envisioned possibilities for ourselves beyond the limited boundaries of self-service, segregation, and the Southern style of social life."

Mays the professor and Thurman the student gravitated toward each other at Morehouse and shared the lifelong bond of two black men, raised in poverty in South Carolina (Mays) and Florida (Thurman), who became intellects and educators of great distinction. With Mays and others as models, Thurman honed his teaching skills as a professor at Morehouse and Spelman. He became one of the most popular teachers at these flagship southern black universities; students felt they could discuss their intimate problems with him. Thurman always was as much counselor and personal mentor as professor.

Some of Thurman's earliest oratorical efforts from his days as a Morehouse undergraduate contain seeds of thoughts that he would develop for years, even decades, to come. In "Our Challenge," given at the annual Emancipation Celebration (held conjointly by Morehouse and Spelman), and later published in a joint Morehouse-Spelman literary publication, Thurman speculated on what progress African Americans had made but also on how far they still had to go. "We have become intoxicated with our own progress," he said. "We have fallen asleep, now we are dreaming, yes, in a nightmare." And during this slumber, hostile forces were shaping the African American future, with the result that "although our chains have been loosed, our minds have been more securely bound." The problem was, the "psychic slavery" of the race was so profound that "though we are victims, we do not realize it." Thurman continued with some florid "uplift"-style prose, urging his fellows to work harder and do better, to bring higher ideals to the black masses and thus soar "above the sordid ruins of our hinderances [sic] and set ourselves free." Within just a few years, Thurman had learned to channel his prose more precisely; it was still sonorous but less sophomoric.

Thurman later remembered himself as a shy and awkward youngster with few friends. But Morehouse had precisely the effect its president and leaders intended it to have—it transformed him into an intellectually and socially ambitious young man, serious but not pompous, well liked and, more than that, well respected. His fellow students already saw him as a mystic, given to flights of contemplation that they admired but were also baffled by. They developed a good-humored but respectful attitude toward the young man who often seemed to be looking toward some greater spiritual experience.

Yet the young mystic was also ceaselessly active. As the Morehouse student representative to the YMCA, Thurman interacted with the generation that would prepare the way for the civil rights movement. And he was regularly corresponding even with such a distant and authoritarian figure as John Hope, to the point of baring his soul a bit about the difficulties and challenges he had experienced. "I thought that my Sophomore year was pregnant with experiences sufficiently exacting to fit me for many of the battles of my early years. But I find that they were but the calm before the storm through which I am now passing," he wrote to Hope in the summer of 1921.

Hope responded to him that the burdens of life had to be borne, for they shaped and tested a man. But in words unusually perceptive for the austerely severe Hope, he told the young Thurman that he was "mentally and spiritually endowed to feel things very keenly, and you will no doubt always have burdens and sorrows, if not your own somebody else's, but you must develop good cheer and great hopefulness as it is going to be your business in life to impart inspiration and to bring relief." Later, as well, during his senior year, Thurman accompanied Hope to an interracial meeting at a local YMCA branch, with some black educational leaders and a handful of white liberals. The black concert singer Roland Hayes was to perform, and one white man announced proudly that the segregated seating had been changed so that it would be divided vertically, with the center aisle as the demarcation line in the main area and balcony. Thurman was disgusted at the "legerdemain" and walked out. Hope followed him and told him, by Thurman's account, "I know how you feel about what is going on in there, but you must remember that these are the best and most liberal men in the entire South. We must work with them, There *is* no one else. Remember." Thurman remembered the lesson; it "helped me grow in understanding," he said.

Thurman's affiliation with the YMCA elevated him into other groups and opportunities, including the young Fellowship of Reconciliation (FOR). The American branch was less than ten years old at the time and generally shared a pacifist, anti-imperialist ideal. In FOR, Thurman later wrote, he found "a place to stand in my own spirit"; and just as important, through his work with whites in FOR, especially George "Shorty" Collins, he discovered "the vast possibilities of reconciliation" between peoples of different backgrounds. Thurman's life and message fundamentally involved exploring these vast possibilities. His heart yearned for reconciliation, even as his daily experience confirmed the relentless assault on the dignity of African

Americans. The gulf between those two would define his career as a thinker and philosopher devoted to unity and as an important religious critic who would attack the social disease of segregation and oppression.

THURMAN'S THEOLOGICAL TRAINING AT ROCHESTER

Upon completing his term at Morehouse, Thurman had a number of opportunities. John Hope thought he could perhaps teach economics at Morehouse after having his degree "validated" at the University of Chicago. ("Validating" a degree at a predominantly white institution was a common practice for African American students, who often did so before returning to black colleges to teach.) Churches were calling him to preach, and there was also the possibility of pursuing a PhD. But Thurman turned down these opportunities; in his initial letter to Mordecai Johnson, he expressed the desire to be a minister of the gospel. Theological training still drew him. And for a young man deeply immersed in the Baptist tradition, there could few better places to go than to Rochester Theological Seminary. Even more so for a young theologian already interested in modernist thought and immersed in the social problems of the day. The home of important theological scholars as well as social gospelers from the recent past such as Walter Rauschenbusch, Rochester cemented and furthered the intellectual directions Thurman already was taking. And Thurman was also following in the footsteps of his first mentor, and later colleague and boss, Mordecai Wyatt Johnson, who had studied under Rauschenbusch.

In the fall of 1923, Thurman came to a northern institution where there was, in effect (according to his own recollection), an unofficial admissions quota of two black students per year, and those students were not to live with white students. Thurman, however, broke such barriers his entire life. Already a democratic socialist in political thought and a member of an international pacifist organization (FOR), he was not likely to follow some petty dormitory rules about racial separation. Soon, Thurman was a roommate with two white students and a friend to many others. Thurman's room soon became a sort of intellectual salon, as a classmate later remembered, where Thurman led devotionals and Bible studies, interpreted the Scriptures for his colleagues, and led them in prayer. "In one of these sessions," the classmate remembered, "I had the feeling that it was not Howard Thurman, but Jesus Christ, so much did his thinking emulate that of the master. I have never had another experience like that."

As at Morehouse, he pursued a rigorous academic curriculum even while speaking and preaching in the area. He participated actively in the YMCA and FOR, published articles in the school newspaper, and immersed himself in the life of the local area. For the first time ever, he was a "minority," living in a white world and realizing the extent to which his own personal "ethical awareness" had been bounded and constrained by the psychic barriers of segregation. He would never be the same for it.

The budding young ministerial candidates took courses such as "Jewish Life and Thought" and "Psychology of Religion" from professors well known to be theological liberals. Meanwhile, Thurman preached at churches around the area. He spoke to the Dewey Avenue Union Church of Rochester, for example, on the topic "The Faith of the American Negro." On other occasions, local chapters of the Ku Klux Klan threatened churches that hosted him, but Thurman simply continued with his plans. He also officially represented the seminary at the Quadrennial Conference of the Student Volunteer Movement, held in 1924 in Indianapolis.

While at Rochester, Thurman spent his summers on the staff of the First Baptist Church of Roanoke, Virginia, where the pastor, Arthur L. James, mentored the young, aspiring minister. The two had a long relationship, dating from James's time as the pastor of Thurman's home church in Daytona; Thurman called him "Cousin Arthur." The church published a sort of monthly newsletter, one of the earliest black publications in Roanoke, titled the *Roanoke Church News*; James ran the paper for the entire term of his pastorate, from 1919 to 1957. Thurman published articles in the paper periodically, including one titled "The Sphere of the Church's Responsibility in Social Reconstruction," in July 1924. In it, Thurman earnestly preached an internationalist social gospel that he had picked up from his years of study and work in the YMCA as well as from the general currents of liberalism from that era. The victors' peace achieved at Versailles, he said, would mean nothing if social institutions were not fundamentally transformed. The institutions that had produced the disaster of the war could not win a just peace. "The conditions resulting from the world war are but a part of the great task of social reconstruction. Our whole social order is shot through with many inherently vicious principles working themselves out in a thousand human ills." What was the role of the church in this situation? Church leaders hardly yet knew what that was. Some still insisted just on saving individual souls—"to give men a sample bliss capsule so as to fire their souls with earnest zeal for the life to come." They insisted that Christian churches had nothing to do with "economic ills, political corruption and social injustice." They could not see the role of the church in the reconstruction of this world.

Thurman reinforced this view with a piece for *Student Challenge* in 1925, where he noted that Christianity had been kept in an airtight container, such that "scarcely a drop of it has been allowed to give strength and vigor to the thirsty, dying plants of Brotherliness in the garden of every day living." Much of the blame for that could be directed at ministers: "The people in the pew have been given a comfortable, one-sided gospel by those who stand in the shoes of prophets but who utter the soft, satisfying words of the Status Quo." The minister was not just there to encourage and comfort but also to "serve as the gad-fly to a slothful, thoughtless, sin-bespattered generation." In particular, the minister should exalt the "sacredness of human personality."

Thurman drew from personal experience. He pointed to the revolutionary potential of the gospel in America's racist culture. Thurman asked, Who would dare preach the true gospel in such a place—that what you did to the "least of them, you did it to me"? "Do those words mean that every time a negro is lynched and burned God is lynched and burned? Do they mean that God is held as a peon in certain parts of this land of 'Liberty'? Do they mean that God is discriminated against, segregated and packed in Jim Crow cars?" Thurman listed an abundance of opportunities for ministers—when they spoke to local groups or to legislators, when they had city council persons as church members, when they delivered talks on religious education and could point to real community issues instead of dwelling "on glittering generalities about loving all men." Such were the opportunities for ministers, although few took them. And thus, "as a general thing . . . Jesus is still unknown in this land that is covered with churches erected in his honor—*absente Christo*."

Thurman kept busy as well with plans for the ministry both by preaching locally and by serving churches during the summer. He received his official ordination in August of 1925 from a former mentor of his at Morehouse, Samuel Owen. Thurman forged his own path in the ordination ceremony, as he did in most things. The examiners at the First Baptist Church in Roanoke quizzed the young, budding modernist warily over a period of four hours, with the questions "running the gamut of religious doctrine within the scope of Virginia Baptist orthodoxy." One examiner later said he hoped one day God, Jesus, and the Holy Spirit "may see fit to meet in your heart." Thurman read them a statement of faith that he crafted, and he initially sought to avoid a traditional laying on of hands. Finally he received it, and it turned out to be a moment of transcendent significance. He later wrote that whenever "it seems that I am deserted by the Voice that called me forth, I know that if I can find my way back to that moment, the clouds will lift and the path before me will once again be clear and beckoning." Always alive to religious experience in any venue he could find it, Thurman reveled in it even though it came (literally) at the hands of elders of a tradition he already had escaped.

Thurman bounced back and forth between his black Baptist southern world and the advanced theological training he was receiving in Rochester. Later during his time there he began studying with the well-known theologian George Cross, a person who, Thurman later said, "had a greater influence on my life than any other person who ever lived. Everything about me was alive when I came into his presence." In addition to the three classes he took with Cross, they also met privately on Saturdays. The young Thurman tried out his own ideas, only to discover that Cross could take his arguments "down to ash." Thurman's other work at Rochester included a close study of John Dewey; one surviving school paper, significant portions of which are plagiarized from sources readily traceable (an academic sin he shared with Martin Luther King, as both were given to unacknowledged borrowing from secondary sources in papers submitted during their seminary training), suggests Thurman's continued effort to balance the rational approach to working out philosophical problems with the acknowledgment of the role of intuition and flashes of inspiration on doing so. These two would form the basis of much of his future work and theological explanations.

Thurman embraced the kind of modernist thought about the Bible he was taught at Rochester. His papers there show he was enthusiastic about historicizing subjects that had been left to the supernatural. For example, he placed the virgin birth (incorrectly, as it turns out) within the context of "the failure or inability of primitive man" to recognize the role of human male-female copulation in creating life. He went through a history of men who were considered gods, ranging from ancient Greek and Egyptian myths to the Buddha and stories that arose from the courtiers of Genghis Khan giving him the title "Son of God." "Familiar!" Thurman commented of this history, because effectively it paralleled the history of Jesus. "From these illustrations and many others, we see how widely disseminated and persistent has been this man-God legend. It remained for the Gnostic philosophers and early theologians to repeat and reapply an old myth to the interpretation of the matchless life of Jesus of Nazareth." He concluded with a note that he simply sought to "trace the permanent primitive element" in the doctrine of the virgin birth as it had come to be applied to Jesus, one that "has its roots back in the dim shadows of a misty antiquity." With this training fully in hand, it was little wonder that, on his first examination for ordination, the elders of a church queried him warily about his beliefs. Within a few years of graduating from Florida Baptist Academy, he developed into a Baptist modernist who had little patience with simply repeating the myths of the ancient worlds as if they were literal truths for the present.

Thurman's longest and most elaborate surviving work from his training at Rochester was a paper, also plagiarized in some paragraphs, titled "Can It Be Truly Said That the Existence of a Supreme Spirit Is a Scientific Hypothesis?" It comes from his work with George Cross at Rochester, and also from summer courses he took at Columbia University while still a student at Morehouse in 1922. In this work, presaging much of his future thought, Thurman considers what might be the scientific basis for religious thought, and how personal experience and rationally derived knowledge could point to the same conclusions. In the paper, Thurman drew fairly extensively from various texts from the era, including from Laurence Buermeyer et al., *An Introduction to Reflective Thinking*, which he had studied at Columbia in 1922. Another work, *Religious Certitude in an Age of Science*, provided Thurman with conceptual ideas and, in places, exact wording. Thurman explains at length what exactly constitutes a scientific hypothesis and then considers that even the scientist engages mechanisms of faith, "from a confidence in the general trustworthiness of the sense perceptions to the dependableness and capability of the external world to be interpreted." But the scientific man dealt only with "external phenomena and modes of behavior," while "the affirmations of the man of religion deal not only with the objects but the subjects of experience." The supposition of the existence of a Supreme Spirit invoked scientific knowledge but also involved "a much larger portion of nature and human nature in its sweep and it touches a wider environment." Thurman concludes his work with deeply personal reflections, speaking of his consciousness that "I make contact with SOMEBODY and I know that I am not alone. Slowly there is taking place in my life a transformation which is more in keeping with the highest things that I keep and feel." He could thus say not only "I believe" but also "I know."

In this paper, Thurman broached ideas he would return to in subsequent decades. As a mystic and naturalist, Thurman loved science, particularly biology, and eagerly sought out scientific explanations. And he was keen to find empirical explanations of religious experience. At the same time, he understood that religious experience transcended science, and that intuitively derived spiritual understanding provided a kind of knowledge outside the bounds of science.

Thurman concluded his work at Rochester with a bachelor of divinity thesis titled "The Basis of Sex Morality," one of his many efforts during that time to apply a modernist and historicized version of Christianity to contemporary social problems. This work is very unusual in that Thurman in his career rarely addressed issues of sex and gender, and nowhere else so explicitly as he did here. The thesis surveys a long history of sex prohibitions from ancient societies to the present, noting the ancient roots of myths about chastity and purity. Thurman continued from there to "the present orthodox attitude," with its emphasis on the protection of virginity among women. Thurman recounted the "social sanctions" that enforced chastity, including an emphasis on the woman as a dependent, and as a dependent, therefore an "*inferior*." Restrictions of dress and behavior arose to enforce the sanctions as well. Religious sanctions further reinforced them: "the sinfulness of everything having to do with sex is the very essence of orthodox religious teaching along this line." A group of women Thurman had interviewed at an earlier conference told him they had been taught that it was "evil even to discuss sex under any condition and the 'marriage relation was a concession made to the flesh.'" The thesis also argues for the connection between prohibitions on premarital sex and laws against miscegenation, a line of thinking advanced for his day.

Ultimately, the sanctions enforcing chastity were "external"; they were "not a part of the inherent respect for personality which one individual should hold for the other. The appeal has not been made to an inner response of the individuals but to a medley of external prohibitions and superstitions. It is built upon a false conception of sex and upon a false conception of woman." Revolt against the artificial prohibitions was inevitable, and healthy, for the prohibitions toward premarital unchastity simply signaled the domination of men over women. Revolt against this was a part of the freedom struggle for women, which paralleled the "general wave of democracy that has swept across the world."

Thurman wrote in his thesis about his long conversations with hundreds of college-aged men and women who could not understand the reasoning behind the old restrictions. They were asking why love itself was not a "sufficient ground for sexual intimacy." Thurman quoted authorities who offered academic and abstract explanations for these prohibitions, but his prose wakened when he recognized "the great gulf between the religion of the 'old Folks' and the religion of the youth." Students learned science, civics, geography, and history at school, while in Sunday school they were taught the old myths. The result was a tendency to rebel and simply throw overboard the antiquated teachings, and thus came the "undermining of the sanction of religion for conduct." The old attitudes toward premarital sex, based on now untenable external authorities, had produced a reaction and rejection, based in part on newfound freedom for women and a more general revolt against external authority. What, then, would be the basis for a new sexual morality?

Here Thurman spoke not just to the topic of his thesis but more generally to his philosophical bent to Personalism. The basis for sex morality came from the individual, and "the authority for the conduct of the individual must be within, if such conduct is to be moral. . . . Whatever sanctions society may evolve must be verified by the individual before conduct." For Thurman, as always, the key was connecting the individual and the social; there should be no conflict between the interests of the two: "If a normal individual has to stretch himself out of shape in order to be proper and acceptable to society, then the standards of society are such that the individual becomes immoral in forming to them." Thurman concluded, finally, that in a properly loving relationship, "the sexual act becomes the highest compliment that the two individuals of different sex can pay to each other"; in any other kind of relation, it would be a "violation." The key was the expression of flesh and spirit in tandem. On this latter point, Thurman gradually developed a philosophy that would permeate his preaching and writing. The "good life," formerly defined by Christianity in a way that accorded with ancient myths and norms, had to be redefined. Original sin had dominated this conception, and within that conception human nature could only be seen as "impure, bad, lustful in the foul sense." Flesh was evil. A healthier, modern interpretation saw the flesh as "the great vehicle whereby the Spirit expresses itself. The good life is the life in which there is perfect harmony, perfect coordination, unity."

Thurman's emphasis on the unity of life defined his career and is evident from the earliest years of his ministry. In 1927, he presented his address "Finding God" to the National Student Conference of the YMCA and YWCA in Wisconsin. Since God is the source of life, he pronounced, out of God comes an "underlying unity" for all. Life is about a "quest for fulfillment" that in reality is a quest for God. And what comes out of that "is an essential kinship of all the creations of all the people in the world, and if that kinship is true, is genuine, then I can never be the kind of person I ought to be until everybody else is the kind of person that everyone else ought to be."

Meanwhile, Thurman's energies were at their height. Sometimes so was his ire at the limitations of the student movements in which he had been so actively involved. Writing to Mordecai Wyatt Johnson sometime later, he wondered why all these conferences and grand meetings had produced so little actual result. He had been reading about quackery, nostrums, and frauds rampant in American society, and saw his task more than ever as releasing "to the full our greatest spiritual powers, that there may be such a grand swell of spiritual [energy] that existing systems will be upset from sheer dynamic." His emerging ideas about nonviolence were evident here, as in later years he used similar language to talk about disturbing the "normal" flow of events.

Thurman's excursions into the academic world of biblical scholarship for his Rochester classes hardly meant he had escaped the world of being a black man in white America. He was reminded of it every day, from the makeup of the seminary, from the interest shown by New Yorkers for his talks on race and religion, and from the hostile interest the New York branch of the Ku Klux Klan took in his doings. In 1924 he published some of his earliest reflections meant for a wider audience. In "College and Color," in the magazine *Student Challenge*, he urged fellow students to cultivate a "sympathetic understanding" that was not patronizing or sentimental; by the phrase he simply meant "an attitude which says that a man of another race is essentially myself, and that I feel toward him fundamentally as if he were myself. His needs and cravings and the drives which lie behind his actions are similar to mine in their essentials."

Thurman carried this message with him the rest of his days. He did so even when, as was most often the case later in life, he turned down offers specifically to speak on race issues, preferring to focus on what his teacher George Cross referred to as the "timeless issues of the human spirit." Thurman asked the students to consider what would go through the minds of the black students at the universities when they were segregated in seating at the local theater, or when crowds of students laughed at racist jokes from a speaker. Black students, he continued (and the words ring true for much contemporary writing), encountered a bewildering variety of responses from their fellows, from a sense of paternalistic protection of unfortunates, to a kind of false sense of fairness from those who would say, "I have no prejudice"—"as if mere words meant much," Thurman pointedly commented—to outright hostility. At least the latter group had the advantage of lacking any hypocrisy; their racism was unadulterated. The "steady, unswerving hand of tradition and custom" governed and shaped all these attitudes—"it is simply a question of what has been and what the particular environment will endorse." But, in fact, any attitude that "strangles personality and inhibits its highest growth and development is wrong. For a Christian believer to have that kind of attitude is a crime against God."

Given the dismal situation on most college campuses, what could be expected of social life more generally? What could be expected of "the great masses who never come under the stimulating influences of collegiate life? If we do not find tolerance in the colleges and universities, where liberal thoughts and democratic ideals are supposed to be fostered, where shall we go?" Indeed, "What a hard time Jesus of Nazareth would have if he matriculated at one of our colleges today!" Thurman asked the students to consider one simple course of action: *"Think of the other fellow as essentially yourself and feel towards him fundamentally as if he were yourself."* This principle grew into one of Thurman's fundamental concepts; he developed it into a fuller philosophy of human personality as sacred.

In 1925, still at Rochester, Thurman encountered the work of the South African writer Olive Schreiner. It remains one of the great curiosities of Thurman's life that a South African writer who was occasionally given to racial epithets in her writing should have exercised such an influence, but she did. Some scholars have pointed out that Schreiner's influence came not so much from generating new ideas for Thurman as from clarifying and supporting ideas that Thurman in effect already had. Surely this was true of Schreiner's sense of the mystical in nature, something for which Thurman needed little encouragement. It was also true in Schreiner's thought about the unity of life as well as the way in which individuals could fundamentally affect the fate of all humanity. Schreiner's influence on Thurman was great enough that he named his daughter Olive after her. Thurman quoted Schreiner for decades afterward in sermons, speeches, poems, and prayers. Something in Schreiner's unusual combination of traits simply touched a deep chord in Thurman and never stopped affecting him. Later in his life, Thurman put together an edited volume of Schreiner's writings, titled *A Track to the Water: The Olive Schreiner Reader.* In a lengthy and moving introduction to that volume, he discusses Schreiner's limitations as a "universalist in outlook" but at the same time "a member of the exploiting and colonizing community," and a feminist and pacifist who could not extend full humanity to Africans. And yet, Schreiner gave Thurman one of his earliest languages to understand the "instinctual sense of the unity of all of life." On reflecting upon his own encounters with nature as a boy, Thurman realized that Schreiner's work allowed him to "make the experience itself an object of thought. Thus it became possible for me to move from primary experience, to conceptualizing that experience, to a vision inclusive of all of life. The resulting creative synthesis was to me *religious* rather than *metaphysical*."

She also influenced Thurman's thinking on sexuality and gender relations. It was not a topic he addressed often, but he did so in his seminary work "The Basis of Sex Morality," which was in effect a sort of modernist view of healthy sexual relations between men and women. When people achieved "spiritual unity" in sex, it mattered little whether it was premarital sex. Thurman shrugged off conventional shibboleths about sex, just as he was doing in theology.

In 1926 Thurman graduated as the valedictorian (again) at Rochester, in a class of twenty-nine men. He received the bachelor of divinity degree (something not very common, which not even Mordecai Wyatt Johnson had achieved at the time of his graduation), which mandated the completion of a thesis during his term in school. Before moving on from Rochester, Thurman had a talk with his primary mentor, George Cross, and Cross's words, both encouraging and admonitory, stayed on Thurman's mind for decades to come. Acknowledging that he, Cross, was a white man who could not know what it was to be a Negro, he nonetheless urged Thurman to "give yourself to the timeless issues of the human spirit" instead of focusing his efforts on social questions of a "transitory nature." It would be a waste if Thurman simply devoted his attention toward the race problem or put his energies fully at the "disposal of the struggle of your people for full citizenship." Patronizing through they were, Cross's words hit at a fundamental division in Thurman's life and thought.

Thurman justifiably was dismayed at Cross's lack of understanding and empathy. Cross simply could not see, for example, that "a man and his black skin must 'face the timeless issues of the human spirit' together." In some ways, Thurman's lifework was all about exactly that. In other ways, though, Thurman put into practice Cross's advice at various points in his life, often rejecting speaking invitations that asked him specifically to represent the race in some capacity or another or to explain how "the Negro" viewed one issue or another. Such requests were equally patronizing, he felt, precisely because they did not ask him to speak from his training as someone with a broad exposure to many currents of spiritual thought, past and present. In other words, Thurman really did want to—and did—speak to timeless issues of the human spirit. Sometimes he did so (particularly later in his life) to the point of being bafflingly abstract and ethereal. In his best work, though, Thurman combined the tough realities of living with a black skin in America with the broader spiritual truths he gleaned from his deep study in myriad religious traditions. His most important work married the lived experience of people with grand truths of religious encounters.

THURMAN'S EARLY CAREER

Meanwhile, in 1926 Thurman was planning his own marriage to Katie Kelley, a graduate of Spelman and of a social work program at the University of Chicago, who had moved back to Atlanta in 1921 and worked closely with Lugenia Burns Hope, the wife of Morehouse president John Hope, in combating tuberculosis. Devastatingly for Thurman, Kelley eventually died of the very disease she had committed her life to defeat. In 1926, before the tragedy, Kelley was an accomplished young woman who seemed the perfect match for Thurman as he took his post at Mount Zion Baptist Church in Oberlin, Ohio (he also hoped to continue his academic studies at Oberlin College).

From early in his pastoral career, Thurman moved his congregation at Oberlin in experimental and modernist directions, sometimes to the dismay of his own parishioners. Thurman experimented with new forms of thought, worship, and expression that he would bring to his leadership of the chapels at Howard and Boston University, and later to his nine years leading the Church for the Fellowship of All Peoples in San Francisco. He was intent on liberating the inner spirit, to express the "meaning of the experience of our common quest and journey"; he was much less concerned with theological fidelity to any one particular tradition. And at Oberlin, he discovered as well some of the possibilities of interracial and intercultural fellowship. The church attracted various members of the Oberlin community, including a local Chinese-born man. Of Thurman's services, he said, "When I close my eyes and listen to my spirit I am in a Buddhist temple experiencing the renewing of my own spirit." For Thurman, this was early evidence that "the barriers were crumbling," and that he was "breaking new ground," even though it would take him years before he fully understood the results of this spiritual breakthrough.

At the same time, he continued his higher academic studies at the Oberlin School of Theology and carefully considered whether he should pursue a PhD. Eventually he determined that he was more interested in nourishing the "inner regions of my spirit" than in pursuing the highest academic degree. Thurman's thoughts and ideas were turning inward. He described himself as undergoing "a veritable upheaval in my thinking."

In these years, Thurman found his mature voice. He moved away from the YMCA pieties of his younger years and the formalism of his academic work. He developed a decidedly critical edge, something that fed into some of his more explicitly political essays during the 1930s and 1940s. That kind of work always was unusual for him. But in his correspondence and speeches in this era, he developed a blistering critique of American materialism and of the impotence of the churches in the face of it. "We are clothed and fed by a vast system built upon deceit and adulteration," he wrote to Mordecai Wyatt Johnson. It would be the job of religious institutions, properly conceived, to release "such a grand swell of spiritual energy that existing systems will be upset." He also tellingly understood the role of black religious leadership to be cultivating a sense of "ethical meaning" such that the mere building of institutions would not suffocate the spirit of Jesus.

In "Higher Education and Religion," written in 1927 for the *Home Mission College Review*, Thurman expressed some of his earliest analyses of the legacies (both positive and negative) of African American religion, as well as the necessity of establishing "some sort of helpful relationship between young minds and religion"—exactly what he had written about in a more formal academic way for his bachelor's thesis at Rochester. "We have as our heritage to-day a religion which is pretty largely apocalyptic," he began, with a "procession of early Negro preachers [who] found themselves leading their hosts through a wilderness of suffering, oppression, and cruelty." Somehow, with an intuitive insight, those "prophets of patience turned their attention to the hope beyond this world and found great refuge" in the Bible, something Thurman thought to be "apocalypticism at its best. God is the Real, the present world can give no peace." Such a dire view, however, had placed a "barrier between life and religion," and "the manifestations of religion under such circumstances tend to be more theological than ethical." Here, Thurman repeated a common critique made of African American churches, and religion more generally: it had produced a powerfully affective theology but had neglected certain ethical issues of everyday life. But Thurman found these contributions of "apocalyptic faith" the most important: first, this faith "made for the development of creative and vicarious imagination under the aegis of religious symbolism," and second, "under the powerful influence of religious zeal and emotion it made bearable an otherwise unbearable series of experiences without attempting to justify them."

For Thurman, the conflict between modern education and older myths could prove dangerous; the resulting consciousness could result in "profound bitterness and cynicism because of the injustice of the present order," with "little left of the apocalyptic hope to comfort and to bless." This left students vulnerable to a "religion of materialism." To those who preached a religion of economic uplift and power to African Americans, Thurman replied that such a philosophy could reproduce the same problems it was designed to solve. Ultimately, those who could save the civilization would be "those who have learned to *live* so as to reveal the superiority of the human spirit to the domination of things. . . . But we are rapidly forgetting it as we embrace the religion of materialism, a religion that has already made you drunk with power and might." In the great debate from the earlier twentieth century between advocates of liberal arts education and practical training, Thurman definitively sided with the former.

Likewise, in "The Task of the Negro Ministry," from 1928, Thurman presented his vision of African American religion as exalting not economic power but a spiritual insight into deeper things. The slave was not, and could not be, entrapped by the "tyranny of things," for such things were denied to him or her. And thus the Negro minister of the present day, learning from this history, could see that "where the highest premium is put upon the possession of things, human life is relatively cheapened. And where life is cheap, ideals languish and the souls of men slowly die." Thurman here also explored an idea that long attracted him, that religion operated more by "contagion" than by organization. As he said of the religion of Jesus, "we must put a vast faith in the contagion in the Spirit of Jesus rather than in the building of organizations to perpetuate his Spirit." Black churches themselves could fall prey to this, the same disease that had consumed white church organizations. That would be a bitter irony given that black churches historically had been built with the sweat of lowly laborers who brought their hard-earned small coins, and for that reason had a "sense of possession" of their churches. The dynamic idea of African American religion inevitably took institutional forms after emancipation, and to some degree that was good and necessary. But "it is also true that just as a dynamic idea is conserved in some form of organization, it is also destroyed by the very organization that preserved it. Hence the paradox: The power that makes it breaks it." Most important, the "Spirit of Jesus grows by contagion and not by organization. . . . In the final analysis a man's life is changed by contact with another life."

Thurman spent much of the next twenty years revisiting the topic of the spirituals, which were then being rehabilitated and understood as great American literature, initially by W. E. B. Du Bois and then by writers such as James Weldon Johnson and others from the Harlem Renaissance of the 1920s. Thurman later wrote that he addressed "a generation which tended to be ashamed of the Spirituals, or who joined in the degrading and prostituting of the songs as a part of conventional minstrelsy and naïve amusement exploited and capitalized by white entertainers." In these early lectures, delivered at the chapel of Spelman College in October of 1928, Thurman worked out his ideas about the meaning of the spirituals. The germ of the ideas here, although more overtly theological and Christian than in later iterations, carried him forward for much of his future work. The "religious message" of the songs, he thought, had been forgotten or else "lost in the beauty of the melodies for which they are distinguished." He began with "We Are Climbing Jacob's Ladder," a song he thought expressed the idea that no situation was "so depressing, so devoid of hope, that the human spirit cannot throw itself into a realm in which these conditions do not exist, and live in that realm despite all the hell about them." Through such songs, enslaved people said that their circumstances could not crush them, that they could live in a purer world amidst the hell among them.

The spiritual "Heab'n, Heab'n," with its famous lines "I got a shoes, you got shoes, All o' God's chillum got a shoes," and parallel lines of "I got a crown" and "I got a robe," suggested that the true test of the religion of Jesus was "made in the intimate, primary face to face relationships of people who live together day in and day out." For if the religion of Jesus could not "purify human relations," then it was meaningless. The spiritual also suggested the difficulty of maintaining normal human relations of honesty in situations of radical inequality, which "robs people of the ability to be straightforward, honest, courageous" and "[turns] everyone in such societies into 'monumental hypocrites.'"

Other spirituals explored the dilemma of human suffering, a theological problem acutely felt among slaves. Thurman used them to explore his own answer to the question of why human suffering existed. He knew that "there is something in the human spirit—to me, it is God—which makes it possible for the most tragic experience to be transformed into that which is sacred and beautiful and blessed." Thurman's lectures on the spirituals delivered at Spelman bore fruit later in his published works on the subject. In these lectures, Thurman demonstrated a keen sensitivity to the universal messages of hope contained within the particular form of Negro spirituals. Thurman resisted any overt politicization of the songs, seeing them more as vehicles of spiritual expression than as direct commentary on what should be done in the here and now. For him, the spirituals exalted human personality over oppressive conditions designed to crush the human spirit.

In these same years, Thurman also grappled with ideas of what nonviolence could mean in American society. Thurman's most important work of that era, published originally as "Peace Tactics and a Racial Minority" and then in expanded form as "'Relaxation' and Racial Conflict," marked his debut as a thinker of considerable influence on American social movements. Thurman centrally injected race into questions of pacifism and nonviolence, a major jump for many early proponents who held more generically philosophical ideas of pacifism. For Thurman, the daily violence directed at African Americans exemplified the damages wrought by violence more generally. Thus, addressing racial oppression would have to be central to American pacifism. Writing for readers of the religious Left and pacifists, he pointed out from the beginning that a kind of pacifism that ignored racial inequality in American society "becomes a mere quietus to be put into the hands of the minority to keep them peaceful and controllable." Part of that involved empowering a small minority of the minority, giving them enough privileges to allow them to identify with the majority and thus look down on the rest of their class. In general, it was all too possible to "hate people so bitterly that one becomes like them. The man who *attends* to evil that he may not fall heir to it becomes like it." At the same time, the Negro lived in a world where everything spoke to the will of the majority; "everything that he possesses tends to lose its significance if it is not validated by those who are in control."

What did this mean for pacifism in America? Thurman concluded: "First, it means that white people who make up the dominant majority in American life must relax their will to dominate and control the Negro minority. Second, Negroes must develop a minority technique, which I choose to call a technique of relaxation, sufficiently operative in group life to make for vast creativity, with no corresponding loss in self-respect." On the side of the majority, the will to dominate came "utilizing all of the machinery at its disposal to that end. Nothing is spared: the press, including the comic sheet and the highbrow journals; the church, including the pulpit; much that goes by the name of charity and many of the *materials* of religious education; and for the most part, the technique and the philosophy of education." Thurman here recounted again his grandmother's stories about plantation life, about how every day was an education in "where she fitted into the scheme of things . . . that she was a slave and that the will of the mistress must be the desire of her heart." It may seem that relinquishing this will to control, the will to dominate, would be difficult, but in fact it could be just the opposite: "When the will to dominate and control is relaxed, then the way is clear for spontaneous self-giving, for sharing all gratuitously. This new spirit finds its direction in the *will to love*." And through that the "relaxation of the will to control and to dominate becomes something very positive and dynamic."

Thurman was addressing specifically educated African Americans, those who lived in the kind of veil described by Du Bois, with a double consciousness, and as a result with some bitterness toward whites and possibly contempt for those of their own group who were beneath them. The key was developing the ability to get away from the "class of minority and majority sufficiently to interpret the relationship between them in the light of a will to share and a will to love." Thurman concluded: "all our attempts to bring about brotherhood, sympathetic understanding, and goodwill are dashed

to pieces against an adamant wall. On the one side it is labelled: The Will to
Control and Dominate. On the other it is labelled: The Will to Hate the Man
Who Tries to Dominate and Crush Me. When there is relaxation, then the
way is clear for the operation of the will to share joyfully in the common
life—the will to love healingly and creatively." Thurman explored this insight
in numerous forms over the next decades.

By the late 1920s, Thurman had developed a national reputation as a
speaker and thinker, and he received job offers of prestigious black pulpits
and academic positions appropriate to his stature. The First Baptist Church
of Charleston, West Virginia, tried to recruit him to replace Mordecai Wyatt
Johnson in that prestigious pulpit. Various black universities sought him
to be a chaplain. But Thurman and Katie Kelley Thurman needed to be in
a place where Katie's health could best be protected, and that was back in
Atlanta, where she spent considerable time at the McIvar Training Hospital
on the campus of one of her alma maters, Spelman College. Thurman took a
position as professor of philosophy and religion, teaching both at Morehouse
and at Spelman. During his time there, and in spite of Katie's failing health,
Thurman wrote and delivered his lecture series on the spirituals. During this
time, as well, as he taught philosophy and religion at Morehouse and courses
on biblical literature at Spelman, he developed his particular modes of classroom teaching, which were less concerned with imparting knowledge and
more consumed with leading students through deep explorations of both
the course material and their dreams and visions for their lives. He developed personal relationships with students as well through his cooking, an
avocation he delighted in. He enjoyed bringing students over on a Saturday,
serving them his special roasted peanuts or homemade sherbet, and exploring with them questions both philosophical and practical. Over the subsequent decades, Thurman exercised a profound influence over his students.
He honed his own personally quiet but charismatic style as a young professor
in the late 1920s. At the same time, he also clashed with the white president
of Spelman, Florence Read, a foretaste of his frequent battles with academic
administrators (black and white) in the years to come. As Thurman saw it,
Read patronized students and faculty alike, arranging their schedules and
activities to her own liking. He also saw that Spelman students "lacked models for themselves as black women." In later years, Thurman spoke kindly of

Read (and vice versa), but in the late 1920s and early 1930s, the paternalistic white administration of African American colleges in general, and Spelman in particular, left him seething.

But the central event of his younger intellectual life came in the first half of 1929. Using funding provided by the National Council of Religion in Higher Education, he embarked on a six-month plan of study with Rufus Jones, a leading Quaker thinker and author who taught at Haverford College. Jones's book *Finding the Trail of Life* had captivated Thurman when he stumbled on it at a bookstore while a minister at Oberlin. He read the book entirely in one sitting and immediately "knew that if that man were alive, I wanted to study with him."

It's easy to see what captivated the young minister. Jones wrote of how "mystical experience is much more common than is usually supposed" among children, which certainly fit Thurman's experience, and how "they are more sensitive to intimations, flashes, and openings. The invisible impinges on their souls and they feel its reality as something quite natural." For Jones, natural beauty was the surest evidence of God; "I *felt* His presence in my world rather than thought out how He could be there. When I was moved with wonder, awe and mystery, I was always reaching out beyond what I saw and touched, and I had a religious feeling even if I did not have a sound theory to go with it." As he finished his schooling, he felt himself "in the condition of the wild geese whom I had so often watched migrate. They kept a fixed *direction* but they did not know where their terminus was to be." Jones concluded the memoir of his youth with this line: "there are no more important epics than those of the inner life."

Finding the Trail of Life captured Thurman's spirits, sentiments, and youthful philosophies and experiences perfectly. Along with George Cross, Jones would be Thurman's closest white intellectual mentor. Thurman came to Haverford for the semester, met with Jones for discussions of readings, and used Jones's library on mystical thought on religion, a virtual intellectual playground for the intellectually voracious Thurman. This was a "watershed" period, as Thurman later described it, from which "flowed much of the thought and endeavor to which I was to commit the rest of my working life." Those days reinforced his "deepest religious urges" and "framed in meaning" what he had learned in his studies to date.

Much as he did with Olive Schreiner, Thurman returned repeatedly to the inspiration Jones provided him. Most important, Thurman's future work carried on Jones's emphasis on uniting mysticism as an internal practice with social activism and public experience. Jones, he later said, "gave me confidence in the insight that the religion of the inner life could deal with the empirical evidence of man without retreating from the demands of such experience." Jones's mysticism was more Christian than Thurman's, but Thurman took his lessons and applied them broadly in his work over the next decades, always emphasizing that the point of mysticism was not simply internal insight but also involved external action toward ethical ends. "The distinctive feature of Jones's mysticism," writes Thurman scholar Walter Fluker, "is that it provides the basis for social transformation." Thus, in their conversations, they spoke not just of the mystics of the past but also of contemporary conflicts, wars, inequality, and poverty. They apparently did not talk about race, but it was no problem for Thurman to extend those conversations toward his own life experiences. Some years later, in his lecture series "Mysticism and Social Change," Thurman put much of what he learned in this era from Jones together with his own developing work on the religion of the disinherited. In the process, he created a theological structure and framework of critical social thought that allowed him to connect abstract theology and concrete social realities in a way very few others could.

Thurman returned to Atlanta intellectually enriched. But nothing could prepare him for the loss in December 1930 of Katie, then just thirty years old, with their daughter Olive just two years of age. It is a time of his life nearly unrecoverable for the biographer, as he said or wrote little about it then or afterward. It's even difficult to tell, really, how close he was to Katie; he evidently later told Sue, his second wife, that Katie really had not been the love of his life. Sue later told him that Katie had assumed a certain mythic place in Thurman's own well-worn recounting of his life for his fans and disciples, because Katie suffered a "Tennysonian" tragic death, like a figure in a nineteenth-century European novel. Notably, Sue wrote this in the early 1970s, in some notes she quickly scribbled in reviewing a manuscript of a potential Thurman biography. In these notes, Sue expressed some exasperation at her husband for implicitly, and perhaps unconsciously, subsuming Sue as a separate person into accounts of his own life he gave to interviewers and biographers. Mostly, however, the extant materials, and Thurman's relative silence about the events of those years, are just too sketchy to draw many conclusions about the relationship between Howard and Katie.

Following Katie's death, together with his close friend of many decades Herbert King, Thurman wandered through England, Scotland, and parts of Europe in early 1931, living at one point on a sheep ranch in Scotland. What little evidence survives from this period and from Thurman's later reflections suggests that it was a dark period of brooding and recovery. He returned to Atlanta to teach in the fall of 1931 and found himself borne down by the sheer weight of racist oppression in the city. It was also, of course, a dark time in America more generally, as the crushing weight of the Great Depression sank in. Somehow, Thurman found in the time some of the beginning inspirations for what became his most important life's work in terms of theological writing: understanding Jesus as a member of a "despised circumscribed minority group." As Thurman later remembered it, "The racial climate was so oppressive and affected us so intimately that analogies between His life as a Jew in a Roman world and our own were obvious."

Thurman's darkest time coincided with the beginning of the relationship that would shape his life most fundamentally in the years to come. For some years he had known Sue Elvie Bailey, the daughter of Isaac and Susie Ford Bailey, from Arkansas. Her parents had been well-known educators and political activists in the state, and Sue thus came from a family deeply rooted in the black Baptist tradition. Sue went to Spelman (and spent one year at Morehouse, taking particular courses not available for Spelman women) for high school and college, finishing there in 1921. During that time she roomed with the mother of Martin Luther King Jr. and first met Howard Thurman. In 1922, she moved to Ohio to attend Oberlin College, where she served as cochair of the World Fellowship committee of the YWCA and pursued her interests in arts and music. She also made friendships with white women, which "opened up to me a window where I could look out, and see a much larger world that was opening up. I had the duty to . . . open windows, and break down walls." Sue spent the rest of her life (she lived until 1996) doing exactly that.

Sue Bailey Thurman was the first black student to graduate from the school of music there. Her musical talents already had garnered her notice. She ended up on the faculty of music at Hampton Institute, another black Baptist institution, in Virginia. Bailey soon emerged as the leader of a student revolt at Hampton after the Virginia legislature passed a bill ending integrated seating in the public auditorium in the town of Hampton. The administration at Hampton, led by a white president, clamped down on the students, and Bailey left with a friend for New York City, where she became a national secretary for the YWCA, traveling the country organizing for it, and developing the intense interests in African American social history and international relations that would mark her life. She spent the rest of her life making good trouble. Sue Bailey Thurman was herself a veteran of battle with paternalistic white administrators of black colleges; she understood Thurman's frustrations at Spelman.

Sue Bailey and Howard Thurman reconnected at Spelman in 1931, when Thurman was there delivering an address and Sue was on the stage with him as part of the event where he was speaking. Friends had forewarned Sue that Howard, known for some personal peculiarities and for being an absent-minded-professor type, might be doodling on paper and showing little awareness that she was even around. And indeed, he was doodling, as she recalled, but he managed to send her a note inviting her to breakfast (some friends later remembered this slightly differently, basically as a setup engineered by those who recognized the potential for this match). Later, she came to his home, still darkened and the shades shut. She opened the curtains to let the sunshine in.

The effervescent, outgoing, and also fiercely outspoken Sue Bailey would spend much of the rest of her life doing the same thing for other people. She was not afflicted with the kind of melancholic brooding that sometimes tormented Howard Thurman; yet, at the same time, the two shared a joy and zest in life that they communicated to others. And their love and joy in each other are evident, to some degree, in Thurman's published papers, and even more so in unpublished correspondence, scraps of paper where Sue scribbled brainstormed thoughts, family memorabilia, and letters from Sue's mother (who evidently shared with Sue an outgoing personality given to vocal and often playfully spontaneous expressions of love for those close to her). In his public writings and in interviews, Howard was not given to revealing himself in deeply personal ways; he tended to repeat a particular set of life stories that exemplified for him intellectual turning points or themes he explored in his intellectual journeys for the rest of his life. But it's clear that he and Sue had an open and egalitarian relationship. Howard would become an intellectual celebrity, but Sue's lifework of major intellectual contributions and social/political activism came with Howard's enthusiastic support.

The two married on June 12, 1932, and did so, fittingly enough, following mutual attendance at a YWCA and YMCA conference in Kings Mountain, North Carolina. It was the place where Thurman had seen his first intellectual hero outside of his teachers at Florida, Mordecai Wyatt Johnson, and where he first felt a larger inspiration that led him to his understanding that shaped his younger years: "my people need me."

He was about to move to Howard University in the nation's capital, where he, Sue, Olive, and the new daughter of Howard and Sue, Anne Spencer, quickly assumed a central place in the life of the university, and really in black America more generally. There, Howard and Sue spent twelve of the most intellectually and socially fulfilling years of their lives. Sue, especially, thrived in the intellectually and socially adventurous climate of Washington during the New Deal years. She began the work of recovering materials for African American history that would become one of her most important contributions to twentieth-century African American life, and she also cultivated international relationships that fundamentally shaped her vision of the African American connection with international movements for freedom. Sue Bailey Thurman deserves her own biography, and some of the scholars listed in the bibliographical essay have sketched a path toward this aim. But such a project will be difficult. Sue's careful pruning of the Thurman papers after Howard's death, including the disposal of much personal correspondence and more intimate details of the interaction between them, demonstrates both how much she cared about the Thurman legacy and her understanding of what might interest snooping scholars and biographers. Still, her central place in twentieth-century African American history, as a figure separate and distinct from Howard, has yet to be fully appreciated.

Shortly after submitting his resignation from Morehouse and Spelman in February 1932, a few months before his marriage to Sue Bailey, Thurman spoke to the First Congregational Church of Atlanta on a Sunday evening.

The pastor, William J. Faulkner, wrote him appreciatively: "God is bountifully blessing you as a teacher and prophet in pointing the way to the light for our people in these troublous times. It will be a keen personal loss to me to have you leave this community. I regret now more than ever that I have denied myself a closer fellowship with you during the past few years. But I shall always count it a source of genuine hope and inspiration that I have known you." Thurman had grown and matured as a college student in Atlanta, later as a husband and father, and then had suffered his greatest personal trauma. By the time he left Atlanta for good, he had come into his own as a nationally respected minister and author. He embraced larger visions and a bigger public and national audience in his next fourteen years in Washington, DC, and in India.

2

"The Unadulterated Message of Nonviolence"
Howard University and the Voyage to India

> From a 10,000-mile perspective, this monumental betrayal of the
> Christian ethic loomed large and forbidding.
>
> —Howard Thurman, Footprints of a Dream

Mordecai Wyatt Johnson, president of Howard University, was a skilled re-
cruiter of academic talent and a hard taskmaster once the talent arrived.
In Thurman, he found just the right person to become part of the team to
take Howard University into its years as a center of black intellectual life in
the country. There were some casualties in this process, though. One was
the formerly affectionate relationship between Johnson, once the esteemed
adviser and mentor of Thurman, and Thurman himself, who chafed (as did
others) under Johnson's adept autocracy. But Thurman also thrived under
it, as did the institution as a whole. And during Thurman's term as dean
of Rankin Chapel at Howard, his six-month tour in India (and later visits
to South Asia by other faculty members and colleagues of Thurman's) led
to the establishment of a relationship between the Indian and American
nonviolent moments for freedom.

Thus the fall of 1932 was a new start for Thurman in ways both professional and personal. Newly married, soon to be a father to Anne Spencer
(his daughter by Sue), he assumed a new position as a faculty member in the
School of Religion at Howard University. Johnson had tried for some years
before to recruit Thurman. This time, with Thurman's personal circumstances changed, Johnson got his man.

As Sue later recollected, she and Howard had both learned, in the YMCA
and YWCA, "to make things happen for students, to sort of nurture their
hopes and dreams," and they took that to Howard University: "We were

young, the sky was the limit. Then we went to India, and that did it indeed. We came back and we were so full of what was needed for . . . the races of men living side by side in this country." She further reflected, "We used to say to each other in those early days, because we marveled at this, that he was a masculine expression of my thought, and I was the feminine expression of his. It was one thought."

The next fourteen years would see the full development of Thurman's powers. Sue's energies likewise shot out in multiple directions. This included her first efforts at collecting documents and archival materials of African American history, a vital work of social history done in collaboration with the National Council of Negro Women and with the professional counsel of Mary Beard, the wife of and coauthor of books with the Columbia University historian Charles Beard. Anne Spencer Thurman recalled this period, in fact, as the happiest of her mother's life, as she kept busy with myriad activities and entertained a steady stream of guests in her home. Howard, meanwhile, exploded with powerful sermons, addresses, letters, talks, and statements on matters both spiritual and political. These later fueled his career as the author of numerous books. But nearly everything he put into print later is present in some form or another in the work he presented mostly as orations and addresses during this period.

By that time, Howard Thurman already was a well-known figure nationally. Black papers referred to him as "one of the greatest thinkers of the age," one who could hold an audience "spellbound and awed" with his "characteristically profound and inspiring addresses." His trip to Asilomar, California, in 1932, and a subsequent month of sermons and lectures through the Southwest, constituted one of his first extended experiences in the West. It must have been a salve after the wounds he had suffered in Atlanta, a city claustrophobic and diseased in ways both physical and spiritual.

The newly married couple moved out of the Deep South, away from Depression-era Atlanta, and joined Howard University at a time when it was the brightest star in the black intellectual firmament. There, young lawyers trained under the legendarily tough legal scholar and mentor Charles Hamilton Houston; sociologists honed their skills under E. Franklin Frazier; and historians learned from the likes of Kelly Miller, Alain Locke, and William Hansberry. Howard University's Department of Religion was, to put it charitably, undistinguished. Thurman's job in part was to raise its stature. That he certainly did, with the help of some impressive colleagues. There, too, Thurman preached sermons that left people in awe of his intellect, his quiet yet forceful delivery, and his quest to search for a truer Christianity, the religion of Jesus that could supplant the religion of Christianity. Gradually he developed the ideas that led to his classic work *Jesus and the Disinherited*, published in 1949.

Thurman's first published sermon, "Barren or Fruitful," came from this time, the late summer of 1932, just as Thurman was moving to Howard. He preached it at the church of his best friend, the Reverend Herbert King, who had counseled and consoled Thurman during his period of depression following the death of Katie. Thurman asked the crowd, "In what do you find your security?" His answer: "Your fundamental security then is not family, training, piety or the like but rather the supreme quality of your dedication to the highest there is in life—God. To say, 'I affirm my faith in God with my total personality,' is one of the supreme affirmations of the human spirit." Thurman always was someone for whom God was the lodestar; everything pointed to him. "God is here," he said that evening in his sermon. "In the midst of life, breaking through the commonplace, glorifying the ordinary, the Great, High God is near." The key was the presence of God in the everyday, the ordinary. "Do not wait to hear His spirit winging near in moments of great crisis," Thurman advised. "Do not expect Him riding on the crest of a wave of deep emotional excitement—do not look to see Him at the dramatic moment when something abnormal or spectacular is at hand. Rather find Him in the simple experiences of daily living, in the normal ebb and flow of life as you live it." Thurman reworked this theme through numerous sermons from this period and later. He wanted to connect people with the voice of God within them.

THURMAN'S EARLY TENURE AT HOWARD UNIVERSITY

From his post at the flagship black university, he crisscrossed the country on speaking engagements, began some of his first significant writing, and struggled to balance his thoughts on both the potentialities and the limitations of Christianity. As well, he investigated the dilemmas of the universal message of Christianity and the particular expressions of it within the American racial hierarchy. Howard Thurman used his role at Howard University to develop a program of religion that drew national attention, and in these years he carried on a correspondence with an impressive array of national figures. As dean of the chapel at Howard, he recognized that he was in an unusual situation, with few precedents in other places. There were only two other deans of a college chapel, in Princeton and in Chicago, and thus, as he wrote to the president of Howard, "the functional significance of the job is loosely defined."

He proposed to Johnson that the dean of the chapel should run the preaching services and personal consultations with students, and "with these two there follow very closely the responsibilities for the development of the religious life of the University generally." The dean should be the head of the undergraduate religious groups. Thurman consistently opposed having the college chapel used for any sectarian purposes or groups, once objecting most strenuously to a Wesleyan student organization that managed to secure chapel space for itself.

Thurman's work also took on a more explicitly political bent in these years than it would have later. As a member of Fellowship of Reconciliation since the 1920s, he already had declared his pacifist sentiments. In his writings from this time about private property, he declared himself effectively a socialist, albeit never a doctrinaire one. Communism never had the same deep appeal for him that it had for many other notable black intellectuals and writers of the era. He was a humanist and an internationalist but was suspicious of the motives of communist-related groups. He took his YMCA training in directions considerably to the left of what the YMCA itself had taught him, but he kept its strong emphasis on peace and brotherhood at home and abroad. And his continued work with the Y and with the Christian Student Association set the stage for the great personal and intellectual event of his early professional career: his voyage to India in 1935–1936 and his challenging encounters there with those who saw the Christianity in which he had been steeped as fundamentally part of the problem of imperialism and oppression.

From his first days at Howard, Thurman moved immediately into the intellectual and social orbit of Washington. The capital was still a very southern, segregated city at the time, but it was about to experience the revolution of FDR and the New Deal. Thurman took to an intellectual environment free of the overbearing paternalism and stuffy evangelicalism of the Deep South. The dean of the School of Religion, D. Butler Pratt, advised Thurman that "each teacher is absolutely free to express his opinions and to teach the truth as God gives him to see the truth," provided that the professor respect those holding other views. But, he added, "our faculty is distinctly modern in its attitude toward the Bible and theological questions, which means, as I understand it, that we have the attitude of searchers for the truth rather than of the closed mind, even of some so-called modernists." That fit Thurman's conception of himself exactly: a modernist, a searcher after truth, and a seeker for reconciliation with those of other views. At the same time, because Thurman was going to be teaching young students who had grown up with literalist and traditional biblical training, Pratt advised him to keep his first-year teaching "elementary" and "adapted sympathetically to some who hold to the literal views of tradition and need, by actual study of the facts, to open their minds to the historical method of approach." Thurman also took on the responsibility of chairman of the University Committee on Religious Life, a role that suited him perfectly. He seized that opportunity to bring Rankin Chapel at Howard into the forefront of black religious life in Washington, DC, and to national attention.

A brief look at the range of Thurman's correspondence and short writings from this era suggests the extent of his national contacts. He reviewed books by the likes of George Bernard Shaw and Benjamin Mays (although he was, in truth, mediocre at book reviewing; his heart seems not have been in it), and he corresponded with the following: Vernon Johns (later the famously cantankerous predecessor to Martin Luther King Jr. in the pulpit at Dexter Avenue Baptist Church in Montgomery); John Hope (who was then ill, and to whom Thurman wrote of what he had learned during his time with the "long terrible illness" of his deceased first wife, Katie); Reinhold Niebuhr (with whom he was a close enough friend to address him as "Reinie," and to assure him that when he came to visit, their daughter Anne Spencer's "crying will only disturb you until three in the morning, after that you may sleep"); black labor leader A. Philip Randolph and luminary intellectual W. E. B. Du Bois (writing to let him know he planned to attend a conference on the Negro Youth Movement that Du Bois was organizing); Winnifred Wygal, executive secretary of the National Student Council; Channing Tobias of the YMCA; Ralph Bunche, his colleague at Howard and head of the Department of Political Science there (and later an important figure in international relations and winner of a Nobel Peace Prize); white southern activist Howard Kester, then in the midst of his investigation of the lynching of Claude Neal in Florida and soon to author his classic work *Revolt among the Sharecroppers*; John Nevin Sayre, chairman of Fellowship of Reconciliation, who wanted Thurman to serve as the field representative of FOR among African Americans; Muriel Lester, a British critic of British imperialism; Frederick Patterson, newly named president of Tuskegee Institute; James G. St. Clair Drake, an important black sociologist who led a group of black Philadelphians interested in applying the ideas of Gandhi to the racial situation in the United States; and a variety of close friends from his Florida years and his academic circles, notably Benjamin Mays (later president of Morehouse) and Mary McLeod Bethune (then a member of FDR's "Black Cabinet" and founder of what later became Bethune-Cookman College in Florida). And that's just a very short and partial list. In fact, Thurman later remembered watching Bethune working with Sue, looking into a mirror, and saying, "Howard, black is beautiful!" As Thurman put it in an interview from 1971, "The expression is now in current use but she was saying it even back then. This is why her contagion was so persuasive. She had identity and projected it. I was caught up in this along with a lot of other people in the town."

Thurman remained active in various organizations that were involved with students, including the National Student Council. But Thurman expressed some skepticism about the future of any united student movement. "In all of the movements there is a lot of deadness," he complained. He had "no faith in the future of a unified student movement in America that is simply a combination of the existing units." Student organizations sponsored Thurman's journey through India. But Thurman, already in his thirties at the time, was no longer a student, and gradually moved out of the orbit of the YMCA and other like groups that had provided so much of his training and first experiences in addressing larger audiences. This estrangement would grow more marked later, when his friend Herbert King was removed from his leadership position with the student movement, deeply offending and angering Thurman.

In the year before his trip to India, Thurman corresponded with religious leaders throughout the country, soliciting their advice and responding to invitations to speak everywhere. One came from the southern white activist Howard "Buck" Kester, who was at that time forming what became the Fellowship of Southern Churchmen (a collection of left-leaning, mostly white, ministers interested in racial progress in the South). Kester pleaded with Thurman to speak at one of the group's founding conferences, where the theme would be "Religion and the Struggle for Social Justice," with the intention to "go at things with gloves off." Kester already had advertised Thurman's talk as "one of our main drawing cards. People do want to hear you and meet you personally. The conference is to be interracial from beginning to end and it will be something new under the southern sky." Not for the first time, Thurman had been advertised as a chief attraction before he had committed to come.

Meanwhile, John Nevin Sayre recruited Thurman to be the African American field representative for FOR, which he agreed to do. Unlike the various organizations within the orbit of the YMCA, FOR more closely fit Thurman's more radical vision of pacificism and interracialism. He represented FOR regionally, recruited new members, "and generally served as a field worker for the Fellowship, making connection between local groups and national headquarters." Allan Hunter, a Congregational minister in Hollywood, learned of Thurman's appointment and wrote him in hopes of meeting with him on the West Coast and discussing placing FOR "on a more spiritual basis." Thurman replied that he could not come at the moment but hoped to stop off on the West Coast on his way home from India. "You must know that I think of you very often, and feel that knowing you provides a great source of strength to me, as the struggle between Negroes and white people in this country becomes more terrible every day," he wrote back to Hunter.

Shortly before his tour in India, in February 1935, and with news of his upcoming visit well known among his friends and colleagues in universities and in the student movement, Thurman spoke to the Intercollegiate Missionary Conference, held at Gammon Theological Seminary in Atlanta.

More explicitly Christian than was his norm (possibly because it was altered to suit the publication needs of Gammon, a center of black Christian theological training), Thurman's address showed the direct influence of Reinhold Niebuhr. "The Kingdom of God will never come by a moral appeal to people who must always live in an immoral society," he said, a direct reference to Niebuhr's ideas that groups were more immoral than individuals. The search for God, he continued, must begin with an individual's realization that "whatever he condemns in society does not exist in his own heart." And the kingdom of God could not be identified with society, "because it is beyond anything that man's society can produce." That could be seen in the recent war to "make the world safe for democracy," when "Christian Ministers asked God's blessing upon men going out to blow out others' brains, to slaughter them with bayonets, machine guns and poison gas. Now we are passing through a period of critical quiet like the man who has been hit on the head with a club, and the physician is waiting for him to pass the crisis." And the victorious nations had not "asked the church, which had blessed their wholesale slaughter, what they should do with the spoils."

In "Good News for the Underprivileged," delivered at Boston University in the summer of 1935 and published later in the journal *Religion and Life*, Thurman fleshed out the ideas that would take form later in his classic *Jesus and the Disinherited*: that the "religion of Jesus" was a "technique of survival for a disinherited minority." For Thurman, the central question of Christianity was what message it might give to the dispossessed, the poor. The key fact here was that Jesus was a poor Jew. "Is it too daring," Thurman asked, "to suggest that in his poverty he was the symbol of the masses of men so that he could truly be Son of Man more naturally and accurately than if he had been a rich Jew?" But growing up as poor Jews, he and his family could enjoy none of the rights and privileges of citizens of the Roman Empire. "They were a captive group, but not enslaved." True, the apostle Paul also was Jewish, but he was free. But "if a Roman soldier kicked Jesus into a Galilean ravine, it was merely a Jew in the ravine. He could not appeal to Caesar." And so Jesus's message was intended for Roman and Jew, free person and slave, set against the "agonizing realities of the struggle of his people against an over-arching mighty power—the Roman Empire." And thus the birth of Christianity as the survival technique for the disinherited minority, as the great defense against fear, which Thurman described as the "lean, hungry hound of hell that rarely ever leaves the track of the dispossessed."

The plight of the dispossessed, Thurman said, was to be left without political or economic status as a "fundamental *fact* of psychology." The role of religion for the dispossessed was to "establish for the individual a transcending basis of security which locates its center in the very nature of life." To put it more simply, "it assures the individual that he is a child of God." Religion also demanded clarity and transparency, something difficult for the weak, who had learned to depend on deception for survival. This was particularly true for black Americans, for whom "self-deception has been developed into an intricate subtle defense mechanism." Religion, though, brought to the forefront the virtue of sincerity, which "inspires the individual to become increasingly aware of, and sensitive to, the far-reaching significance of many of his simplest deeds, making it possible for him to act, in time, as though his deeds were of the very essence of the eternal." Part of that involved absorbing violence with an exercise of love. The admonition of love too often had been perverted to serve the purposes of the powerful, but in reality, it meant accepting the "inherent worth" of others: "It says, meet people where they are and treat them as if they were where they ought to be." It allowed the underprivileged to "meet the enemy upon the highway; to embrace him as himself, understanding his limitations and using to the limit such discipline upon him as he has discovered to be helpful in releasing and purifying his own spirit." Jesus, the emblematic underprivileged man, the man without citizenship or status, "speaks his words of power and redemption across the ages to all the disinherited."

In the summer of 1935, as the time for his voyage to India neared, Thurman corresponded with numerous people, seeking their advice for his trip. In this correspondence one sees how Gandhian thought already had begun to influence African Americans. In a letter from J. G. St. Clair Drake in August 1935, Thurman learned of a group that had been looking at pacificism, non-violence, and social change and sought to bring a "group of Negroes together for discussion and study of non-violent coercion as used in the Satyagraha movement and the philosophy of non-violence. This group would attempt to relate the philosophy to our American Negro-white relations." Drake sought Thurman's advice for this group in Philadelphia before Thurman's trip, and hoped to bring Thurman there the summer after he returned. Thurman thereafter maintained a relationship of several years with nonviolent activists and interracial worship communions in Philadelphia. That experience prepared him for his coming "great adventure" in San Francisco. Drake would soon be part of a generation of African Americans alive to the idea of bringing Gandhian ideas to the United States.

Just before he left, Thurman wrote a letter of appreciation to his high school principal, Nathan W. Collier, then president of Florida Normal and Industrial College in Saint Augustine (previously Florida Baptist Academy in Jacksonville, when Thurman attended there). "I count my four years at the Academy as the four most significant years in my academic career," he wrote to Collier; he had received a "much more cultural and much more thorough" training even than in college. And now he would be putting it to use on the largest international stage, setting sail on September 21 as guests of the Indian Student Movement; he was to "interpret the significance of the religion of Jesus as over against Christianity in the life of people who have their backs against the wall and in the light of the background of the social struggle in American life." Thurman's whole life had prepared him for this task.

At this time, black Americans already had established a relationship with India, and with Gandhi. Through Thurman's voyage there in 1935–1936, that relationship would be strengthened immeasurably. Gandhi and news of the nonviolent resistance to imperialism had appeared in the pages of the *Crisis*, the newsmagazine of the NAACP, then edited by W. E. B. Du Bois. Mordecai Johnson in 1930 had urged Howard students to study Gandhi's example carefully and had pointed to Indian nonviolent movements as an example that black Americans could follow. The black Americans Julie Derricotte and Frank Kelly had traveled there in the late 1920s, cultivating relationships with Indian students. Kelly Miller, Thurman's colleague at Howard, explained, in "Passive Resistance of Gandhi" (published in the *New York Amsterdam News*, an African American newspaper, in 1930), the connection of the Indian leader to the teachings of Jesus and to the situations of African Americans. Articles in the *Baltimore Afro-American*, the *Norfolk Journal and Guide*, the *Chicago Defender*, and other venues furthered the connection. Once the Negro delegation who traveled in 1935 had been constituted, their forthcoming trip drew considerable notice in the black press. In short, Howard and Sue Bailey Thurman's encounter with India came at a propitious moment, a time when black America was hungry for a message of inspiration for a struggle emanating from dispossessed communities living under oppressive regimes. Thurman traveled in the midst of a rich ongoing discussion of, and excitement about, the subject.

THURMAN AND THE NEGRO DELEGATION

The turning point of Thurman's life, and the key to much of his later influence, came in 1935–1936. During a six-month period from September 1935 to March 1936, he traveled with his wife, Sue Bailey Thurman, as part of the "Negro delegation" of the American Christian Student Movement. His preparation for the trip was extensive, and it was preceded for some years with exchanges between India and America.

Thurman involved himself with, but also was ambivalent about, the Student Christian Movement (SCM), which he had considered too willing to tolerate segregation and mouth pious platitudes. But it was through the SCM that he arrived at this crucial moment. The main impetus came from the Reverend Augustine Ralla Ram, executive secretary of the Student Christian Movement of India, Burma, and Ceylon. Ram had met Thurman at Spelman in 1931. In his trip to the United States, Ram had noted the parallelisms between the de facto caste system for Negroes and the one in India. And Ram and others in the international wings of the Christian Student Movement had moved that organization into a critique of the relationship between traditional missionary work and colonialism. Ram was a second-generation Christian, vice president starting in 1932 of the World Christian Student Federation, and committed nationalist. He had once told an audience at Spelman College in Atlanta that "Gandhi's outlook is like that of Christ, many think of him as second corporate Christ, the living spirit of Christianity." The SCM in India wanted members of the Negro delegation to combine a "philosophical, mystical approach of personal religion" with a "practical and ethically compelling demand for social justice."

Ralla Ram was keen to host black Americans who could express a universalist vision of Christianity, apart from its connection in the mind of young Indians simply with Western imperialism. "They all think that Christianity is part and parcel of a western cult," he wrote to Frank T. Wilson, one of the delegation's organizers and a longtime friend of Thurman and colleague in work with the YMCA and the Christian Student Movement in America. He hoped the delegation could show that "Christianity is universal in its sweep," and that members of the delegation, who had suffered at the hands of whites, could bear witness to the meaning of Christ even amidst that suffering. He suggested also that political questions could be discussed, but in smaller groups and out of the earshot of journalists who might broadcast such discussions and poison relations with the British government. But Ram felt much confidence that the "mission from America will do this country an immense amount of good in not only dramatizing the wide sweep of the Christian faith, but will also be a great adventure in healthy internationalism."

Initially, Thurman was reluctant to participate, and along the way once withdrew his consent to participate due to his fury at how the other participants were selected (more on which later). Matters were no easier, given that the Thurmans had two young children (Olive and Anne Spencer). As well, Thurman still carried a large debt from paying for Katie's health care during her declining years, and Mordecai Johnson had made it clear that Thurman's absence would have to be voluntary and unpaid. Thurman eventually financed his year, in fact, by taking out a loan against a life insurance policy. The debt he carried from that was a heavy weight for years afterward.

But more important (as always with Thurman) than the practical considerations were the philosophical ones. Thurman rejected any idea that he would be defending indefensible practices in American Christianity. And he certainly had no desire to be a missionary or proselytizer. Thurman complained, often with unusually blunt and harsh words, whenever he sensed he was being put in a position of serving as the shining icon of some American evangelical missionary project. Fears about just that very thing almost persuaded him to call off the trip entirely, and in India itself he resented it even when Indian Christians expected him to perform that role. When American and British missionaries peddled the standard evangelical line, it only worsened the situation. In April of 1936, for example, Thurman wrote to Mary Jenness, the author of *Twelve Negro Americans*. He was to be featured in the volume but wrote objecting to how, as he put it, "in writing up the material which was at your disposal it has been necessary to give to it a propagandistic flare," with that material used to "make a case for a particular theory of missions." Thurman added, "I find it impossible to entertain the idea of having my life considered as the product of any particular enterprise however good and noble it may be. For such a picture makes the complex life of the Negro too simple." Thurman's words here recall one of the central ideas of Ralph Ellison's novel *Invisible Man*, published about fifteen years later; like Ellison, Thurman hated the idea of being turned into a symbol, a projection of the ideas of others about the nature of "the Negro" as a character in American life. Thurman also had extensive discussion with organizers of the journey, including Winnifred Wygal, until finally he was persuaded that the pilgrimage "fell within the range of my own life and purposes."

As plans progressed for the delegation, Thurman worked hard to educate himself on India. He solicited a wide range of views from black Americans to transmit. Before then, as well, Thurman had been corresponding with friends and associates of Gandhi, including Madeline Slade, an English follower who had spoken at Howard University, and Muriel Lester, the British pacifist who was in close touch with Gandhi and suggested that he meet with the black delegation when they were in India. In September, Thurman wrote to Gandhi that he was "exceedingly anxious to spend some time visiting you in your Ashram if this is convenient for you," and asked him to correspond with A. Ralla Ram of the Student Christian Movement. Some weeks later, Gandhi responded by inviting them to visit, assuring them that if the "western amenities" of life could not be provided, "we will be making up for the deficiency by the natural warmth of our affection." Thurman persuaded Lester to speak at Howard University in 1934, and traveled cross-country to meet with the English pacifist. He wrote to Henry Burke Robins, one of his former seminary professors from Rochester, asking his advice and summarizing his preparations: "During this winter the group is making a careful study of: First, comparative religion; second historical Christianity; Protestantism in America, primarily with reference to minorities in America; the relationship between Christianity and capitalism; the life, career, and teachings of Jesus; finally, the history of the British and the Indian."

Most important of all, he had been "making a study of religion of the under-privileged," the most "searching" question Christianity would face and the question he confronted on his journey. Robins responded by acknowledging Thurman's most fundamental point: "by and large, religion down to date, has been administered and even formulated by privileged classes in the various cultures." He continued that "when we put the acknowledged principle over against the prevailing practice, our western religious life stands condemned." And thus the Christianity of the privileged had little to offer to the underprivileged except empty words about being "content with the lot into which they are born." But the actual Christianity of Jesus went straight to the original principles of fraternity and brotherhood, and Robins felt that "by and large the Christian missions, around the world, have gone to the underprivileged."

Thurman also arranged to have Sue spend about ten weeks in Mexico, to give her experience in the kind of trip she would later make to India. She prepared to be, in effect, a cultural ambassador. The lengthy and cumbersome process required to get a tourist permit for Sue, and the possibility that the Thurmans would have to post a bond to the Mexican government (part of a discriminatory immigration policy enforced by Mexican authorities against black travelers), required considerable diplomatic correspondence and eventually a talk with the Mexican embassy before being resolved. Sue made her way without suffering the embarrassment of other black American visitors.

As Thurman explained it to another correspondent, he was not going as a member of the delegation in any sense to represent "American Christianity," in which he had no confidence; rather, as an underprivileged man, he was "interested in religion from the point of view of the needs of underprivileged peoples." Starting with that perspective, he had discovered that Christianity was "not a world religion, but a technique of survival for an underprivileged minority. The technique that it worked out was so fundamental that it became the basis of a world redeeming faith. In America it had its greatest opportunity since its beginning, because here it started on the ground floor with one of the most audacious political experiments in the history of the world."

Before traveling to India, Thurman had written to a Boston physician and Unitarian activist on racial issues named Richard Cabot, expressing his desire to see a program that would send black students abroad. Thurman presented the advantages of sending a "young, socially-minded, sympathetic, intelligent Negro" who could make a "profound contribution in the interest of justice and cooperation between the races in America." Such a person, with proper training and experience with diverse groups abroad, could publicize at home what he had learned abroad about techniques of struggle for equality and bring a greater sense of the international dimension of the Afro-American struggle. The pilgrim could also advise colleges on how to make greater and more effective use of people from other cultures who were already in residence here. And finally, that person could warn black Americans traveling abroad how to deal with discriminatory laws in other countries, and at the same time put black scholars in "direct cultural relationships with scholars all over the world." Thurman already was acutely aware of the problems faced by black Americans on cross-ocean voyages that were de facto segregated, with blacks relegated to third class. Shortly thereafter, Thurman warned that "The testimony of some white person as to how he was treated crossing the Atlantic means absolutely nothing. He can only know the other side if he happens to be a Negro traveling without connections."

But the theme most evident in Thurman's correspondence was the composition of the delegation: Who would be with the Thurmans on this critical journey? The group organizing the trip, representing the SCM, considered a variety of candidates and asked Thurman's opinion on several of them; Thurman gave a decidedly negative view of a few and said one person "would have no definite contribution to make." By contrast, Thurman endorsed Marian Minus, a recent graduate of Fisk University and covaledictorian of her class together with the future great African American historian John Hope Franklin. But the India Committee wanted someone with explicitly Christian convictions and was concerned with Minus's apparently heterodox views. Minus wrote to Elizabeth Harrington, of the India Committee, that she was interested in all forms of human behavior as related to Jesus and did not lean toward any one organizational form of religion as the "only [medium] of religious expression and opinion." (Minus ended up with a career in black left-wing political organizing.) Perhaps a larger problem was her relative lack of involvement in the national student movement more generally. In any case, some combination of the two left her off the final list of the Pilgrimage of Friendship.

A few months before departure, Phenola Carroll, wife of the Reverend Edward G. Carroll, then pastor of John Wesley Methodist Church in Salem, Virginia, received the nod as the fourth member of the delegation. Howard Thurman was furious at what he perceived to be broken faith, and Sue Bailey Thurman resigned from the delegation (Thurman considered doing the same). Thurman wrote in fury to Harrington that he had not been consulted on the decision, and while he felt Phenola Carroll was a "lovely" person, she was not nearly as qualified as others being considered (especially Thurman's personal choice, Minus). Phenola would be, he felt, coming along as the wife of Edward, without much of a contribution to make on her own and certainly without the sense of those "who hold the venture to be of a two-fold sacredness to the millions of Negroes in America, to American students in general and to the advanced guard in the Student Movement whose vision has led us all to make such an undertaking at tremendous sacrifice." That sacrifice, for Thurman, included taking a year of absence without pay from Howard, something that nearly crushed him financially. But Phenola's selection came just three months before the voyage and could not be reversed. Thurman soon found that she had talent in "dramatics," and he put her to work reading black-authored poems and giving talks on cultural topics.

The delegation of four black Americans, Thurman's sister Madaline, and Thurman's two girls set sail on September 21, 1935; they were compelled to accept third-class accommodations on the cross-Atlantic voyage. After leaving Madaline and the girls in Geneva, Switzerland, they continued on to Colombo, Ceylon (present-day Sri Lanka), arriving on October 21, 1935. The fact that the group obtained visas without much problem was a surprise, given the initial reaction of a colonial bureaucrat to the request: "If an American educated Negro just traveled through the country as a tourist, his presence would create many difficulties for our rule—now you are asking us to let four of them travel all over the country and make speeches!"

From there, after a brusque introduction with a colonial officer upon landing, for the next 140 days the group traveled virtually without stopping (with local authorities monitoring them, possibly reading their mail, and periodically quizzing them on trains as to their plans). Thurman took charge of scheduling, financing, and keeping the group records. What struck him immediately was the experience of living in an overwhelmingly nonwhite world: "The dominant complexions all around us were shades of brown, from light to very dark; and more striking to me even [than] this were the many unmistakable signs that this was *their* country, their land. The Britishers, despite their authority, were outsiders. I had never had an experience like this." That being said, signs of that British authority were everywhere, and after more than one encounter with it, Thurman could only be reminded of the infantilization of black people in the United States.

Howard and Sue ("Mrs. Thurman," as he always called her in public) traveled extensively, fought off various illnesses, struggled at times with the spiciness of Indian cuisine, and sought out audiences with prominent Indian thinkers and writers, including Rabindranath Tagore (with whom he did not really connect well, one of the disappointments of the trip) and Mahatma Gandhi (with whom he did). He did not defend indefensible practices in American Christianity. Further, he sought to distance himself as far as possible from those who would place the delegation of four in an evangelical context. He fought against the idea that the group would be seen as "the spearhead of some kind of evangelistic movement from the West," something worsened by the fact that Stanley Jones, a well-known American missionary in India, had publicized it as such. Further, Thurman and others in the planning process feared being put "on exhibition either as singers or anthropological specimens"; the Indian sponsors had to be told that "sending a good tenor or bass to India was no concern of ours." Still, for all these precautions, Thurman discovered that some of his audiences expected more explicitly evangelical addresses, and complained when they didn't get them.

After arriving in Ceylon in late October, the group set out on an epic and exhausting journey, visiting fifty-three cities. They gave more than 260 lectures and informal talks. Beyond that, there were countless smaller group interviews, discussions, and chats over tea. Howard Thurman himself gave no fewer than 135 addresses, the most by far of the group. The group traveled the entirety of India, moving from Colombo in Ceylon northward to Madras, then to Calcutta, and from there inland in the northern part of India to Agra and eventually to the Khyber Pass, in present-day Pakistan, bordering

Afghanistan. Then they traveled back inland to Delhi, southward to Nagpur in the middle of the country, west to Bombay, and eventually terminating back in Ceylon. The group also explored parts of Burma, including Rangoon. Thurman gave some radio addresses while in country (he later loved giving radio addresses on WBUR in Boston), and the group sang spirituals (led by Sue, who was talented musically in a way Howard was not) while being filmed. By previous agreement, Thurman avoided explicitly political questions in his public talks (seeking to avoid trouble with the British authorities), but he never hesitated to address questions of race and politics in America, giving talks such as "American Negro Political Questions" and "Education of the Negro in America."

Thurman spoke to Indians of various religious backgrounds and persuasions, including those who saw him specifically as carrying a traditionally Christian message of the meaning of Jesus's life, and those who understood him to be carrying a political message of the unity of colored peoples around the globe. Everyone probed him, or challenged him very directly, on the question of race in America. One Indian journalist in Madras wrote of Thurman's talk "The Faith of the American Negro," that the audience felt a "thrill" because they recognized "the articulation of their own deepest and unexpressed feelings." They could see and feel their "linking up with another race as the lecturer proceeded with his interpretation of his people, defending them against false judgment, proclaiming the grit and character that was evolved under great stress. . . . It was no cold intellectual presentation of the incidents of a complex social history, but the soulful expression of the faith of the meek that rose conqueror over trials and suffering."

The group also faced delicate decisions about when and how to present Negro spirituals to Indian audiences that were eager to hear them but unaware of the contexts in which these songs had been appropriated in America, much less of the ugly minstrel traditions of the United States. They performed the spirituals to multiple audiences, featuring the excellent singing voice and artistic talents of Sue, but Howard made sure to accompany the performances with lectures that formed the corpus of what later become his books on the subject. As one missionary wrote to a delegation organizer, "Burmese Christians love to sing these spirituals because they express to them Christianity more congenial than Western music does."

Despite his initial reluctance, Howard came to accept this as part of their intercultural work.

The schedule of the group while in Madras during the first week of December 1935 gives one an idea of the nature of the visits. Edward Carroll delivered addresses to a high school and to the Madras Christian College Union, and another (with Phenola) to a Methodist church on "Negro's church." He also preached at a Baptist church and gave a devotional. Phenola Carroll read poetry and gave interpretations of the work to a group at Women's Christian College. Sue Bailey Thurman spoke on the "Negro in American civilization," part of her interest in African American history more generally (a topic that became one of the primary labors of her life). Meanwhile, Howard Thurman spoke on numerous occasions, on topics ranging from the Negro spiritual to Negro education, and gave general speeches titled "What Shall I Do with My Life?" and "Faith of the American Negro."

We have a brief account, from Thurman himself, of his experiences upon arrival and the first days in Ceylon, where he had his important encounter with a young barrister who challenged his being a representative of a Christianity that was so tied into white supremacy in America. After he had arrived and got settled, newspaper reporters came to interview him, although already he had been "tipped off by an Indian to go easy on the interviewers and do not say anything to offend the white man lest our journey be cut off before it started." The reporters asked about black American life and the usual list of celebrities. "True to the mentality of the white world," Thurman sighed, they mentioned only Booker T. Washington and George Washington Carver.

Thurman compiled notes on his meetings with reporters, church members, and government officials. One surprise was a worship service led by a student that seemed to be Pentecostal in nature. "He was Pentecostal in his emphasis and said that the second coming of [Christ] was universal because we had come in fulfillment of the word, thus before the end of time the gospel would be preached to all people." For Thurman, such an evangelical emphasis was a "wretched disappointment and I saw trouble ahead if there were many like him ahead." Thurman appreciated his sincerity, "but it was all so sad because he had been completely duped," presumably by the missionary that Thurman distrusted, Stanley Jones, who had given the students his "insights." On another occasion, a correspondent from Judson College in Rangoon, Burma, specifically requested that the Negro delegation sing spirituals (even though he had been informed that they did not want to) because "our people here have been greatly helped by the Spirituals and have been using them in our evangelistic campaigns. We realize that we cannot do justice to the deep religious experience which they express for we cannot enter into the soul of your people. Therefore, we are most anxious to hear them (sung) by the people to whom they are the natural expression of their religious experience." That sort of response simply made Thurman cringe, even though, in his meeting with Gandhi, he submitted to the Mahatma's request.

There were two key moments during Thurman's trip, by his account. While in Ceylon, a lawyer peppered him with questions concerning the racial hypocrisies of American Christianity, and whether other religions (particularly Islam) would better express the aspirations of black Americans. His journal presents the shortest account. Later he elaborated on it at greater length, repeating it again late in his life in his autobiography. Here is the account from the journal, perhaps the freshest and most immediate rendering, without some of the elaborations that came later:

What are you doing here? This is what I mean—Africans were taken to America as slaves, by Xns—they were sold in America to other Xns—they were held in slavery for 300 years by Xns—They were freed as a result of economic forces rather than Xn idealism . . . and I understand that you are lynched in America by Xns. In the light of all this, I think that for a young intelligent Negro such as you to be over here in the interest of a Xn enterprise is for you to be a traitor to all the darker peoples of the earth. Such I consider you to be. Will you please account for yourself and your very unfortunate situation?

Thurman responded that he had not come as some kind of museum exhibit of the Christian faith, nor was he there to

bolster up a declining or disgraced Xn faith in your midst. I do not come to make converts of Xny nor do I come as exhibit A as to what Xnity has done for me & my people. I am a Christian because I think that the religion

of Jesus in its true genius offers me very many ways out of the world's dis-
orders. But I make a careful distinction between Xnity and the religion of
Jesus. . . . I am dead against most of the institutional religion with which
I am acquainted. I belong to a small minority of Xns who believe that society has to be completely reorganized in a very definite egalitarian sense
if life is to be made livable for the most of mankind.

A few years after the India journey, in writing his final report, Thurman
fleshed out the story a bit more. His interlocutor challenged him to explain
what he was doing in India representing Christianity, a religion so burdened
with a history of white supremacy in the West. In the name of Christianity,
slavers stole humans from Africa. And then "you were sold in America to
other Christians. You were held in slavery three hundred years by Christians." Abraham Lincoln then freed the slaves, a result not of Christian belief
but of "certain political, economic, and social forces, the full significance
of which he himself did not quite understand." And then, even worse, "for
seventy years you have been lynched and burned and discriminated against
by Christians," with the so-called Christians even interrupting their services
to join lynch mobs. The barrister, while he did not want to seem rude, nonetheless had to state the point directly: "in my opinion you are a traitor to all
the darker peoples of the earth and I wonder what you, an intelligent man,
would have to say for yourself." Thurman understood his challenge and knew
it would come from the audiences he talked with in India. It was a test of
what really was his true faith: "Believing as I do that the Christian religion
has a fundamental significance for the underprivileged and the disinherited,
that has been my approach to the whole study of the history of the faith."

For Thurman, the key question remained why the church was "so powerless before the color bar? . . . From a 10,000-mile perspective, this monumental betrayal of the Christian ethic loomed large and forbidding." Much
of the rest of Thurman's life was in effect an attempt to answer the challenge
presented to him there.

Later Thurman traveled along the Khyber Pass. While looking into
Afghanistan, where trains of camels were bringing goods along the road-
ways used by ancient conquerors, he said, "All that we had seen and felt
in Indian seemed to be brought miraculously into focus. We saw clearly
what we must do somehow when we returned to America. We knew that

we must test whether a religious fellowship could be developed in America that was capable of cutting across all racial barriers, with a carry-over into the common life, a fellowship that would alter the behavior patterns of those involved. It became imperative now to find out if experiences of spiritual unity among people could be more compelling than the experiences which divided them."

Sue later remembered him telling her at the time, "I know what I have to do when I get back to America. I've got to try to make an assault on this segregated church in America." The word "assault" here is probably Sue's paraphrasing—it doesn't sound like a word Howard would have selected—but the idea remains the same. Thurman's memory of his epiphany later led him to a major experiment in Christian interracialism. Typically for Thurman's life and experiences, it was an encounter with nature that gave him insight into his own life and formed his own plans and philosophies. The nature mystic remained just that during the arduous travels through the South Asian continent.

Also during the trip he met with Kshiti Mohan Sen, a scholar of Sanskrit. They spent a morning, as Thurman put it, "sparring for position—you from behind your Hindu breastwork, and I from behind my Christian embattlement." Calling it a "watershed experience of my life," he perceived the two of them fusing religious souls. Thurman saw in him what he saw in the Quaker mystic Rufus Jones: the purest form of religion, a simple and direct communication with God. Sen's Hinduism, exemplified in lives of the humble, had much in common with Thurman's religion of an outcast, downtrodden, and politically marginalized Jesus. Thurman's Jesus became an honorary Hindu. From that point forward, Christianity remained Thurman's starting point but not his destination. He was more interested in a search for fundamental unities in human life and religions.

Thurman also found his initial days in Colombo depressing, ironically because much of the social structure there reminded him of home. The colored classes and servants referred to as "boys" performed manual labor and were constantly demeaned. "We were thrown into the arms of a people expecting us to be evangelical, to win souls. . . . We did not see much of the students. Stanley Jones had prepared the way for us and what a preparation—we were to be singing soul-saving evangelists full of the grace of God."

At least, he mused, they had spread some knowledge of the life of blacks in the United States and dispelled "suspicions in the minds of the native people that we were here to fit into the schemes of Western Civilization of which Xnity is a part."

Thurman preached his most popular address, "The Faith of the American Negro," several times during the journey, at times preceded by Sue singing "We Are Climbing Jacob's Ladder." No exact manuscript of the talk survives, but several newspaper accounts of it do. In one of them, Thurman suggests how people in India might well imagine "how difficult it was to plant in the minds of Negroes the free ways of thinking and feeling and looking at their lives as endowed with responsibility and to make them think that they had their own destiny to fulfill in the life of the country." In another account, of an address delivered in Bombay in February 1936, Thurman explained how black Americans after emancipation had to develop a "constructive outlook—a way of thought in new relationship," in order to relieve the "feelings of insecurity and inferiority caused by the system of slavery." Education had been a key part of providing that. Further, Thurman explained that the faith of the Negro was balanced by a kind of "elemental laughter. Rumour and propaganda had made the America Negro the greatest clown of all, but there was something much deeper, and that was the laughter in the heart of the group life. It was the laughter of the strong man who struggled out of defeat to struggle again."

Everywhere they traveled, Thurman later wrote, crowds gathered to hear them (and, much to his embarrassment, they had to take up collections to help finance their trip, as the travel funds provided by the committee beforehand were not sufficient). They were expected to speak to a full range of issues, sometimes to things that stretched their knowledge base and preparation. Particular audiences were keen to hear about "rethinking the whole problem of National education in India." The varied responses Thurman and the delegation received ranged from the challenge issued by the lawyer in Colombo to the evangelical enthusiasm of some Indian students and others in attendance. The latter dismayed Thurman; this was exactly the opposite of what he wanted to accomplish. One English woman in attendance, who remembered seeing the Fisk Jubilee Singers when they were in Calcutta when she was a girl, said to Thurman, "It came over me that you are a proof to the non-believing world that Jesus is alive and divine, and that yours is a unique opportunity to witness to the worth of Jesus Christ as you and your companions address our non-Christian brothers and sisters; for in spite of wrong interpretations of His Gospel, the all powerful influence of His personality has finally triumphed." She hoped they would see the value of the Christian environment in America "as against almost 2000 years of heathen surroundings in India." On the other hand, an attendee at one of Thurman's lectures and leader of the Dhamric Hindu Mission in Madras told Thurman that God had given every race a "peculiar and distinctive instinct of self-preservation materially and self-elevation spiritually . . . towards the attainment of . . . God-Realization and self-emancipation." And thus, what he really wanted from Thurman was a talk on the "traits of a pure and original non-Christian negro," what was the "instinctive religion of the Negro, American or African, uninterrupted and untainted by the Christian missionary encroachments." Thurman struggled to present a realistic portrayal of "the Negro," given how audiences came to his addresses with such varied but equally stilted stereotypes and preconceptions.

Another kind of response (one that particularly irritated Thurman, who knew white paternalism when he saw it) came from Henry W. Luce, a longtime missionary in China and later in India, and father to Henry R. Luce, the American publisher who founded the *Time* and *Life* magazine empire. Writing from Lahore, Luce said he had heard Thurman speak at a YMCA on the faith of the American Negro. Luce presented himself as an "ardent internationalist and inter-racialist" who, from his boyhood, had (together with millions of whites in the country) been "interested in doing all I could to assist your group to attain the highest possible best." Luce left the address with the feeling, shared, he believed, by some others, that Thurman had given the impression that "the Negro race in America had suffered all it has suffered at the hand of the American whites—that they had not lifted a finger to help, and that your people, so far as they had gone, and attained all by their own inherent power." It was not what Thurman had said, exactly, but more in what he had "omitted." Even worse, Luce alleged, Thurman had omitted how many black Americans had received white philanthropic dollars to aid their education; that Muslims were really the culprits in the slave trade; and that few Africans had risen to the level of black Americans. Luce wrote, he said, "with all good will, solely to suggest as an older man to a younger, that your work . . . would be more vital and creative if it touched upon the emphasis which I seem to miss." Once again, Thurman had hit a sore spot with a white sympathizer, simply by pointing out, even if indirectly and allusively, the long-lived economic and psychological effects of white supremacy. And not for the first time in his life, an older white adviser had tried to corral the younger Thurman. Unfortunately, no record exists of Thurman's reply. Surely, he must have seethed as he read it.

On the other hand, many in the audiences simply recognized the parallels between black Americans and Indians under British colonial government. One head of a Christian school, writing to the delegation in November of 1935, noted that he had followed the plans of the group since before their arrival and had long followed black American publications and the exploits of leaders such as Booker T. Washington. "I have the great heart and head sympathy for you Brethren & Sisters," he explained, "for the treatment accorded to you in U. S. A. particularly in Alabama, Florida, South Carolina, [Georgia], at the [egregious] imperialistic animals of the white Americans. Your economic exploitation, political disfranchisement, Educational inequalities, lynching etc are a sheer mockery to the brute force of the White race." He continued, "You are well qualified to speak to the Indian situation, because of the comparable position to which you are subjected in your own country. Like the Indians you are concerned with the liberation of your people. White Americans on the other hand was just one more example of patronizing [oppressors] preaching love."

Thurman assimilated all he experienced and drew from it lessons that guided the rest of his life. He felt keenly too the absence of any black American student on the delegation. The Indian students complained that "there is no one in the delegation who can see life at their level and hobnob with them in their hostels and dormitories as fellow undergraduates." Students had no real chance to take leadership roles, as even student organizations often were led by the president of a college or someone similar. For that reason, Thurman sought to organize exchange programs to bring Indian students to the United States and also to exchange professors.

Finally, at the end of the trip, in February 1936, the Negro delegation conversed with Gandhi for three hours. Arguably, the conversation changed the course of American race relations from that time forward. "Never in my life have I been a part of that kind of examination," Thurman later reflected on the visit, with "persistent, pragmatic questions about American Negroes, about the course of slavery, and how we survived it."

As reported by Mahadev Desai for the *Harijan*, Gandhi's own publication, Gandhi came to his meeting with the delegation with much curiosity about black American life and asked Thurman questions, which Thurman answered with "the cautious and dispassionate detachment characteristic of a professor of philosophy." Thurman mentioned the different philosophies represented by Booker T. Washington and W. E. B. Du Bois, and mentioned Du Bois's new work *Black Reconstruction* (a book that, although ignored at the time, revolutionized the study of Reconstruction after the Civil War). Thurman gave a then-prevalent view of the history of the South since the war, how poor whites who "smarted under the competition of the Negro" had come to be in control. Turning the tables, Thurman asked Gandhi a series of questions, beginning with whether black South Africans had participated in his movement. No, they had not, Gandhi replied, because "it would have endangered their cause," nor could they have "understood the technique of our struggle nor could they have seen the purpose or utility of non-violence."

Much of the conversation hinged on the meaning of the word "nonviolence," originally *ahimsa* in Sanskrit. Gandhi explained how the word did not come across fully in English, with the negative "non-" at the beginning. In reality, nonviolence was a metaphysical force, a truth that underlay the seemingly endless violence of human life. Always given to a love for the mystical, Thurman was fascinated. Thurman asked Gandhi if nonviolence was a "form of direction," to which he replied that it was "not just one form, but the only one." Because it was not possible to be "passively non-violent," it necessarily required action. Rather than a negative force, it was a "force which is more positive than electricity and more powerful than even ether. At the centre of non-violence is a force which is self-acting"; it was a "force superior to all the forces put together. One person who can express Ahimsa in life exercises a force superior to all the forces of brutality." Indeed, Gandhi could have used the word "love," but since it contained so many other connotations in English, he had to search for a word with the negative particle.

For Gandhi, one true exponent of *ahimsa* could turn back the exploitation of his whole people, and if that person could not, then he had not yet expressed *ahimsa* "in its fulness," for it was the "only true force in life."

How then, Thurman wondered, could individuals or entire communities be trained in such a difficult concept as had not yet even been realized within a single person? It could take several lifetimes, Gandhi replied, but it was the "only permanent thing in life," the only thing that counted. For truly, "The Kingdom of Heaven is Ahimsa." Sue challenged him about how she was to act "supposing my own brother was lynched before my very eyes." For Gandhi, the answer was a metaphorical self-immolation, a refusal to participate in any way with the lynching community, even to the point of refusing to touch the food offered.

The delegation asked Gandhi to come to America, not for the whites, but because African Americans suffered under a problem that cried out for a solution. Gandhi demurred, saying he had to perfect himself and his movement in India before he could consider taking his message to others. The meeting ended with Sue singing "Were You There, When They Crucified My Lord?" and "We Are Climbing Jacob's Ladder," which, to the reporter, "gave expression to the deep-seated hope and aspiration in the breast of every oppressed community to climb higher and higher until the goal was won." Thurman told Gandhi that, when he looked through the annals of Negro spirituals, "striking things are brought to my mind which remind me of all that you have told us today." Gandhi bid them farewell, by this account, with his famous line: "If it comes true it may be through the Negroes that the unadulterated message of non-violence will be delivered to the world."

By Thurman's account, Gandhi ended the meeting by pointing out that the greatest enemy of Jesus in the United States was Christianity itself. Either version plausibly expresses Gandhian sentiment, but the former became the tagline in an account of the meeting published the following year. Leaders at the founding meeting of the Southern Christian Leadership Conference two decades later remembered it; they understood themselves to be carrying out Gandhian principles of social struggle. Both Thurman and Gandhi saw social change coming less from mass movements than "from a handful of persons who had realized the proper techniques for self-mastery and could, by their example, show others the way." Both believed that "without the quest for personal spiritual development, genuine social change becomes impossible."

In a more immediate sense, the pilgrimage of the Negro delegation had an impact both in forming Thurman's own personal conception of religion and in influencing black Americans' perceptions of the world. Thurman certainly was already a religious modernist, far away from the religious ideas of his upbringing, but his time in India (and his resistance to being "used" in any evangelical sense as a missionary) pushed him even further in the religious directions that he would take the rest of his life. Certainly his vision at Khyber Pass became one of the touchstones of his life, something he came back to spiritually and mentally very often in charting his own path. Further, Thurman's visit was soon followed by trips to India by his friends and colleagues Channing Tobias and Benjamin Mays, who traveled to India in 1937 also as part of the Student Christian movement. They also visited with Gandhi. Black students from various universities soon followed in their wake. Such personal contacts were no longer possible with the advent of World War II, but a link between the black American struggle for freedom and the Indian struggle for independence had been established. After World War II and during the early years of Indian independence, it would strengthen even further.

Like many on the pacifist Left, Thurman was not a proponent of a mass movement of nonviolent civil disobedience. Ironically, in this sense he also heeded the words of Gandhi, who felt that the masses were not yet ready, not schooled in the spiritual discipline necessary for such a movement. Instead, Gandhi and, later, Thurman looked to (in the words of scholar Walter Fluker) the "small bands of dedicated followers of nonviolent resistance who by the strength of their beliefs would be able to bend great historical forces to their will." If one source of the belief in the power of small-scale transformation came from the apostles and the call of discipleship, another was certainly Gandhi's ashrams.

Through Thurman, and through Mordecai Wyatt Johnson, Benjamin Mays, and others, ideas of pacifism and nonviolence were percolating through the Left. This included one Sunday school teacher in Indianola, Mississippi, who told the black scholar Hortense Powdermaker that Gandhi had the right idea and "has Christ in him. . . . It is through love that we will conquer." Few did more than Thurman to advance Gandhi's message. And so the American mantra became, "It may be through the Negroes that the unadulterated message of nonviolence will be delivered to the world." But for Thurman, this would be through small groups of dedicated activists, what he called "apostles of sensitiveness," rather than through a major mass national movement. But later, when the latter actually arose, he was delighted by its advent and threw his spiritual resources behind it.

THURMAN'S CONCLUDING REFLECTIONS

Thurman served as head of the India visit. Along the way he negotiated travel arrangements, kept the financial books, negotiated the speakers' schedules, and generally worked himself to a state of nervous exhaustion. His work was not done, though, until he filed his final report, which finally happened in 1938 when he sent in his reflections to the National Student Council of the YMCA. For years afterward, Thurman grappled with his complex set of responses to all he had seen and experienced on his journey through South Asia, his numerous talks, the intellectual and cultural challenges presented to him, his delight in being in a country overwhelmingly nonwhite, and his disgust for the everyday acts of imperialist violence that he had seen. The report is frank and, at points, sharp-tongued (by Thurman's standards, anyway). "I tried to be honest and objective, bearing in mind my obligation to my own religious convictions," he explained to the report's recipients.

Thurman began by reviewing why he was so reluctant to head the delegation in the first place—his unwillingness to represent American evangelicalism or to be seen as "the spearhead of some kind of evangelistic movement from the West." "Organized religion, for the most part, feels it necessary, so to make its peace with the powerful of the earth," he said, and thus tended to side with the strong against the weak. But once assured that he "would be completely free to make any interpretation of the meaning of the religion of Jesus Christ as I, myself, had discovered that meaning, my course was clear."

"India was great, inspiring, and depressing," he wrote to his friend Samuel Archer, the successor to John Hope as president of Morehouse College. Thurman himself was then under consideration for the presidency of Shaw University in North Carolina, an idea he flirted with for some time but eventually rejected (as he did all other offers to become a president or an administrator at an institution—the role just did not suit him). Similarly, later in writing to Max Yergan (at one time a YMCA activist, but by this time a communist and associate of Paul Robeson, before later defecting to anticommunist activism), he commented that "the only thing that I can say in passing is that I did not know what it was to wrestle with hate until my experience in that country [India]." He was not referring to any personal experience but rather to "the complete futility that is present in the mind when one sees what it is that Imperialism truly involves." Later, in writing to another correspondent about beginning a scholarship fund to foster student interchanges between black Americans and Indians, he explained that Indians had been so influenced by "anti-Negro propaganda that their minds were made up about us long before we appeared on the scene. Much of the propaganda was deliberate and thought out and has been going on over a long period of years." Thurman indicated that he and Sue could see that their presence had helped to shift views considerably, and thus a fund that would provide a means for other Negro students to spend some months in Indian institutions would serve as a continuous "flesh and blood answer to propaganda." And the influence would work both ways, as Negro students would gain an international perspective on their own struggles, and with an extended stay would "get even more first-hand insights than we were able to get and would be in a position to provide a great deal of inspiration to college students" upon their return.

Thurman struggled with the place of Christianity in India, because it was inevitable that the Christian missionary would be identified with the colonial ruler (regardless of the individual missionary's political sentiments). His faith inevitably was embedded in the culture of which he was a part, and thus the conversion of Indians meant wresting them out of their own culture. Indeed, the missionary's message was necessarily limited by his identity, race, or connections with the ruling class. Thurman saw many self-sacrificing missionaries, admirable in many respects, who were at the same time increasingly orthodox in their religious expressions. The comparatively rigid presentation of Christianity in India arose because "it cannot afford to countenance the political effects resulting from a very liberal interpretation of the social implications of the Christian message." But as a result, Thurman found few instances where the Indian Christian was accepted as a brother. Thurman noted how acutely aware he was of this, coming as he did from a culture where he had been "victimized by racial separateness and segregation within the Christian Church." Thurman concluded that it would not be possible to impart the true religion of Jesus within the existing institutional structure of Christianity, given the way the church was embedded in the vested interests of the world, in contrast to the life of Jesus of Nazareth, "who was a member of an underprivileged disinherited group in a Greco-Roman world." There were individual Christians in India who transcended their institutional contexts; they came not from any class in particular but were "part of an invisible kingdom for which the bleeding heart of a stricken world languishes, not only in India, but everywhere." They were part of the class of the "apostles of sensitiveness," the kind of spiritual elite that Thurman looked to as the ideal carriers of the true message of human brotherhood.

But the majority of Indian Christians remained dependent on Western expressions of Christianity, and money too. Being a Christian in a Hindu culture usually meant adopting Western clothes, singing Western hymns, and thinking of the Christian God "in terms of the ideology of the dominant controlling European of his country." And thus, the "economic dependence of the Indian Christian upon the West tends to rob him of independence of thought, and action based upon the dictations of his own heart and mind." Thurman was encouraged by the movement toward increasing independence among Indian Christian churches, but still felt the Indian Christian was "singularly a man who is half way between two worlds." The missionaries he encountered were earnest and generous as individuals but tended to be afflicted with a kind of love wrapped in condescension. The missionary faced an impossible task. He was to represent humility and servanthood in a land where he could have as many servants as he wanted; he came from the ruling class and strived to serve a Jesus "whose teachings cannot be compatible with much to which the missionary must give his approval in order to function"; and he was to "live without arrogance, even as he is called upon to uphold the dignity of the white man in that part of the world." Such a task could only be accomplished by the best, and such was not the character of the average missionary, Thurman implied.

Thurman concluded his report with a searching analysis of the differences between the caste system of India and the racial system of the United States, and in particular the place of "in-between" people, mulattoes in America and Anglo-Indians and Eurasians on the South Asian continent. But the basic difference, the one that gave Thurman hope for social movements in America, was that "the political ideal of America is in favor of practices that are democratic in genius and before which undemocratic practices such as discrimination can be condemned as antithetical and immoral." Such a democratic dogma was lacking in India. And because both whites and blacks claimed allegiance to Christian brotherhood, the actual existing social practices of America could be exposed to the "searching judgment of the most radical social teachings in existence." The United States certainly was not a Christian country in its practices, "but the ideal which is accepted provides the more underprivileged members of the society with a powerful weapon of defense," one not available to the underprivileged in India. Indeed, Christianity's great hope in India was a message of redemption for the untouchables, but it could never realize that potential as long as it remained "impotent in the presence of the color bar and in the presence of all kinds of racial and class distinctions in the West."

The visit to India fundamentally shaped Sue Bailey Thurman's ideas as well. Like African American male religious intellectuals, Sue saw that the black freedom struggle had to be tied into a larger international struggle, what the scholar Dennis C. Dickerson has referred to as "black women's internationalism." In speeches to black women's clubs and church groups, Sue deployed her deep historical understanding and her own pioneering work in African American women's history to connect struggles past and present, ranging from Harriet Tubman and Sojourner Truth in the nineteenth century to the present struggles of women of color at home and abroad. "We fight on all fronts," she said, to "establish ourselves in all parts of the world as people to be respected." Of Tubman, a particular hero of hers, she told one audience,

I think these days of Harriet Tubman, of whom I hope I am a descendant. She was so anxious for the future of America, that all men would find ease of mind here and opportunity to live that she gave her days and nights to the liberation of her fellow bondsmen that slavery would soon die and America become the first real democracy in the modern world. She worked without benefit of organization. She was a fierce voice that pierced the night. . . . And no DAR can claim a heritage greater than that she left every other American.

For Sue Thurman, it wasn't possible to function as individuals "until we see ourselves as part of a great whole, of whom the women were the beginning, and of whom we are the continuing line of succession." Her pioneering work in vitalizing the collecting of African American historical documents, and of pressing the case for the public presentation of African American history, grew directly from this philosophy.

Like her male counterparts, Sue Thurman insisted that Gandhian techniques and philosophy could be applied to the situation of black Americans, and that the oppression facing darker women around the globe knew no national boundaries. Sue Thurman fostered that connection through developing the Julie Derricotte Foundation, designed to place African American students in India and female Indian students in black colleges. Thurman had been Derricotte's friend when Julie made her journey to India in 1928 to attend a YWCA conference, and later became involved with the World Christian Student Federation prior to her tragic death in an auto accident in 1931 (one possibly caused by the need to drive her an extra distance to Chattanooga, Tennessee, to find a hospital to tend to her).

The journey of Howard and Sue Thurman and Edward and Phenola Carroll was not the first visit of African Americans to Indian independence leaders. But thanks to the national influence of Thurman and his ability to translate Gandhian ideas into an American idiom, this visit was a turning point. Two years later, in January 1937, Thurman's lifelong friends Benjamin Mays (who had taught him psychology at Morehouse and later served as president of Morehouse for many years) and Channing Tobias traveled to the YMCA world conference in Mysore. Before the conference, Mays spent two hours with Gandhi, exploring the meaning of nonviolent resistance and the possibility that nonviolence could be practiced on a mass scale. After returning home in March, Mays published a series of reflections, originally for the *Norfolk Journal and Guide* but soon widely republished, in which he explained that nonviolence came from the idea of *ahimsa*, and that it tied together ideas of Jesus, Tolstoy, and Hinduism. Mays concluded: "The Indians have learned what we have not learned. They have learned how to sacrifice for a principle. They have learned how to sacrifice position, prestige, economic security and even life itself for what they consider a righteous and respectable cause." For Mays, Gandhi had "given the Indian masses a new conception of courage. . . . To discipline people to face death, to die, to go to jail for the cause without fear and without resorting to violence is an achievement of the first magnitude. And when an oppressed race ceases to be afraid, it is free." Mays's companion on his journey, Tobias, added similar reflections in the *Chicago Defender*.

These travels in India and meetings with Gandhi, together with a growing sense of the international dimensions of racial oppression, took further hold in Thurman when the dean of the Howard School of Religion during the latter years of Thurman's term there, William Stuart Nelson, spent a year in India in 1947. There he witnessed, at Gandhi's side, the beginnings of the terrible events that led to the partition between India and Pakistan, as well as Gandhi's efforts to quell those disturbances. His wife, Blanche Wright Nelson, worked to further the objectives that Sue Bailey Thurman had pursued following her visit, to forge connections between black American women and women in India. Afterward, the Nelsons returned and lectured about Gandhi at numerous black educational institutions. In 1947, William Stuart Nelson compiled a group of essays published as *The Christian Way in Race Relations*, a symposium from the likes of Thurman, Mays, and other black religious intellectuals. The volume distilled the growing theological argument against segregation, including Thurman's understanding that "implicit in the Christian message is a profoundly revolutionary ethic," precisely because "the norms it establishes are in direct conflict with the relationship that obtains between men in the modern world." Segregation violated the spiritual relationships between men ordained by God, meaning it was a sin; and thus the struggle against segregation mandated moral means to a moral end.

Thurman and others blended the ideas of Gandhi with their own Christian conceptions within the American context. The question was really how (or whether) these ideas could be applied in America. A friend and correspondent to Thurman in late 1935, attending teaching sessions at the Quaker Pendle Hill community near Philadelphia with the theorist of nonviolence Richard Gregg, wondered how the gap could be bridged between two races, when their entire bases of social visions were so radically different: "When a whole community, for example, sanctions a lynching, how could nonviolent resistance change the image that those white people carry around in their minds about the Negro's 'place.'" Gregg had pointed to India as an example of how it could work, and Thurman was just then exploring those ideas in India, but to this correspondent, "the Indian against the English and the Negro against the American white man are distinct and different cases."

Thurman and others in the black intellectual world explored such difficult questions over the next two decades. Thurman used his classes and his pulpit at Howard to diffuse these ideas. Thurman and others spread their notions through the 1940s and 1950s. Eventually, that synthesis of ideas, joined to political organizing and grassroots mobilization, became fundamental to the most important social movement in twentieth-century American history.

3

The Affirmation Mystic in Action
Thurman's Philosophical Explorations, 1936–1944

You must live and proclaim a faith that will make men affirm
themselves and their fellowmen as children of God. You must lay
your lives on the altar of social change so that wherever you are
there the Kingdom of God is at hand.

—Howard Thurman, "Religion in a Time of Crisis"

Coming home from India, Howard Thurman was physically and mentally exhausted—and broke. Yet he also was infused with new visions for what would be required for racial transformation in American life. During and after his sojourn in India, Thurman came into his own as an intellectual, an idealist, and a renowned preacher. His experience there taught him that sacrificing everything for the right cause could be the key to finding one's meaning in life, that men and women were "under great obligation to find something in our world, some cause or purpose to which we may give ourselves in utter devotion." He urged young black people to accept his new visions for what would be required for racial transformation in American life. At North Carolina College for Negroes in 1942, he spoke of the gulf between democracy and the American way of life, and that blacks were acutely aware of "the loss of democratic principles of life. We must constantly be calling to these ideas," for blacks would be "largely responsible for the soul of America. We are called at this moment of crisis in our nation's history."

A reporter who interviewed Thurman in 1942 called him a "mystic with a practical turn of mind." He represented a "Christian likeness of many of the best qualities of Gandhi and Nehru," one of the few men "around whom a great, conscious movement of Negroes could be built," like the Indian one. But that was not Thurman's role. Thurman's primary influence always was that of a teacher, preacher, counselor, and mentor. And at no time was that influence greater than during his last eight years at Howard, when his intellectual powers took flight in sermon series, talks, addresses, and speeches throughout the country. In those years, he taught students and interacted with figures such as Pauli Murray and James Farmer, younger people who stood at the forefront of the civil rights struggle to come. They looked to Thurman for inspiration and guidance.

Sitting in his class at Howard in the late 1930s, where he was a divinity school student under Thurman's tutelage, James Farmer remembered Thurman's penetrating philosophical questions, queries that challenged students to think beyond becoming complicit in the American racial system of oppression. "We would leave the class with no answers," Farmer later reflected, "but many intriguing questions that had not occurred to us before. It was Thurman's belief that answers must come from within, from the bit of God in each of us."

Born to a family of Texas Methodists, Farmer grew up witnessing the scars of segregation around him and determined to do something when he could. Thurman loaned books on Gandhi to Farmer. Later, Thurman connected Farmer to Fellowship of Reconciliation. Farmer subsequently decided to veer away from a projected path of Methodist ministry and instead focus on destroying segregation. When his father queried him about it, Farmer replied that he would have "something to do with mass mobilization in the use of the Gandhi technique." For him, the key was mass nonviolent action, "not an individual witness to purity of conscience, as Thoreau used it, but a coordinated movement of mass noncooperation as with Gandhi. And civil disobedience when laws are involved. And jail where necessary. . . . Like Gandhi's army, it must be nonviolent. Guns would be suicidal for us. Yes, Gandhi has the key for me to unlock the door to the American dream."

With his training from Thurman and others, Farmer became one of the founding members of the Committee (later Congress) of Racial Equality (CORE) in Chicago in 1942. From its beginnings, Farmer later remembered, CORE determined that people, not experts or professionals, should lead the struggle for racial justice based on the principles of nonviolent direct action. CORE members pioneered the practices of nonviolent civil disobedience in the 1940s. They initially focused their efforts on segregated institutions in

Chicago, which garnered limited attention nationally but set a model for future use. The missing ingredient was the "mass" in "mass mobilization," something that could occur only with the active involvement of African American church people. The radical legacy of Thurman, Farmer, and CORE eventually found its way to the ministers and church communities in southern cities, who began organizing boycotts and crusades early in the 1950s. Later, Farmer and a group of others from CORE organized the Freedom Rides of 1961, when groups of integrated passengers boarded buses traveling through the Deep South, intending to test Supreme Court cases mandating segregation in interstate travel. The violence and bombings that met some of the travelers dramatized the brutality of segregation.

During his years at Howard following the sojourn in India, Thurman traveled tirelessly, preached constantly, lectured to myriad groups, and spread the gospel of nonviolence. He planted the seeds of what would become the gospel of nonviolent resistance. He worked out his ideas, expressed later in *Jesus and the Disinherited*, that Jesus spoke specifically to the oppressed in American society. Thurman had come to see that segregation was in effect a will to dominate, and that it could be defeated only through powerful forces of resistance. His goal, as historians Peter Eistenstadt and Quinton Dixie explain, was to "rip people from their complicity and complacency with evil. Only in this way would people in power relinquish 'their hold on their place.' It is not until something becomes movable in the situation that men are spiritually prepared to apply Christian idealism to un-ideal and unchristian situations." Full preparation to do nonviolent battle with Jim Crow, Thurman said, would require "great discipline of mind, emotions, and body to the end that forces may not be released that will do complete violence both to one's ideals and to one's purpose." Nonviolence was fundamental in both the means and the ends of the struggle for social justice.

Thurman himself embodied this quest for internal spiritual enrichment and external engagement with the world. He understood that making the church a social service organization would rob the church of the spiritual energies that made it what it was in the first place. He also understood that disconnecting the church from the world was heresy of a different sort. As always, his vision incorporated the internal and the external together. One must tend to the state of the soul and the state of the world together. In doing so, he universalized certain African American Christian traditions and blended them with theologies and ideas he had picked up from Gandhi, from Quakerism, from his natural propensity to see God in nature, and from poets and authors whose words he wove into his sermons. Thurman's synthesis of ideas reached its peak of expression in this era. Thurman felt called to broadcast his ideas, and his speaking fees supported the family. For Thurman, necessity was the mother of intellectual inspiration.

THURMAN AND BLACK EDUCATION

Thurman stood in special relation to the institutions of black higher education that he attended and worked for. His mentors and colleagues, and those in the administrations of academic institutions when he was younger, recognized his talent immediately. For years they attempted to recruit him as dean or president of numerous institutions, ranging from Florida Baptist Institute (where he had gone to high school) to Morehouse College. As well, churches pursued him for pastorates. But consistently, until the opportunity for his "great adventure" in San Francisco arose, he turned down opportunities and offers. Whatever his other flaws, Thurman knew his own strengths and weaknesses. His training was in religion, and his strength lay in preaching and mentoring. He had little interest in fund-raising and administrating. Prior to the appointment of Benjamin Mays as president of Morehouse in 1940, the outgoing president, Samuel H. Archer, for whom Thurman had a deep personal affection, tried mightily to recruit him to the post. Thurman replied, kindly but firmly, "I am not at all sure that such a thing would be in keeping with the will of God, for my own life." That was a no, in Thurman-speak.

Thurman also developed his tough critique of the nature of black educational institutions, joining colleagues in criticizing their tendency to reproduce the status quo. Thurman himself was about as good an example as can be imagined of the talented tenth that Du Bois had in mind when he critiqued Booker T. Washington and the rise of industrial/practical education as a primary focus of black institutions. Thurman had received a rigorous academic training starting in high school and continuing through his college and seminary days, and was a proud Morehouse man. But when speaking at Shaw University in Raleigh in 1938, he attacked the tendency of education simply to reproduce and "perpetuate the established order." Institutions did this for a good reason—they needed to survive, and could not do so outside the framework of what was required by state governments, philanthropic institutions, and wary whites. Black students in both the North and the South learned the same attitude white students did, but upon graduation, they soon discovered that they were still part of the disinherited class: "For this reason I have never seen an educated Negro who was not discouraged in a very definite sense. He stands ever in the presence of an overwhelming frustration."

Whatever his critique of black education in general, the cohort of scholars at Howard aimed to change what they themselves had experienced. Thurman, E. Franklin Frazier, Rayford Logan, Charles Hamilton Houston, and other professors were among the black scholars of that generation given just enough opportunity to experience first-rate graduate and legal educations but not yet afforded the opportunity to pick where they would make their careers. One of the ironic effects of segregation was to concentrate black educational, economic, social, and intellectual power in bases within the black community. Howard served that purpose, but did so only through skillful leadership and a generation of dynamic teachers and scholars. For example, by 1938 there were thirty-nine college graduates in seminary training in the School of Religion at Howard. By the end of 1939, Howard had more African American college graduates in master's-level religious training than any other institution in the United States, forty-three, all with college degrees. The mysteriously charismatic Thurman drew in interested students.

Meanwhile, Thurman and others pursued new ways of expressing a religious vision in the real world of an America that segregated and demeaned African Americans, a symptom (for Thurman) of a larger denial of human personality in the modern world. As the scholar Anthony Siracusa has expressed it, Thurman "articulated how a religious way of being could become a powerful way of practicing the politics of nonviolence," one defined by an "insurgent, nonviolent action." In doing so, he provided an intellectual foundation for a way of being that underwrote the nonviolent struggle against Jim Crow.

Thurman's work on Jesus as political insurgent inspired others under his tutelage. Thurman supervised master's theses exploring his favorite theme of Jesus and the disinherited, and the meaning of active nonviolent resistance that he taught to his students. One of his students, for example, prepared a thesis titled "An Examination of the Thesis That Christianity in Its Genesis Was a Technique of Survival for an Underprivileged Minority." The argument about Jesus paralleled Thurman's argument about whites needing to "relax" the will toward domination and violence, and the necessity of creative action by the minority. This was not simply "protest" but rather a way of being in the social world that valorized human personality. Another thesis produced under Thurman's tutelage, from 1941, "Educating Young People on the Philosophy and Technique of Nonviolence," took Thurman's lessons from Gandhi and applied them to young black Americans. The key again was the marriage of religious being and nonviolent political action.

At the base of Thurman's thought was his understanding of the meaning of the life of Jesus, and its relationship to the contemporary social world. He was to present those ideas in full form in lecture series in the late 1930s. Here he made fundamental contributions to American religious philosophy.

THE SIGNIFICANCE OF JESUS:
THURMAN'S FIRST SIGNIFICANT LECTURE SERIES

Thurman's lectures and addresses from the time he returned from India to the beginning of the Second World War marked one of his greatest periods of intellectual ferment and national interest. These were unpublished addresses; his books and publishing career arrived some years later. But much of what he then published came from the material he developed during the second half of the 1930s and early 1940s. He inspired a generation of Howard students and other frequent attendees at his addresses at the Howard Chapel, which regularly drew crowds of five hundred or more to hear his careful, deliberately delivered orations. Thurman had no evident interest in jazz in his life, but he knew how to use silences in his addresses just as Miles Davis knew the same in his tunes—the implied note that wasn't there, or the silence that left the audience anticipating what was to come, was indispensable to his oratorical repertoire, just as were silences to Davis's jazz modes. "Most of all people are overwhelmed by his silences," a writer for *Crisis* said. One young Episcopal woman and student at Howard who frequented Rankin Chapel to hear Thurman said that he was the "first really exciting person I met in the area of theology. I always characterized him as a mystic, the only black mystic I know"; Thurman portrayed Jesus as a "model, not Savior," a revolutionary thought for many. His student James Farmer later remembered (with some sly humor) that Rankin Memorial Chapel "was packed" when Thurman preached, and that "though few but theologians and philosophers comprehended what he was saying, everyone else thought if only they *had* understood it would have been wonderful, so mesmerizing was his resonant voice and so captivating was the artistry of his delivery. Those who did grasp the meaning of his sermons were even more ecstatic."

Much of Thurman's thought that he had developed in seminary and in his early years at Morehouse and Howard emerged most clearly in a series of lectures he gave in early 1937. Sponsored by the Student Christian Movement, the same organization on whose behest he had toured India, Thurman lectured on "the significance of Jesus" before crowds of college students in Canada. Thurman approached these lectures differently than usual. He wrote out most (five of the six) lectures carefully, rather than extemporizing from notes. He wanted to make his most coherent statement to date, weaving together the various strands of his thought and his career. Thurman's addresses drew interest from publishers such as Scribner's, but they were never published fully in any definitive form. Rather, bits and pieces of them found their way into Thurman's work for years thereafter. Moreover, in the lectures Thurman brought together parts of his intellectual world derived from modernist thought and higher criticism, and from his work with groups such as Fellowship of Reconciliation and other Left and pacifist groups on the American political spectrum.

Thurman spent much of the rest of his career balancing the diverse parts of his intellectual background and career, and his thoughts in "The Significance of Jesus" put them clearly and forthrightly. Thurman still felt called to speak to African American audiences and minister to African American students in particular. From his own travels (including a trip later that same summer of 1937 to St. Louis, a segregated city), he well understood the enraging and humiliating struggles African Americans faced. No doubt he used the Green Book, as did other African American travelers, even as he yearned for the day when friendly men would meet under a friendly sky.

Thurman also had received thorough training in modernist interpretations of the Bible and had used it in his sermons, including those he delivered in Canada in 1937. Thurman comes across as more of a Christian in this series of talks than in many he gave later, simply because of the emphasis on Jesus as a figure. He began by requesting his audience to "approach the life of Jesus stripped bare of much that is metaphysical and theological and mystical." Instead, the starting point simply was Jesus the poor and underprivileged and disinherited Palestinian Jew, shorn of power and citizenship in the Roman Empire, who nonetheless had fundamentally changed the entire direction of the world. But that left a fundamental question: What distinguished Jesus from the other Jews of his time? What made Jesus into Christ?

"There is one overmastering problem that the underprivileged always face," Thurman continued. "What must be their attitude towards their master, their oppressor?" Ancient Judaic traditions offered various responses to this dilemma, including violent revolt (the solution of the Zealots), alliance with the ruling authorities (the response of the Sadducees, Thurman said, basing his arguments on historical assertions that have been undermined or discredited in more recent scholarship on the ancients), withdrawal into communal asceticism (as did the Essenes), and others. Jesus offered another answer, but only after facing his period of temptations. Jesus saw that he could be a "creative harmonizer" and "interpret the world and life in terms of some creative purpose out of which life arose and that all aspects of society are constantly under the judgment of such a purpose." And thus his teachings would remain "simple, direct, always under this inexorable scrutiny of God." Everyone, no matter their social station, had to live "under his Divine scrutiny." There could be no escaping that.

In his lectures, Thurman explored the balance between individual and social transformation. Thurman insisted that pursuing individual righteousness would not be sufficient to ensure social transformation, but also that a social transformation in and of itself would not produce righteous people. As he expressed it, "Experience reveals one of the potent fallacies of Orthodox religion, namely, that that world can be made good if all the men in the world as individuals become good men—after the souls of men are saved, the society in which they function will be a good society." That was at best a "half-truth," because in fact people were caught up in "a framework of relationships evil in design," meaning that their gestures toward the good could be used as instruments of evil. Such was the case with the segregated South, for example. Thurman summed up his view in his second lecture: "The two processes must go on apace or else men and their relationships will not be brought under conscious judgment of God. We must, therefore, even as we purify our hearts and live our individual lives under the divine scrutiny, so order the framework of our relationships that good men can function in a good framework to the glory of God."

Thurman also developed a sustained argument about economic relationships and the role of private property. Here, with unusual clarity, Thurman's economic and social radicalism became clear. "When property becomes sacred, personality becomes secular," he argued. Property as an end in itself blocked the expression of love shorn of self-interest, because the sacralization of property "renders individuals in society who are without property, without security. It makes individuals possessing property identify their status and their significance with the amount and value of the property they possess. They seek to organize themselves for defense against all efforts toward distribution and confuse all sharing with those outside their property class as either charity or philanthropy." Thurman never joined the Communist Party and was more of a sympathizer than an activist for socialism. A socialist by sentiment, he upheld human values over the rights of property. But he was not involved in any organized socialist movement.

In Thurman's view, the Good Samaritan story should be normative rather than exceptional. The response of Jesus to those in need exemplified this world. When confronted with a woman who had committed adultery, Jesus responded with his famous words about casting the first stone. For Thurman, this showed how Jesus "met the woman where she was and treated her there as if she were where she should have been," a variation on a basic philosophical maxim of Thurman that he repeated frequently in various forms. Loving people involved meeting people "where they are, and we treat them there as if they were where they ought to be, and by so doing, we believe them into the fulfillment of their possibilities and love becomes an act of redemption. We place a crown over their heads that they are always trying to grow tall enough to wear."

Thurman returned to these words frequently; they became something like his trademark. In speaking at the seventy-fifth anniversary of Morehouse College in 1942, he noted how this philosophy had been put into effect by the school's founders after the Civil War. They referred to it as a college, even when it was something like a primary school for newly freed African Americans. The founders had followed the philosophy Thurman advocated. They had met the freedmen, "many of them fear-stricken, chronologically old, and they treated them there as if they were where they should be, where they were destined to be. By doing that, they buoyed them into the fulfillment of a possibility that staggered their imagination, by putting over them a crown that for the rest of their days they are trying to grow tall enough to wear."

In preaching about the cross of Jesus, Thurman emphasized Jesus as a man without full knowledge of the meaning of his sacrifice. And the resurrection was not a part of the meaning either. Instead, Thurman was primarily interested in the symbolics of sacrifice. Jesus provided the model for the religiously inspired activist against social evil. Jesus exemplified the life of those willing to risk everything, including their lives, in the pursuit of social justice. What could be learned from the cross of Jesus? "There are some things in life that are worse than death," Thurman responded. It was Jesus's death, more than his life, that turned him into a Savior: "For here is revealed that a man's life becomes meaningful and whole to the degree that he is willing to stake everything on a conviction that what he does when he is most himself has the approval and the imprimatur of the Highest."

That did not exempt the Christian from conflict. The Christian projected "his ideal into the midst of a world that is organized on other than principles of kinship and brotherhood. He demonstrates that he cannot escape conflict." Thurman saw little reason for the church other than to commit to "struggle in the world." Thurman saw "too much agony, too much hunger, too much poverty and misery everywhere, too many flagrant denials of kinship and brotherhood all along the line." There was no time to wait for some imagined divine intervention in the future: "Something concrete must be done *now*," because "to wait for moral pressure to work its perfect work may be too late. The oppressed may be annihilated meanwhile."

Thus, the Jesus follower might employ some form of shock therapy to tear people away from their "alignments in the kingdom of evil, to free them so that they may be given a sense of acute insecurity and out of the depths of their insecurity they may be forced to see their brotherhood with the oppressed." Thurman could not understand those who saw Jesus simply as an ethical teacher but "cannot be bothered very much with his religion. They are inseparable as I think of it; for Jesus knew, as did Aristotle, that for man to see the right thing is not for him to do the right thing." The world presented so much organization of evil, with much to depress and little to uplift or inspire. Loving involved doing, for the sake of love itself, "what no power in heaven or hell could make me do if I did not love." Love allowed one to encounter and appreciate the brilliance in the world: "when I love the sun seems to shine more brightly, the colour of the leaves is a richer green, for somehow I have tapped a source that whispers to me the secret of the mystery of existence. Whatever else God is He must be like this." The defining characteristic of God was not power but love. And so the meaning of Jesus was that he placed before us "an impelling dream, growing out of a fundamental interpretation of the meaning of life—human life—all life; a methodology by which that dream might be translated into living power—in a living community." And he showed us a power to work out love within community, "without inner defilement and without self destruction."

Thurman's own philosophy came under a severe test later that year when he traveled to St. Louis to deliver his address "The Sources of Power for Christian Living" at the National Methodist Student Conference. One organizer suggested to him how important it was that, at the Methodist event, the black speakers would not be confined to topics of race relations. This appealed to Thurman's desire not to be slotted as a "race speaker" before mixed-race or white audiences. As Thurman explained to another correspondent a few months later, "My training and main interest are in the field of religion. I do not accept invitations to discuss the race question; not because I do not think the race question needs to be discussed, but I am determined to make my contribution along the lines of my preparation and my chosen field of activity. I cannot do this if I become merely a propagandist or a sociologist."

Thurman was not aware that the hotel where he thought he was staying would not accommodate him that evening. Thurman returned to the event for his address and explained to the audience what had happened. He left the event after his talk and made his way directly to the train station, sleeping on the train to Oxford, Ohio (his next speaking engagement), his fury no doubt resulting in the migraine headache that plagued him en route. Thurman normally flourished in environments such as the one in St. Louis, where he could address a mixed-race audience on his preferred themes of religion in general and not race in particular; but his experience at the hotel reminded him again of exactly where he was in the American racial system. The sponsor of the Methodist conference, H. D. Bollinger, apologized to Thurman afterward, indicating that "the best that I can do is to pledge myself all the more to the practice of Christian brotherhood" in future Methodist assemblies. Thurman responded with appreciation but indicated that "recovery from such things is most difficult." He drew one main lesson from the incident. Trust between blacks and whites was nearly impossible to achieve because "the framework of the relationships is so completely without high ethical quality that even the most simple ethical advances challenge the entire society."

"As a Christian," Thurman said, "I must see to it that what I condemn in society, I do not permit to grow and flower in me." That was a struggle for a black man of Thurman's intellect and sensitivities. Incidents such as those in St. Louis filled him with a rage that he internalized (manifested in physical symptoms) and, only occasionally, externalized in sermons and addresses directly commenting on American racial politics. Simply waking up and going about one's business constantly confronted black Americans with their status as disinherited noncitizens, American untouchables. How could one avoid cultivating an internal rage? One could not, Thurman responded. But one could channel rage constructively.

Following this humiliation, Thurman somehow summoned the will to deliver his best and most original addresses. Speaking to the National Assembly of Student Christian Associations in late December 1937 or early January 1938, Thurman advanced a critique of the relationship of traditional Christianity with nature. It was one of the earliest-developed statements of African American Christian environmentalism. In this work, Thurman draws most extensively on one of his primary intellectual influences, Olive Schreiner. The South African author, essayist, poet, and nature mystic reinforced Thurman's ideas, expressing them in a poetic language that appealed to Thurman's love of that genre. Thurman's talk, "Man and the World of Nature," at the National Assembly draws from Schreiner and other recent work in science. In it, he presents a kind of early eco-humanism emphasizing "reverence for all expressions of life." It certainly was true that nature was "red in tooth and claw," Thurman acknowledged, but traditional Christianity had radically (and falsely) separated man and nature. This was a false dichotomy that ended in the destruction of nature and the fueling of human aggression. Man prepared himself for a battle with nature, and then one day discovered that nature was not the enemy, but instead that "he is a part of nature and that every judgment that he passes upon nature is a judgment that nature passes upon itself."

In this way, humans could understand both the beauty and the harmony, as well as the brutality and the aggression, in nature—and that this was a part of human nature as well. Seeking to understand the contradictions of human nature, people turn to psychology, theology, or other fields of inquiry that might provide insight. But the "ethical insights that we have are built for the most part upon the false line that was drawn in the past between man and nature." In the future, theologians would work toward a reintegration of man and nature in their own work toward an ethical synthesis. The result would be a new respect and reverence for life and a recognition that a proper understanding of nature provided the key to comprehending ultimate significance.

Thurman followed this short but fruitful address with another, "Christian, Who Calls Me Christian?" In this speech aimed at a student audience, he presented, in a more pointed fashion, ideas that he had worked out in his series on the significance of Jesus.

In what way, he asked, should Christians act in a world that demanded moral compromise? First, as he had argued elsewhere, he insisted that "I must not permit to grow and flower in my own heart and life what I condemn in society or in my fellow man. . . . I must be rigorously honest with myself there. I must not permit my mind to do clever tricks with me so that I shall give to my own sin and my own weaknesses high and holy names as I pour out invectives and condemnations upon those same things in society and in other people around me." But that alone was not enough. For to be a Christian was to seek and "devise methods and techniques and ways, personal and group, by which it will be possible for an increasingly large number of people to live the good life in time and space without external limitations." The Christian was in brotherhood with both the powerful and the weak, but how could the committed person best approach the question of inequality and ruptures in human relations? Perhaps "some form of pressure more drastic and more immediately devastating than moral pressure" would be necessary, a point of action that might loose the oppressor from his security "so that for one breathless moment or for one breathless week he becomes the brother in experience with the insecure and the weak; and while he is in that condition it may be that the spirit of God can take advantage of the looseness of his situation and effect another combination before he settles down again." And perhaps it could even come to the point of offering one's life as a sacrifice against the workings of evil regimes; indeed, it could be a "great spiritual act to know when the moment for martyrdom has arrived."

What would be the sources of this kind of certainty or commitment? And how could one distinguish it from fanaticism? "There is the freedom of mind that comes with a great commitment," one that causes an "orderly recklessness of action" but could be difficult for the intellectual person to reach. Fellowship with Jesus was one answer, for "he becomes for us not the product of any age or any race or any school of thought, but a great benediction to all the races of men." And other goals could be accomplished with a "sustained relationship with an inner group of like-minded, like-dedicated people." Both in fact may be necessary, but neither was sufficient. Only a relationship with God, the infinite power, accomplished through meditation and prayer, was equal to the task. In a critical passage, Thurman expresses it this way:

> But in the great task which involves the transformation of the world, and the redemption of the individual human spirit from evil, only primary releases from God may apply. For the task is infinite, and only an infinite power can address itself to an infinite need. We get this in the life of meditation and prayer and discipline; in moments of quiet I hold, at the center of my spiritual focus, the cause to which I am dedicated. This gives an abundance of freedom and joy because it destroys fear—fear of failure, fear of death, fear of being misunderstood, fear that I am mistaken in the thing

that I am undertaking, fear that all my life long I might live for a cause only to find at the end that the cause is wrong. *In moments of profound meditation I become sometimes for one transcendent moment only a central part of the purpose of life.*

Such a discipline was both clarifying and cleansing, because through such practices "against the darkness of the age I can see the illumined finger of God guiding me in the way that I should go." Above the clamor of daily life and the struggle for power and status, "I can hear speaking distinctly and clearly to my own spirit the still, small voice of God without which nothing has meaning."

During these years, as well, Thurman thought deeply about what it meant to practice pacifism, on the one hand, and actively combat racial prejudice on the other. And he was bitingly critical of reformist groups, such as the Commission on Interracial Cooperation. They had attempted to amend or ameliorate, rather than annihilate, segregated institutions. "The time has passed for the theoretical and the merely discussional approach to the question on group conflict in the South," he wrote to John Nevin Sayre of the International Fellowship of Reconciliation (FOR) in May of 1936. Thurman worried about the peace movement in the United States being "essentially a 'high brow' movement. Its effectiveness among the masses of the people is not as great as the energies put forth would justify." He hoped FOR would not be another group slowly tilling the ground of "education . . . to bring about reconciliation and harmony," but would take an approach more "in the area of action including propaganda." Thurman remembered fondly his relationship with leaders such as George "Shorty" Collins, a student pacifist leader he met while at Morehouse and who became his friend over the subsequent decades. Thurman later praised "Shorty" (so named because he was six feet five inches tall, towering over Thurman, who was about five feet eight inches) for encouraging him to "stand in my own spirit—a place so profoundly affirming that I was strengthened by a sense of immunity to the assaults of the white world of Atlanta, Georgia." And during these years, Thurman carried on a correspondence with Howard "Buck" Kester, whose daring actions in going undercover in Florida to investigate a particularly brutal lynching there had won him admirers. The Kester of the 1930s was precisely the sort of white ally that Thurman wanted to enlist to take on segregation as directly as possible.

Through these years, Thurman elaborated at length on his ideas of the nature of American Christianity and the relationship of African Americans to it. Blacks in America, the disinherited minority, faced a profound crisis of self-confidence. It came from the fact, he told one audience in Nashville in 1938, that "we have been so consistently despised we have at last begun despising ourselves." And it was worsened by the place of blacks in an American system set within a broader world of imperialism and colonization. The imperialism of their era, Thurman argued, came not so much from a struggle to dominate resources. Rather, it continued because the powerful sought connection with the powerless, who still had some connection to "the roots of life" and could then suck the vitality, the life, out of the powerless: "That is the psychology of imperialism: It is not because one man wants to kill another man so much, but because people who have grown up as powerful people in the world have grown mean and emaciated and sterile and they are looking around for a luscious people of the earth and laying on them to suck their strength."

And yet, Thurman continued, this is also why the soul, the spirit, of enslaved people could not be defeated. The slave could not be killed "because he laid hold on life, elemental life, with such an abiding enthusiasm that the only way you can destroy him was to destroy life." And it taught the enslaved to laugh in the face of these circumstances, to have the laugh of someone who knew he was not, and could not be, spiritually defeated, to mock the spiritual pretension of their oppressors.

Here, and through much of his writings about the spirituals that came from this era, Thurman proposed a fundamentally psychological interpretation of the sorrow songs. The depth and profundity of his writings from that era were matched only by Du Bois's essays in *Souls of Black Folk*. Thurman resisted the tendency of others to fit slave culture into some kind of neo-Marxist resistance framework. Instead, he was more interested in the root psychology of a situation. Thurman certainly had a strong moral critique of contemporary economics and power dynamics, and held fundamentally socialist economic views. But ultimately, those were not his primary animating focus. Rather, Thurman fixated on the question of the relationship of the dispossessed to Christianity. He queried why his forebears had "embraced the religion of the men and women and of the civilization primarily that had victimized them."

He proposed a variety of answers through his writing but always returned to his fundamental insight: the disinherited of America had seen in Jesus "a messenger and a signal for the underprivileged and dispossessed," a vision unavailable to those in privilege, those having power. And thus they had the wisdom and the maturity not given to the powerful, to effect a "great creative spiritual inspiration" and to redeem the religion "that had been disgraced in their midst." They found a hidden spiritual truth, that being "a confidence of God that belongs very essentially to the hearts and minds of the people," without which there could be no peace. Thurman vividly portrayed the spiritual struggles of the disinherited: "When you can absorb, make room for our spirit, squeeze all of the violence out of all the things that meet you, it is then you are a master of life. And if you can't do that you will be a slave of life. Now, that is a confidence in God stated in simple language. That is the great ghost that drives you on. Drives me on, drives you on; and everything you touch, everything, if it is to have meaning, must be summarized in terms of some kind of absolute meaning."

Similarly, as he told an audience in Northfield, Massachusetts, that same year, prayer was a vehicle through which "we who pray the prayer become channels—literally channels—through which the knowledge, the courageousness, the power, the love, the endurance needful to meet the infinite needs of the world may flow. For only infinite energy is able to meet infinite need, and we who pray this prayer become channels through which God's life of healing and redemption may flow. We must search more and more creatively how to devise methods by which good may supplant evil, by which the hearts of men may be redeemed, and by which the world in which those hearts must function may be redeemed." As always, for Thurman, the personal was both spiritual and social at the same time.

THURMAN AND MYSTICISM

Through the 1930s, Thurman championed the African American spirituals; he preached around the country on the significance of Jesus most especially in the lives of the disinherited; he held audiences captive at Rankin Chapel at Howard with his weekly sermons exploring the connection between the intellectual and spiritual dimensions of Christianity; and he compared the oppression of power in imperialism abroad with segregation at home. Already, just in this short list, Thurman brilliantly wove together numerous threads of American religious thought and practice. And he brought another intellectual tradition to the discussion as well: mysticism.

Here, Thurman drew directly from American nineteenth-century mysticism, originating with the generation of Emerson, Thoreau, and others. Emerson defined religion as "the emotion of shuddering delight and awe from perception of the infinite." Thurman never quoted that line, and yet his thought on mysticism explores that concept, refracted through his study with Rufus Jones and the tradition of Quaker mysticism.

"Fundamentally, the mystic rests his case upon the meaning of a primary contractual experience of God," Thurman began. "It is first hand. He considers himself as standing within the experience itself. . . . The assumption is that the finite and the Infinite are not two fundamentally separate universes of discourse but that they are grounded in a transcendent unity." The contradictions of life were not ultimate; below them lay a fundamental unity, one that could be grasped in a mystical experience that then pointed the way toward social engagement.

Thurman distinguished between rational and intuitive knowledge, discursive reasoning and more immediate realizations. But even while the two were different, they could work in tandem, because "even in discursive reasoning there is a leaping quality in the mental process. In the moment of intuition the mind leaves behind the process and its grasp of knowledge is immediate and comprehensive." Here, Thurman actually forecast some developments among intellectual historians of the future, notably Thomas Kuhn's *The Structure of Scientific Revolutions.* Like Kuhn, Thurman emphasized how knowledge advanced over time with incremental gains and then, in one massive, intuitive leap, an entire new understanding of something, a new paradigm, came alive. Kuhn and others were not exploring those ideas in any religious context, but they were structurally similar to Thurman's ideas as presented here. Except that, for Thurman, that intuitive leap had to emerge from spiritual insight.

The problem for any form of mysticism was how to verify the experience as something more than just a figment of one's imagination. After that leap of intuition, the knowledge could be made secure with logic, the "road map that can be reproduced indefinitely and made available to all intelligent travelers." Thurman pointed out that "in intuitive knowledge more of man's personality is involved than in more rational knowledge." Intuitive knowledge was "more personal," and thus in effect was more real and could be a deeper take on reality. The mystic's deepest religious knowledge came through such intuition, arriving to him "with overwhelming conviction and certainty," striking him "with the vividness and clarity of a sensation. He sees the vision; for the vision breaks in on him when he is ready to receive it. All of his disciplines are preparatory to his moment of vision."

The mystic's vision was immediate, and "only when it is broken down into manageable units of intellection" did it become part of the "sequential totality of experience." The mystic, too, was "always looking for one symbol that is sufficiently inclusive of meaning" that it could serve as a direct route to God. For the Christian mystic in particular, that symbol came in Jesus Christ. For some Christian mystics, Jesus essentially dissolved into God, while for others, including (he implied) Thurman himself, Jesus was an "inclusive symbol of God," the "fullest expression in time of what is disclosed to him in his own moment of illumination." The ultimate goal was to be "unified with but not dissolved in God."

The result of the mystical experience bore elements of regeneration, or conversion, a "profound recentering of the personality." Often it came as a result of an "excruciating agony of spirit and mind." For Thurman, such experiences had come through nature. He remembered, here for one of the first times and later recounted in his autobiography, his encounters with nature as a boy:

> When I was a boy I was always driven to worship when I saw a storm come up on the shores of the Atlantic Ocean on the Florida Coast. A stillness pervaded everything. The tall sea grass stood at attention. As far out as my eyes could go the surface of the sea was untroubled, quiet, but expectant. I could almost hear the pounding of my own heart against my ribs. Then, as if by magic, there came a stirring of the wind, increasing in intensity and ex-

pansiveness until the sea grass, the loose dry sand, the surface of the ocean were all caught up in an increasingly maddening fury—the storm had come.

It was, for him, the last bit of silence before the arrival of God. He now could intellectualize how forces of nature placed "solar and phallic symbolism" at the end of "the whole language and literature of religion." Thurman recounted how his religious experiences as a youth were tied up in the sun and the sea, the rebirth of spring, summer thunderstorms, and all the manifestations of nature that "have somehow united with certain powerful inner urges of the human spirit." But Thurman rejected a mere mysticism of pantheism, because for the truest Christian mystic, the struggle and pain evident in nature were a "symbol of the moral struggle of human life."

And for this reason, true knowledge of other people came through intuition, just as was the case with God. "We cannot expect to find the meaning of another person at the end of a syllogism," is how he expressed it in his lectures, and "We cannot expect to find God at the end of a syllogism." True knowledge of God could not come through strictly discursive reasoning but only through "knowledge of love. We must approach Him along the same avenue by which we seek a deeper knowledge of each other's personality." Knowledge is power, but so is spiritual intuition.

But then, what distinguished the knowledge that derived from spiritual intuition from a "vague glowy feeling about the world of nature and man"? Thurman asked. How could we know if we had experienced the truths of the mystics and not just the shallow warm glow of a false sense of oneness? Here he injected the key component of ethics into mysticism. A mere "diffused transcendency" was not enough, because the "Christian mystic in his experience of intentness, intensity, ineffability and passivity, is conscious of being grasped by a reality that is focal and frontal." How, then, could a mystic "carry the reality of his vision which is monistic in its very nature into the ordinary commonplace experience of life"?

Thurman's third lecture in this series specifically approached the question of mysticism and ethics. What most critics of mysticism failed to understand, he said, was the simple reality of evil, something the true mystic first discovered in his own spirit and then found in the social world around him. The mystical experience of alone-ness, that sense of unity with God, the moment of spiritual fulfillment when tensions were resolved, did not absolve the mystic of the question of how to manifest that unity in the social world of "time-space relationships," and how that would influence the conduct of his life.

The challenge for the mystic was to maintain the sense of unity, the kind that had completely penetrated his soul. Over time, inevitably, conflicts and blocks would arise: "the struggle with impulses, with inner divisions, unworthy desires, purely self-regarding tactics including the whole world of egocentric manifestations, all these are regarded by him as an indispensable part of the defect of his vision." For many, asceticism was the route to control the struggles of the flesh and maintain the original spiritual vision. The ascetics understood the reality of evil; in a sense, it underlay their entire set of practices. The mystic-ascetic sought the "inner equilibrium" so as to be ready at any moment "for the direct visitation of God." And thus "the greatest mystic-ascetics in the Christian tradition have turned the whole stream of Christian thought and achievement into new and powerful channels of practical living." Here was Thurman's crucial tie between the mystical and the practical, the visionary spiritual aesthete and the committed activist for a better world.

And in Jesus, explained Thurman, the Christian mystic could see "the meaning of the triumph of the spirit over the body; the transcending and triumphant power of God over the most relentless pressure and persistence of things that divide and destroy. To know Him in the fellowship of his suffering seemed to the Christian mystic the key to his victory." And thus, the ultimate meaning of mystical asceticism involved not withdrawal from society but instead "a steady insistence that one's human relations conform more and more to the transparency of one's inner graces, one's inner equilibrium in which is his consciousness of the active presence of God." The inner active presence of God could be made visible in the external social world.

In his final lecture in this series, "Mysticism and Social Change," Thurman explained how the "realistic mystic" came to understand that his full personality could "only be achieved in a milieu of human relations." In this lecture, too, Thurman deployed the term "affirmation mystics," a usage he got originally from the Quaker scholar Rufus Jones. Thurman explained how, in the Christian tradition, "social sin and personal sin are bound up together in an inexorable relationship so that it is literally true that no man can expect to have his soul saved alone." And so the affirmation mystic joined the socialist, the political organizer such as Eugene Debs, and those who identified with the disinherited, in joining his destiny with sufferers everywhere. Indeed, Thurman repeatedly turned to the example of Debs, the Christian socialist activist who set his sights on an identification with all who were oppressed.

The problems all mystics faced involved living in a human society dominated by unequal forms of political and economic organization. The mystic could face economic insecurity, and thus be unable to achieve the good "even in his simplest relations with his fellows because of the difficulties involved in establishing a basis of trust between him and them that will not victimize him in his effort to maintain himself in the world."

And thus practical reasons dominated the thought of the affirmation mystic. He was not primarily a humanitarian, nor was he motivated by any particular economic theory. Rather, he took interest in social action "because society as he knows it to be ensnares the human spirit in a maze of particulars so that the One cannot be sensed nor the good realized." He sought a society in which men could freely pursue their religious visions. That could only happen with freedom from the constant, grinding, life-and-death struggle for security. The achievement of economic security, in effect, lessened the "imperialistic will" for power, and thus the spiritual insight of the mystic could have relevance "without seeming to be unrealistic, romantic, or sentimental." The affirmation mystic could not escape in "mere asceticism," but instead he would have to "embrace the social whole and seek to achieve empirically the good which has possessed him in his moment of profoundest insight."

And here the affirmation mystic could make his most profound contribution. The powerful in society naturally would resist any tendency toward equality, toward furthering human community. They would seek to hold the masses in a state of "depersonalized individualism" and use the power of the state to reinforce the status quo. But the affirmation mystic would then refuse to give in to violence and coercion as a response. He (Thurman always used masculine pronouns to refer to humans in general) would work toward the achievement of human community, even while waiting patiently for its realization in the social world; he could see that "working and waiting are two separate activities of the human spirit."

Thurman explored this linkage between the natural, internal, and social worlds in numerous addresses and sermons during this era. He wanted people to explore what it meant to enact and realize God's vision for the natural and social world, accomplished in concert with groups of like-minded individuals. Men's physical environment did not match God's desire, nor the "conscious end to which I think Jesus Christ calls the human spirit." The physical environment was one of imperialism, war, and ecological degradation. And so the challenge remained, for Christianity, "to make the physical environment become the very agency of self-conscious creative material and spiritual ends." The same could be said for the social world. The Christian should demand that his inner self be brought in line with an "inner harmony based upon a profound consecration to God," and the same with the "resourcefulness and the harmony and beauty and richness of nature."

Thurman's structure of imagining God's vision also encompassed the Christian's relationship with the social world. As a self-conscious act of will, the Christian would consecrate the social world. That involved crying out against injustice. But doing so required personal penitence. The affirmation mystic would see that one was a part of the "manifestations of evil and injustice that are not under the control of the will and the purpose of God, but represent the unrestrained manifestations of creative egoistic impulses in man." And so even the seeker, the holy individual seeking justice, would participate in injustice simply by virtue of belonging to an unjust society. "I cannot continually restrain myself in the presence of the challenge to do good and to be good without paying for it in terms of moral and spiritual disintegration. Much of the cynicism of modern life hinges upon the fact that moral man has not been willing to recognize the relationship that exists between the amount of moral and spiritual atrophy in his own spirit and the things that he is willing to do from day to day." The consecrated individual would seek to minimize his participation in evil social arrangements and in all cases identify with the dispossessed; here he returned again to Debs, the same source that inspired a famous passage in *The Grapes of Wrath*, the famous novel from exactly this same time (later 1930s): "I must see that while there is a lower class I am in it, where there is a criminal element I am of it, while there is a man in jail I am not free." And he would look for ways to implement practically some means of social transformation. He would do so without giving in to hate, the flammable toxin that "burns up the moral and spiritual bearings of the hater and leaves him with a stranded corpse on the shores of his desolate experience."

Jesus's central concern was "the realization of a kingdom of friendly men upon the earth. A kingdom of friendly men in which the security of one man is guaranteed by all men." At every point, Jesus was concerned to alter the nature of relationships "so that any individual man would feel free to relax his tension and fear of insecurity and even of death. . . . For Jesus has identified himself primarily with the best that the mind of man can dream of as man contemplates the good life for himself, and for his age, and for his generation." Thurman looked to the great power that "comes from meditating upon the life of Jesus Christ, and then the strength that comes out of that fellowship of men and women of a common dedication around a great purpose."

Still, the "ultimate source of power is God." And the method of contact with that ultimate power was "worship, meditation of prayer," the time when one became "fully conscious of the ultimate source of power." Prayer allowed for a renewal of the spirit, by freshening the spirit and touching the center of one's "spiritual focus."

Thurman developed similar themes in his sermon "Fellowship with God and Prayer," in February of 1943, part of a series investigating how individuals could summon strength in demanding times. Thurman's focus remained on contact with God, the source of all strength, the "ultimate spiritual resource for human life." Only that was sufficient "in the task that calls for the faithful transformation of our individual lives and the redemption of man and society from evil," when "only an infinite energy can meet the exhaustive demand. . . . Anyone who has faced the abysmal churnings of evil in his own spirit out of which come in crimson stream deeds that fill the life with shame and the days with anguish, knows that only God is sufficient." Only God could move our desire such that one could "*desire* to desire the right." And that could only come from prayer and meditation, bringing the mind to focus on God, "centering down" on God (as the mystics put it). The detritus of daily life, the trivialities ordinarily filling the mind, would be replaced with a focus on the essential, the profound. And in doing so, "One's *will* to act the Kingdom of God and to make life everywhere yield its maximum weal for every man, takes on a new dynamic."

In his sermons, addresses, and shorter publications on Jesus, the natural world, and the nature of an affirmative mysticism that engaged fully with the social world, Thurman linked together key themes of his thought and career. And he found an audience, both black and white, eager to hear those themes. The Depression years were a time of broader ferment, from various sides of Christianity. Fundamentalists railed against Franklin Delano Roosevelt and the New Deal as a kind of harbinger of the antichrist of socialism, a theme obviously picked up with even greater force following the Second World War. Meanwhile, progressive Christian activists, some of them linked to New Deal ideas and programs and others well placed in seminaries, explored new ideas of what Christianity could mean with the old shibboleths destroyed by the great storm of the Great Depression. Black people, disproportionately affected by the Depression, migrated, struggled, and organized through churches, labor unions, NAACP chapters, Communist Party cells, and in colleges and universities.

Thurman himself trained a cohort of young scholars who would take his teachings directly into the early civil rights struggle. Thurman was thus part of, and yet a singular figure within, the broader world of the liberal Left of American Christianity in these years. And he balanced his more abstract and ethereal sermons and addresses with more direct commentary on economics, race, migration, and war. Although not ordinarily given to direct political commentary, sometimes it simply was necessary. On those occasions, Thurman spoke plainly and powerfully about the insidiously evil nature of American racism.

THURMAN'S VIEWS ON RACE IN URBAN AMERICA

In 1940, addressing a Chicago meeting of the Conference of Christians and Jews, Thurman delivered one of his more memorable speeches specifically directed to racial inequality in the United States, and more specifically in northern cities. "The Negro in the northern city is not a citizen and his position is a perpetual threat and constant disgrace to democracy," he insisted. The problem for northern blacks was simply "crass, elemental, physical survival." Thurman summarized the roots of racial inequality from slavery to the present and reinforced the conclusions of early black sociologists of that era. And he anticipated much "whiteness" scholarship in examining how immigrants to northern cities learned to secure their place in American society by differentiating themselves from Negroes. Nonetheless, black Americans sustained an interest in Christianity; they had taken up the task of "the redemption of a religion that has been disgraced and prostituted in a new world." The earlier world war had brought some opportunity for citizenship for blacks, for then "the future of democracy was dependent upon [them]," but then the situation was radically reversed after the war. "In my opinion, not until churches, schools, governing boards of all kinds, political, secular and religious, guarantee the Negroes' right as a citizen to belong and to participate in the common life will he [cease] to be merely an individual, eating, occasionally sleeping, breathing but remaining the perpetual threat and condemnation of democracy. He must be given responsibility and the incentive to exercise a free initiative if life ultimately is to be sane and secure for us all."

World War II presented a massive challenge to American pacifists in general, and certainly to Thurman. But Thurman was perhaps less agitated intellectually than many of his peers, because he knew a part of his ministry involved counseling young black men destined for the military. He thus maintained pacifist views as a personal philosophy, but, as he explained repeatedly, he was not absolutist in those views. He would not simply withdraw from his responsibilities to assist students and black servicemen and servicewomen, nor would he forsake his role in the "Double V" campaign—victory against racism abroad and at home.

Thurman explained to one correspondent, regarding the war in Asia in 1937, that he did not share her view that if China did not surrender to Japan, it would simply fall under the power of the white man. The correspondent had written to Thurman, "I am a Negro, and I want to see the darker Races become as strong as possible," especially since "I feel that the white Races have been congenitally united against the dark Races." Thurman replied politely, but firmly, restating his opposition to imperialism in any form, "whether the imperialist be black, yellow, white, or any other color." He thus opposed Japanese aggression in China. As a "member of the darker races," he understood the sympathy with Japan, but since he was foremost a pacifist, "I am opposed to the whole sordid struggle that is going on between China and Japan." But he understood the point of view of the correspondent—there was, after all, an effort "on the part of the white race as a whole to hold the darker races in subjection if not in complete servitude." This was in 1937, but it was the first of many letters in which Thurman explained the dilemmas he faced as someone who advised many young black men who were going into the military, while retaining his status as a pacifist and conscientious objector. As he wrote to one correspondent in 1941, "Now that we are at war and the plight of Negroes becomes increasingly more tragic, in the army and out of the army, something like a great blight has settled upon us everywhere. Every waking moment, I am involved in this at one point or another."

Thurman held no illusions about what might come in the "good war," or what had resulted from the wars in the past. He viewed all wars as connected to imperialism and exploitation. "If nations for hundreds of years can build their empires out of the blood and vitality of millions of defenseless and so-called backwards peoples," he wrote in one sermon from 1940, and if they could "exploit and abuse and torture human life and squander their resources until there is nothing left but a mockery of decency and self-respect— if nations can do this as they have done in Europe for several centuries and not be bathed in the blood they themselves have caused to flow up on the earth, then the moral order itself is an illusion. The history of a nation is the judgment of the nation." The consecrated mystic would seek ways to maintain his light in the darkness, because "Your light becomes darkness when you lack the courage and the will to do what you know to be right."

In his correspondence with A. J. Muste, the so-called American Gandhi and linchpin of American pacifism for decades, Thurman explained his conflicted position in regards to his pacifism and his service for Fellowship of Reconciliation. In September 1940 Muste asked him to be vice chairman (one of three) of FOR. Thurman accepted but asked him to understand that "my work makes such absolute demands on all of my time and energy that there is simply nothing left" for much additional labor. In particular, as part of the buildup to war, black men and women sought him for counsel, and the "complications of our social order make it very difficult to keep clear of critical conflicts." And indeed, the letters extant in the Thurman papers show the extent of his correspondence with younger black men involved in the military, including his colleague from the India trip, Edward Carroll, who had been posted to the Alaskan islands. He noted how, when black men went into army camps, they could not simply be left to the devices of white men "whose normally weak scruples as to treatment are almost thoroughly routed by the customary moral disintegration opened by war. And yet I know war is not only futile but is thoroughly and completely evil and diabolical." Hence his dilemma, and hence his plaintive comment that "what my duty is as a Christian is sometimes very obscure."

It was a little clearer for Muste, who corresponded frequently with Thurman on plans and ideas for how he could use his time most effectively. At one point, early in 1941, Muste urged Thurman to work on unionizing black workers for Ford in Detroit. Thurman, characteristically, demurred at this kind of direct political commitment. The problem was complex, he told Muste, for blacks saw working for nonunionized Ford as preferable to belonging to unions that previously had excluded them. They had been so "exploited in so many ways that it is hard for them to believe in anybody under any circumstances. Least of all, any group bearing a union label." Much education would be required to overcome that, he concluded.

Meanwhile, Thurman explored other opportunities prior to moving to San Francisco, the most serious of which was the pastorate of Olivet Baptist Church, the flagship Baptist church in Chicago. He visited there in March of 1941 and preached what was in effect a trial sermon before an appreciative crowd. "I was profoundly moved by the response of the rank and file of the people," he wrote to his host in Chicago. "I believe that what our people need is to have the religion of Jesus taught to them in order that they may understand what it is that is required of them," he said. Referring to his style of preaching in contrast to the emotionalism that stereotypically characterized the black pulpit, he noted that "I took a text that belongs to the 'war horses' and the 'whoopers,' but I wanted to appeal to the minds of the people, being confident that the feelings would take care of themselves." Thurman was surprised by the "completely positive impression that the experience made upon me" and asked officers of the church to be discreet if they were interested in offering him the pastorate. As it turned out, ironically, the pastorate went to Joseph H. Jackson, a power broker with the black Baptist convention who later became an enemy and obstacle to Martin Luther King and civil rights leaders.

Thurman's fame as a lecturer continued to grow in the early years of the war. In "Our Underlying Spiritual Unities," an address delivered in Chicago in the spring of 1941, Thurman expressed some of his deepest hopes for that era, in spite of the darkness engulfing the world at that time. It could seem that men were caught in forces beyond their control, he noted, but closer scrutiny revealed a different story. Something in the human spirit insisted that social change could come, and that the "contradictions of experiences" were temporary rather than ultimate: "Sometimes blindly, sometimes with little hope of vindication, often with wild irrationality, the spirit of man dares to affirm that the ultimate end of man is good." Such a hope was an anchor in despairing times. And these were such times. Even as man had greater technical and psychological knowledge than ever, and the ability to conquer diseases as never before, so he had "less confidence than ever in the ability of the mind of man to administer to those deeper needs of the human spirit for faith in each other, for hope, for growth, and security." And the church was deeply culpable. "How dare we undertake to teach reverence to children when we ourselves do not believe in reverence for life in general or life in particular as a valid concept in our kind of world," Thurman said.

Shall we teach lies to children? . . . Can we teach trust when we are bound by a vast network of impersonal social relations which create the kind of climate in which trust cannot possibly thrive? Or can we teach trust even as we confess how little trust we have in each other in our cause and in our God? I wonder. What do we mean when we teach the brotherhood of man? When over and over again we give the sanction of our religion and the weight of our practice to those subtle anti-Christian practices expressed in segregated churches, even in segregated graveyards. Can we expect more of the state, of the body politic, of industry than we expect of the church? How can we teach love from behind the great high walls of separateness?

In "The Will to Segregation," from the summer of 1943, Thurman wrote out (for the magazine *Fellowship*) one of his most complete statements on the effect of the war on citizenship rights for African Americans. The war had extended new citizenship opportunities to those normally shoved into second-class roles. The nation needed Negroes to participate, to buy bonds, to be drafted, and to contribute to the entire range of the war effort. "It is unfortunate that it took a global war with its concomitant effect upon our national life to give the Negro a fresh sense of significance and power," he noted ruefully, but such was the case. And as the war made more clear what exactly the practice of democracy would mean, so rose the frustration of African Americans "in direct proportion to the degree to which the meaning of democracy is made clear and definite."

The war gave the nation the chance to examine, and relinquish, its "will to segregation." In this section of the piece, Thurman anticipated the arguments that soon were to emerge in the *Brown v. Board of Education* decision, with its emphasis on the psychological effect of segregation. "Segregation dramatizes a stigma, and becomes a badge of inferiority," he explained, and those segregated always lost a degree of self-respect and experienced an attack on mental health (surely Thurman had himself in mind here, as his internal rage at being a Negro in a segregated society manifested itself in episodes of depression and physical pain). Those who were the despised of society could not help but despise themselves in turn, and could thus, in equal and opposite reaction, develop tendencies toward their own expressions of chauvinism. But in moments of national crisis, the despised could take opportunities to attack at its root the system that repressed them, a fundamentally "sound instinct of self-preservation" that could lead to constructive ends. On the white side of the color line, the segregation imparted a "false sense of superiority." It simply could not be otherwise, when the white child grew up suffused within a culture that exalted his kind but degraded others.

For Thurman, the solution lay in freedom of choice. Segregation in the church, for example, came from the exclusion of Negroes. Desegregation would not necessarily effect an immediate drastic change, but freedom of choice would be available and thus the will to segregation broken. Thurman concluded with words anticipating the revolution to come over the next decades. The time would come when "I cannot wait for the thing to work itself out." With poverty and misery and oppression everywhere, the call for concrete action would not "wait for moral pressure to work its perfect work"; that could be too late. What should be the answer then? Boycotts, noncooperation, or other shocks to the system that could "tear men free from their alignments to the evil way, to free them so that they may be given an immediate sense of acute insecurity and out of the depths of their insecurity be forced to see their kinship with the weak and insecure." The dominant class would not give up its privilege, and the situation had to be given shock treatment to move men to "apply Christian idealism to un-ideal and unchristian situations." To Thurman, this was exactly what groups such as Fellowship of Reconciliation and others were doing. But, he warned, "action of this kind requires great discipline of mind, emotions and body to the end that forces may not be released that will do complete violence both to one's ideals and one's purpose." Or, as he put it in another commencement address, at Garrett Bible Institute in Evanston, Illinois, that summer of 1943,

> It is your divine assignment to announce that man lives his days under the persistent scrutiny of God—that God is at stake in man's day. How men treat each other, what they do to the environment in which little children must grow and develop, how they earn their living—all things in the making of which they play a significant part stand bare before the eyes of God. You must live and proclaim a faith that will make men affirm themselves and their fellowmen as children of God. You must lay your lives on the altar of social change so that wherever you are there the Kingdom of God is at hand.

Through his other correspondence, addresses, and personal writings, Thurman continued exploring the connection between the struggle for racial justice at home and the anti-imperialist movement abroad. Thurman had objected strenuously to the people chosen to accompany him on the student delegation to India, Edward and Phenola Carroll, but once there he did his best to give them opportunities. In the years afterward, Thurman kept up an occasional, cordial correspondence with Edward, who ended up in Alaska, as chaplain of one of three black units of the US army during World War II.

Carroll found himself in this outpost with "oodles of time to read heavy books, study the Bible, and scrutinize people," and wrote Thurman inquiring about job prospects at Howard after the war.

More important for our purposes, Carroll referenced an address of Pearl Buck that had criticized a certain provincialism among black American leaders. They were, she thought, not fully able to connect their struggle with the struggles of nonwhite peoples abroad suffering under imperialism. "If I have a criticism to make of the colored people of our country," Buck said, "it is that they have been too selfish in their interest in equality. They have thought too often of equality only for themselves in this one country—and by so doing they have limited their own struggle and robbed it of size and force and meaning for the whole human race. You are not simply a group of people in one country—you are part of the great war of the peoples for freedom." Carroll objected, asking Thurman if he agreed that "she doesn't know that Negro soldiers are thinking broadly concerning enslaved peoples all over the world." Thurman agreed, noting that Buck "approaches the problem of Negros from her background of work with the Chinese," which limited her vision.

Buck knew little of the deeply internationalist roots that lay behind the coming civil rights movement, nor of the work of leaders such as Thurman (and many others) in cultivating that. Thurman himself was involved with other educators and black leaders from that era in pressuring President Franklin Roosevelt to press the cause of Indian independence. Thurman felt a special closeness to the cause. They asked FDR to work out a provisional war government for India, leading to independence. "Lead the world boldly to victory," they demanded, "and to the building of a society which befits the dignity of man."

Meanwhile, struggles at home occupied Thurman's attention, including one case in which a Virginia sharecropper was sentenced to death for killing a farmer in a dispute over rights to crops. Kay Beach, a conscientious objector during the war, wrote worriedly to Thurman about the possible consequences of the case. Thurman responded that blacks had been "far too docile," something confused with "meekness and cowardliness." Because of this, many had turned away from nonviolent techniques, thinking that this simply worsened this aspect of cowardice. "The problem, therefore," Thurman said, was to "maintain in non-violent *action* an increment of courage that would be dissociated from the so called 'hat in the hand' attitude." Thurman had seen the possibilities for violence flare up everywhere. He had traveled through the country in 1942 and saw the same thing everywhere—"sporadic outbursts of violence, meanness, murder, bloodshed, and a great paralysis in the presence of it all." That made all the more important the work of "small groups in communities all over the United States demonstrating courageous, peaceful action, carefully planned and carefully executed."

During this time, as well, Thurman appeared frequently before the Young People's Inter-Racial Fellowship in Philadelphia, a kind of precursor to the Fellowship Church in San Francisco. Its cofounder Marjorie Penney had created the fellowship as part of the Friends' Young People's Inter-Racial Fellowship Committee on Race Relations. Thurman was impressed enough to express interest in becoming a full-time pastor if the project turned into a regular congregation. Penney delighted in Thurman's preaching; he expressed a "Fellowship point of view," she told him. And no wonder she thought that, given Thurman's deep immersion in Quaker thought during his time at Haverford College and his talks with Rufus Jones. As well, Thurman corresponded with William Worthy, then the secretary of the Inter-Racial Fellowship. They wrote of the case of William Sutherland, a conscientious objector during the war who, afterward, became an antinuclear activist and active in international radical and anticolonial politics in Africa. Worthy explained to Thurman that they were carrying on Sutherland's work to build an organization with the goal of "total democracy now."

Thurman, James Farmer, and others worked deeply through issues of nonviolent protest action during the war. In late 1942, A. Philip Randolph had proposed initiating a Gandhian campaign, one that would entail African Americans not in the armed forces or in particular situations at work to "disobey any law which violates their basic citizenship rights, such as Jim-Crow cars and all forms of discrimination." But Farmer expressed his worries about the idea, fearing that such a course could lead to massacres of blacks and generally a setback to the nonviolent philosophy. Eventually, Randolph aligned his efforts with Fellowship of Reconciliation and with the Congress of Racial Equality. Thurman explained to Farmer that he too saw dangers in Randolph's plan, because "non-violent civil disobedience is a technique that presupposes very definite discipline. It is an act of the will arising out of a profound spiritual conviction, which by its very nature is devoid either of ill-will, contempt, or cowardice." Thurman reflected back on his experience and talks with Gandhi, who had told him that similar plans for civil disobedience in India had collapsed because "the masses of the people were not able to sustain so lofty a creative idea over a time interval of sufficient duration to be practically effective." Moreover, civil disobedience was a kind of last resort, and black Americans still had access to court challenges. Certainly nonviolent protest and civil disobedience were valuable tools, but they required particular spiritual disciplines and fortitude "so that the masses of the people will not be inspired by fear, revenge, or hate." It would take a future generation and an expansion of the tactics and philosophy of the civil rights movement to modify Gandhian ideas to fit the black American context. When that happened, Thurman was delighted; but in the 1940s, intellectually he could not truly foresee what was to come when his own ideas came to be applied in a mass movement of nonviolent civil disobedience.

In the early 1940s, Thurman was well placed at Howard, had an adequate salary to support his family, and, despite his increasing conflicts with Howard's president Mordecai Wyatt Johnson, was happy in his post.

It was, then, a shock to all when he took a new, highly uncertain position with an experimental church in San Francisco, where he would be a copastor initially with a somewhat difficult white Presbyterian. Thurman's years at Howard had provided him major challenges and epic experiences abroad; now he was to embark on what he himself came to see as his "great adventure": to strike directly at the heart of the disease of segregation thoroughly embedded in American Christian churches. And yet, nothing brought Thurman more satisfaction in his life than his work with the Church for the Fellowship of All Peoples. It was one of the first self-consciously multiracial congregations in American history. It began as a sort of experimental mission run by Presbyterians and ended as an experiment in remaking Protestantism in America, in terms of both its interracial attendance and its worship methods.

Thurman's cosmopolitan vision expressed itself in the church that he served from 1944 to 1953. He took great pride in it, and his face long afterward remained the symbol of the church and its hopes. Thurman also worked to balance church as *church*, a place where people sought spiritual sustenance, and church as a center for activism and working out visions for a new and better world. He envisioned the Church for the Fellowship of All Peoples as a tool to do precisely that. He was ready to lay his life on the altar of social change.

"A Sense of Coming Home"
The Great Adventure in San Francisco

There was kindling in my mind the possibility that this may be the opportunity toward which my life had been moving.

— *Howard Thurman*, Footprints of a Dream

Howard Thurman moved to San Francisco in July of 1944 to pursue his dream of an interracial fellowship. He had visited San Francisco for the first time in the late 1920s and had taken immediately to the city. In his published memoirs, he recalled attending staff meetings of the national YMCA held in California in the early 1930s. One summer, as he recollected, "when I disembarked from the Oakland ferry and walked down Market Street, I had a sense of coming home that I never felt any place else in the world." The city by the bay was, from that point forward, his real home, even during his years in Boston from 1953 to 1965. Little wonder that he moved back west after his retirement from Boston University and lived out his days on Stockton Street, near the north bay and Coit Tower, where he served as a mentor to a small but influential group of disciples who would go on to careers in the church, in academia, and in social activism.

Thurman moved to San Francisco to pursue what he considered one of the great adventures of his life: to establish an interracial congregation in America "that was capable of cutting across all racial barriers, with a carryover into the common life, a fellowship that would alter the behavior patterns of those involved." He wrote to a correspondent, "If Christianity cannot do this, then we shall have to find some other faith, and there is no other faith on the horizon." It could be, he thought, the fulfillment of the vision he had at Khyber Pass. When spirits spoke to him in natural settings, Thurman listened, and remembered.

His work with the Fellowship Church seemed to embody his thoughts in "The Meaning of Commitment," when he wrote: "Commitment means that it is possible for a man to yield the nerve center of his consent to a purpose or cause, a movement or an ideal, which may be more important to him than whether he lives or dies. The commitment is a self-conscious act of will by which he affirms his identification with that he is committed to. The character of this commitment is determined by that to which the center or core of his consent is given." Then in the prime of his powers, Thurman wanted to "find out for myself whether or not it is true that experiences of spiritual unity and fellowship are more compelling than the fears and dogmas and prejudices that separate men."

Leaving Howard University behind, he came to San Francisco during an era of rapid transition. It was a city of 630,000 just before World War II; of those, only about 5,000 were African American. By the end of the war, thanks to westward immigration, approximately 32,000 African Americans lived in the city (and many more lived across the bay, in Oakland, Berkeley, and Richmond). The Fillmore District, just west of Van Ness Avenue, grew into a black neighborhood. Many lived in small rooms and apartments recently vacated by Japanese Americans; about 5,000 Japanese Americans from San Francisco ended up in internment camps. One local NAACP leader in San Francisco noted that "Caucasian San Francisco turned to the machinery already at hand for the subjugation of the Oriental and applied it to the Negro," referring to residential segregation and unequal treatment in nearly all areas of municipal life.

The Church for the Fellowship of All Peoples, originally located in the Fillmore and thus identified as a congregation in a black neighborhood, eventually found its home in the Russian Hill neighborhood of the city. The eventual results of his great experiment suggest much about what Thurman did and did not accomplish with his dream of a cosmopolitan American Christianity. In answering a query about interracial churches nationally, Thurman had written that "there is an increasing concern within the church for interracial justice and fellowship, but I'm convinced that the church is unwilling to solve this dilemma. It is committed to a revolutionary ethic and diluted into thinking that the revolutionary ethic can be implemented in less than revolutionary terms. It is for this reason that the church has been content with various expressions of the missionary impulse." His goal, in part, was to change that, to implement the "revolutionary ethic" in a revolutionary way, and in the context of a permanent church deeply embedded in a multicultural environment. His venture in San Francisco failed to produce the long-term results he hoped for, but his life's work, including his congregation in San Francisco, proved influential in the broader movements of American religion after World War II.

A cautious man generally, and one ever sensitive to financial strain, Thurman was not one to gamble big or act impulsively. And his venture in San Francisco was not an impulsive act.

Months of correspondence preceded the move. The nonviolent activist A. J. Muste served as a sort of intermediary, talking with the Reverend Alfred G. Fisk, chairman of the Department of Psychology and Philosophy at San Francisco State College, about recruiting a black copastor to work for a projected interracial congregation in San Francisco. In 1943, Fisk contacted Thurman about finding a part-time divinity student who might be interested in participating in the experiment. At first, Thurman later said, he did not see a connection between himself and the church, but later realized that San Francisco was the "ideal center" for his religio-racial experiment, "with its varied nationalities, its rich intercultural heritages, and its face resolutely fixed toward the Orient."

Together with Fisk, Thurman helped plan what soon came to be called the Church for the Fellowship of All Peoples. It was one of the first self-consciously multiracial congregations in American history. There were predecessors from the nineteenth century, including Tremont Temple in Boston, and more recently, a variety of interracial religious experiments in Philadelphia, Los Angeles, and other cities. But Thurman had something more permanent in mind. Just before his arrival, Thurman wrote to Fisk that "we must keep in mind constantly that the kind of church that we are building has never been built in the United States before. We must not hamper the creative form that the spirit of God may inspire, by clinging to the patterns with which we are ordinarily familiar."

Initially, Fisk saw Thurman as someone who could recommend good candidates for an African American copastor. "We are committed to a real equality between the races in all aspects of church organization," Fisk wrote, including the church boards, the choir, and in all the other normal church activities. "It should be *of* and *by* and *for* both groups," Fisk wrote to Thurman. The initial post for the copastor would be part time but could grow into full time. "Could you suggest to us the man? We are very anxious not to delay too long, lest we lose the enthusiasm we have now," he pleaded.

Thurman did indeed have some men in mind, most notably his close friend Herbert King. Thurman recommended King as someone with "wide interracial experience"; and in fact, King had just lost his position as national secretary for the Student Division of the YMCA, a bitter split that angered Thurman and motivated him to seek out other opportunities for his friend. But King was a little uncertain about the proposed post. Aside from the low salary, he wondered if he would have to accord with the position of Fellowship of Reconciliation. Though not a "militarist," he explained to Fisk, "I am not a Pacifist." Ultimately, the position was not suited to King.

But more than anyone else, Thurman had himself in mind, initially not so much in a conscious way but in a way that betrayed himself in his answers to Fisk. He felt "excited" about the prospects for the church and wanted to take some time away from Howard University to help out. "It seems to me to be the most significant single step that institutional Christianity is taking in the direction of a really new order for America," he told Fisk in October of 1943.

Thurman connected his experiences to the opportunities opened up by the war. As always, he was horrified by the war itself but understood that it had created breaches in the racial wall that would not be there otherwise. "It is for this reason that war, despite its terror, wreckage and stark tragedy, makes so great an appeal to men, women and even children," he told one audience, because it gave the sense of being "engaged in a total enterprise that is meaningful." For the ordinary individual, war provided a means of counting for something—"his country cares about what he does—all secondary and tertiary citizens becomes citizens, first class."

In Thurman's case, the chance to open the Fellowship Church as a national model for a truer fellowship of Christianity was irresistible. It could be, he thought, both the culmination of his life's work to date and the model and springboard for a national movement that could remake the implicit racial rules that had stifled American Christianity. If such a church could be established in every community, he thought, "the Church itself would once again set in motion those spiritual processes which gave to it its original impetus and power."

Fisk moved quickly to embrace Thurman's enthusiasm. After giving him a brief history of the activities to date, he continued, "And now if Howard Thurman could come, it would be a climax in this movement toward the firm establishment of a socially integrated community. What a testimony it would be to 'the new world a-coming.'" Fisk noted that the church had little to offer yet by way of a solid membership or even a salary. It was probably a place more suited to a seminary student, and even then Fisk would have to tell him, "You must be able to see the invisible, as a prerequisite for coming." Yet Thurman's coming might produce the change they hoped to see in the world. Thurman's star status nationally could draw congregants and thus financial stability for the nascent congregation. "Shall I say that the destiny of San Francisco hangs in your hands," Fisk asked rhetorically. "I must be realistic—but I hope for the best," he concluded.

In their correspondence in late 1943, Fisk hoped to persuade Thurman to come by the end of the year. "San Francisco, so it seems to me now, is doomed if you do not come. . . . There is no one in the nation who could do what you could do here." But Thurman's commitments at Howard as well as family matters—the pressures of caring for his mother, a daughter about to go to college, and a musically talented daughter whose lessons had to be paid for—all detained him. Fisk kept trying, but July 1944 would be the earliest possible opportunity, although Thurman said he could possibly visit during the Christmas holidays.

In the meantime, the two corresponded on matters of both grave and minor importance. One was simply the name of the church; some wanted to call it Neighborhood Church, but that didn't fit with Fisk's broader conception for the role of the congregation; he hoped for something like Fellowship Church, with a subheading "For All People." Fisk also noted the real, albeit loose, connection with the Presbyterian denomination (his home) but admitted he did not even know what denominational connection Thurman had. Later the question of denominational connection would create something of a rift between the two. Fisk was a Presbyterian by birth and training, and he understood the church to be the extension of a Presbyterian mission project—the Presbyterians had loaned them the building and money for the budget, he pointed out to Thurman, without even requiring them to put the name "Presbyterian" on the sign outside the church. Yet younger people in the church sought less of a Presbyterian, or even a Christian, commitment, and thus Fisk sought Thurman's advice and views on the nature of the church affiliation.

Fisk wanted to know where Thurman thought he would fit into the project—as a pastor with a total commitment to the local church or as more of a guest star preacher, speaking to the congregation on occasion but more involved in addressing broader audiences in the area and nationally. Fisk had recruited a young associate pastor to work there temporarily, the Reverend Albert B. Cleage, whose later work in leading black nationalist congregations in Detroit made him well known in the 1960s. But Fisk and Cleage clashed almost immediately, and Cleage's internship at the church ended before Thurman arrived. Thurman and Cleage apparently never met in person.

Fisk went over various possibilities for halls or auditoriums that the church might rent that could accommodate the hoped-for growth of the congregation. The church found its first home at 1500 Post Street, just west of Van Ness Avenue in San Francisco, in the Fillmore District, then a majority black area, next to the formerly Japanese neighborhood of the city.

Thurman responded in early 1944, outlining his plans for working with the church during what was projected to be a year or two leave of absence from Howard. He hoped to see "how well and intimately two men of different races sharing common leadership of a church can work themselves into the life of a community made up of different races." Thurman worried about being consumed by other activities outside the congregation, leaving little time for calm reflection. Yet, "On the other hand I do not want to seem to be some kind of ecclesiastical prima donna." He looked for some medium point between those extremes.

During these months, Thurman kept up his public writing and speaking, including a short essay titled "The White Problem." He published it in 1944 as part of a series of articles on race, inspired by Gunnar Myrdal's work *An American Dilemma*, on the problem of race in America. Thurman explained his philosophical views on personhood succinctly. The race pride and arrogance of the dominant powers that had led to the world war could only be replaced by a "will to brotherhood" that would mean "placing a crown over every man's head and using all of one's powers to enable him to grow tall enough to wear it." The test of true religion, especially Christianity, would be ordering social life on this ideal: "If Christianity cannot resolve racial prejudice, notions of white supremacy and class conflict, it is doomed to become merely an esoteric sect stripped of all power and redemption."

As Thurman prepared for his move, Fisk kept him informed about the doings of the church, fund-raising possibilities, and problems that already were emerging between his rather more traditional view of the church and those of the Sakai group. This was a small group of radical women who lived in a house owned by a Japanese American who had been detained in a camp during the war. They subscribed to the tenets of the British pacifist Muriel Lester. Thurman later also clashed with these congregants, who had a more explicitly political vision of the role of the church itself.

Fisk already experienced philosophical conflicts with the temporary associate pastor Albert Cleage. Their relationship broke down completely shortly after Cleage arrived. As Fisk saw it, Cleage had alienated congregation members: "He is said to stand for Negro 'nationalism'—which I really doubt, but he certainly has a defeatist outlook."

But Cleage's views were close to Thurman's views ideologically, although he was more outspokenly political. Much later, Cleage told a biographer that "an interracial church is a monstrosity and an impossibility," despite the well-meaning attempts of its founders. But at that time, Cleage in fact had asked Angelo Herndon, an African American activist and writer, not to publish a story about his dismissal from the church, for fear that it would impede the work of Thurman, and Thurman expressed his gratitude: "the general opinion is that venture[s] of this sort simply cannot work. Any publicity revealing friction simply jeopardizes the possibility of the fulfillment of the idea." Later, Thurman told Fisk that he was glad Cleage would stay until late June, just before Thurman's arrival, as the appearance that Fisk and Cleage simply couldn't work together would feed suspicions more generally about interracial cooperation. And at the time Cleage indicated that he saw the church as a "live and vital force in the community concerning itself with all problems effecting the rights of the Negro." In October of 1944, moreover,

Cleage had expressed warm support for the church. The next year, in May 1945, Cleage asked Thurman to recommend him as pastor of an interracial church in Detroit: "I am sincerely interested in the inter-racial church idea and feel that its extension during these critical days is a most significant contribution to the building of a more Christian world. My experience in San Francisco might be of value to a new project," he wrote to Thurman, who provided the recommendation, calling Cleage a "socially minded, intelligent young man."

What a "more Christian world" entailed, exactly, differed from what Fisk had in mind. Cleage saw the interracialism of the church as a means of addressing the "socio-economic framework" that kept blacks in submission. And he saw opportunities to cooperate with various political groups. As Cleage saw it, the basic weakness of the church was the lack of a "common social philosophy," because "people cannot work together to accomplish any program, however small, unless they agree in their interpretations of the total world in which they live." This was not just confined to the new church in San Francisco but was the dilemma of liberal Christianity in the United States more generally: "Liberal Christians everywhere can no longer avoid their total responsibility to society by making pleasant and ineffective gestures in restricted and isolated areas of living." The true Christian church could not just be a place where people of different races worshiped together but must "function in every area of life as a united liberal force striking fearlessly out against all forms of oppression, bigotry and inequality. Its friends are the friends of human freedom no matter what the banner beneath which they march, and its foes are the oppressors of mankind, even though they march beneath the banner of Christ."

Thurman straddled the respective visions of Fisk and Cleage; his notion of the church was less traditionalist than Fisk's and less overtly political than Cleage's. But that is not to say that he shied away from embracing figures or causes controversial in the public mind. At one point, Thurman had suggested enlisting his friend Paul Robeson, the talented African American singer and political activist (long associated with causes of the Left and with the Communist Party), to give a benefit concert on behalf of the church, a prospect Fisk found "thrilling." In writing to Robeson to see about the concert, Thurman described for him the vision for the church. "Is it possible to create an island of religious and racial community in a sea of religious and racial tension and animosity?" he wondered. Would it be possible for a white man and a black man to share responsibilities equally, and to minister to all equally "on the basis of their respective gifts rather than their racial affiliations"? Thurman hoped to use the church to explore creative worship possibilities, to host intercultural talks and lectures, and to foster in the children of the congregation an "appreciation of religion as a part of life of other people and their culture as an important increment of democracy."

At the end of his term at Howard, Thurman went over the demands of the previous year at Rankin Chapel, noting that "to the most casual observer it is clear that the collapse of so many stable things in our world has heightened a deeper sense of social and personal stability in the lives of countless people." It was there that the "chapel has rendered a service unique in the university and of profoundest significance." But that too had come at a high cost. As Thurman expressed it, "The demands for counselling grow out of the Sunday Services [and] move in a continuous stream. All of this means that the Dean of the Chapel finds it impossible to get any one single day of complete rest. He has no Sabbath, no day of rest!"

Thurman was to find no rest upon his arrival in San Francisco, either. Although not one to keep personal diaries, Thurman's reflections on his first two months in the city by the bay suggest much about both his excitement regarding his "bold adventure" and his immediate recognition of the challenges that would face him. Thurman got off the ferry after his cross-country trip, and Fisk, whom he described immediately as "a highly nervous and tense individual with a deep sense of mission and a profound sincerity" but one whose "goal tends to stifle his imagination," immediately took Thurman to meetings and conferences lasting most of the day. "This is the kind of zeal that Alfred Fisk has," Thurman commented warily. Perhaps aware of his own propensities toward hyperactivity, Fisk later wrote to Thurman, "I think that I do need your ministry of spiritual quietness."

Thurman also noted the general impression of the church as a haven for pacifists. But Thurman's extensive work with black men in the military had given him a different vision. He may have been a pacifist, but he was not an "absolutist." He was not so "because I do not have the wisdom to be that. The Pacifism of the church should express itself in the quality of life that emanates from the place rather than from pronouncements of one kind or another." Thurman also sensed early on the problems he was going to have with the Presbyterians. "The church is so completely dominated by secularism that it expects to behave just as business does with reference to investments," he noted. The Presbyterians expected to exercise control over the congregation, forgetting that this was a "unique venture" in which God's free and creative spirit should be given ample space to move.

In his first missive back to friends and supporters at Howard University in October 1944 (when he still was on a one-year leave of absence, soon to be a two-year leave), he detailed the kinds of community work he had plunged into in the city, including consultations with the Conference of Jews and Christians, the San Francisco Council of Churches, and other local and national organizations; and for Sue, a whirlwind of activities ranging from the local PTA to serving on the board of directors of the International Institute of San Francisco. Howard's first daughter, Olive, was set to attend Vassar, and the daughter of Howard and Sue, Anne, pursued her musical talents and found her place in the Junior Workshop of the Fellowship Church. But Thurman also enjoyed being a tourist, visiting Fisherman's Wharf and Chinatown, describing the two great bridges of the city, Golden Gate Park, art museums, and other delights: "You will have a gay time in this queen of cities," he assured his friends back east. (Thurman could not have known the double entendre his word choices would imply for readers of later generations.) Significantly, as well, Thurman mentioned Pauli Murray's pursuit of a law degree at the University of California in Berkeley and Thurgood Marshall's service in the Port Chicago incident (an explosion at a munitions-loading shipyard north of San Francisco that killed or injured over two hundred African Americans in the navy, after which a group of survivors received court martials for refusing to load ordnance on the ships).

Thurman arrived in San Francisco during the last year of the war and delivered sermons and addresses around California on the subject of wartime conditions and postwar aspirations. He soon had the church involved with the early gatherings of the United Nations, an organization that seemed to embody many of Thurman's dreams of international cooperation. Dating from the formation of the United Nations, Fellowship Church and its members were actively involved in the work of its constituent organizations, including UNESCO (United Nations Educational, Scientific and Cultural Organization). Twelve members of the Intercultural Workshop, led by Sue Thurman, had attended the UNESCO Plenary Conference in Paris in 1949, including the Fellowship Quintet, under the leadership of Corrine Barrow Williams, the music director of the church. While at the UNESCO house, the delegation had met with Reinhold Niebuhr, a supporter of the church. The group subsequently toured the United States, and Sue Thurman also led workshops on "the Indian in American life." Meanwhile, the church had been involved with a work put on by the San Francisco Symphony Orchestra, held at the War Memorial Opera House (location of the meeting where the UN was born), with Howard Thurman serving as a narrator for a musical setting of the Psalms.

Thurman had called listeners to ask the question, "How can a nation engaged in total war provide for the internal survival of those values with which in its most lucid moments it identifies life itself?" The answer would come from those "who are willing to be Apostles of Sensitiveness for the whole nation." They would be advocates for the "ideals and ideas of democracy," who would never permit those ideals to be subverted and would resist every effort to be labeled as Reds or subversives. They would keep alive "the flickering torch" that would "remain alight in the postwar years," keeping the ideals alive even during a wartime when they "seem most irrational and fanciful." Moreover, minorities were particularly well placed to serve as apostles of sensitiveness, precisely because they were "most directly and immediately exposed to the effects of the breakdown of the democratic ideals in the body politic. The more stigmatized is the minority, the more tragic the plight the keener will be this awareness." In the end, the apostles of sensitiveness would serve as "nerve ends for the body politic," exposing to others the "open sores in the democratic national life."

Just after the war, Thurman further developed his concept of the apostles of sensitiveness, in a sermon delivered at the Cathedral of St. John the Divine in Manhattan. He preached:

There can be no love among men even on the most intimate levels of their experience, if they are not alive to each other, if they are unable to have a sense of what is vital to, and within, another. This is the authentic basis of respect for personality. In essence it means meeting people where they are, *and treating them there* as if they were where they ought to be. By so doing, one places a crown over their heads that for the rest of their lives they are trying to grow tall enough to wear. To have a highly developed sense of fact with regard to other people is the searching demand of our faith, if we are to be in the spot which we occupy—Apostles of Sensitiveness.

The apostles would also have a developed sense of alternative visions of life, of freedom. They would know that what they saw around them did not have to be. "However barren may be the manner or the circumstance," he said, "the growing edge is implicit in the fact of existence and it becomes not only reasonable but also mandatory for the human spirit, brooding creatively over any aspect of experience. . . . The Apostle of Sensitiveness is profoundly aware of what is vital, quickening and alive and becomes the very point at which God breathes into circumstance, the breath of life."

For Thurman, even during the days of dramatic developments in public life, the inner life was still determinative. "What he seeks in the world of activity," he wrote of the spiritual seeker just after the war, "is that of which he is already deeply aware in his inner life. The clue to the outer world of relations is found in the inner world of experience." The advance of the tools of destruction in the modern world meant that "nothing short of a profound revolution in the basic structure of our thought about human life and human destiny can be of any avail." The words of Jesus remained revolutionary two thousand years after he lived precisely because so little progress had been made in realizing them; they were "timeless" only because human inaction had made them so.

THURMAN AS PASTOR

The Church for the Fellowship of All Peoples had a rocky start. Originally connected with, and heavily subsidized by, the Presbyterian Church, the congregation was quickly pushed by Thurman in a different direction. The last thing he wanted was a mission church, and even less so a "neighborhood church," when it was clear that racial segregation defined American neighborhoods. If the church remained in the Fillmore District of San Francisco (where it originally was located), he realized, it would quickly become a black church, and nonblack congregants would disappear; this would defeat the entire purpose of the enterprise. In any event, the church soon outgrew its original location, and it became necessary to move simply for practical reasons of space. He resisted being made the object of "charity and condescension" by Presbyterians, however well meaning they might be, because in that case "the crippling disease that has dogged the vitality and the health of the Christian enterprise would have overtaken us—the deadly disease of condescension. Very quickly we would have become a dumping ground for uplifters and the challenge of the development of an integrated religious fellowship would have bounced off the conscience and hearts of the people. For herein lies the great temptation: *If a man can feel sorry for you, he can very easily absolve himself from dealing with you in any sense as an equal.*"

Eventually, Thurman moved the church out of the orbit of the Presbyterians. It became an independent congregation, subsidized in part by a national group of supporters and also by fees from Thurman's near-constant speaking engagements. Thurman lived on trains as much as he lived in the city itself. His star was in its ascendancy, his presence sought everywhere, his name growing into a celebrity theologian and minister.

As Thurman settled into his new role as pastor of Fellowship Church, first in conjunction with Fisk but soon by himself, he avidly, and uncharacteristically for him, publicized the church by writing articles in journals and periodicals, sending fund-raising form letters to current and potential supporters, and drawing in celebrity supporters such as Paul Robeson and Eleanor Roosevelt. This was exactly the kind of work that led him always to reject roles in academic administration. But for the church, and in support of his great adventure, he struck out on new paths.

The church, he wrote in 1945, less than a year after moving to accept its copastorate, was a dream that had "haunted" him for ten years. He recounted his affiliation with the fellowship congregation of the American Friends Service Committee, the germ of the idea. But the Fellowship Church in San Francisco intended to have a full-time pastor and represented a "creative experiment in interracial and intercultural communion, deriving its inspiration from a spiritual interpretation of the meaning of life and dignity of man." The church was there to show that the God of life and the God of religion were one. Therefore, relationships between men should be based on warm fellowship rather than "distrust, prejudice, and strife." He noted as well the importance of placing this experiment within the "framework of historical Protestantism." To Thurman, if his venture could spread to other cities, then the "Church itself would once again set in motion those spiritual processes which gave to it its original impetus and power. . . . To those of us who have dreamed of it for years, it represents an authentic growing edge for far-reaching social change in making possible communities of friendly men in a world grown gray with suffering and hate."

Thurman consistently resisted several models he had seen in the past: the mission church, which invariably became an object of condescension; the social mission or activist institutional church, which could easily lose its spiritual moorings; and the church with no connection to social life, which could easily lose its ethical imperative. His vision was of a church with strong spiritual grounding that would prepare, strengthen, and fill with God's love those who carried on a struggle for justice in the social world. The church had a social mission, but not one that was direct; it was not the job of the church to organize protests, to become social service agencies, or to directly involve itself in political life. Rather, as Thurman saw it, individuals in the thick of the struggle should have a place to "be able to find renewal and fresh courage in the spiritual resources of the church. . . . The true genius of the church was revealed by what it symbolized as a beachhead in society in terms of community, and as an inspiration to the solitary individual to put his weight on the side of a society in which no person need be afraid."

By 1949, the church numbered about 285 members, with whites composing about 60 percent of the total; a few years later, whites made up about half, and blacks about 40 percent, of its 345 members. Some congregants envisioned the church as a center for social activism and protest, more so than was ever the case with Thurman. The church became Thurman's own, a kind of trial project for his ideas. The initial commitment spoke of congregants seeking "after a vital interpretation of God as revealed in Jesus of Nazareth whose fellowship with God was the foundation of his fellowship with men," and of people desiring "to have a part in the unfolding of the ideal of Christian fellowship through the union of men and women of varying national, cultural, racial, or creedal heritage in church communion."

The black press publicized Fellowship Church as well. During a meeting of the UN Conference on International Organizations, the church brought in speakers such as W. E. B. Du Bois, Mordecai Wyatt Johnson, and others. The church also hosted a dinner for black journalists who were there to cover the opening meetings of what would become the UN; Sue Thurman, representing the National Council of Negro Women, was one of several unofficial delegates to the founding meeting. Characteristically for her, she registered her dissatisfaction with the representation of people of color in the new organization, and the way imperial powers had sought to control the proceedings.

A reporter for the *Baltimore Afro-American* wrote of how the church contrasted with other experiments, communal ventures, and charismatic messiah figures that had arisen in black life:

> Dr. Thurman, working with a white pastor, is operating a church in which the race question has been abolished. The important thing is that the members are not cultists or fanatics, or screwballs—just plain everyday substantial citizens from all walks of life who believe in cooperation and practical Christianity. There are no mystic rites. Nobody thinks he's God, there are no angels and nobody pretends to be blessed with eternal life. This takes the stigma off of interracial mixing. The divisionists have cleverly perpetuated the idea in America that if white and colored work together they are members of the lunatic fringe. This keeps a lot of decent people in the same old rut.

Here, in praising Fellowship Church, the journalist took a swipe at the various new religious movements (most notably Father Divine's Peace Mission Movement), generally portrayed as "cults" in both the white and African American press. Thurman's intellectual sheen and emphasis on high culture in services stood in contrast to other marginalized groups, and drew warm praise for that.

A year into his tenure at the church, Thurman moved to separate it from its Presbyterian affiliation, sending a polite but firm letter of his intention to the denomination's Board of National Missions in July 1945. Before then, Thurman had met with Jacob A. Long, who managed urban mission work for the Presbyterian Church (USA), and the two determined that their visions were simply not reconcilable. Long wanted a neighborhood church serving a very particular (and largely African American) local community; Thurman envisioned something different. Long told Thurman that the Presbyterians could not support independent projects, and that he wished the Fellowship Church could have maintained its "community character" even while retaining an affiliation with the denominational organization. Thurman replied, in August 1945, that the church sought to establish an independent identity, outside the bounds of a mission or neighborhood church. There would come a time, he noted, when "internally the interracial and intercultural core of our Church is so well established that we can do a community job without our becoming a racial Church," but he implied that time had not yet come.

The pride Thurman took in his work is evident in his letter to Eleanor Roosevelt in March 1946, documenting the growth and progress of the church from a small group of 35 when he first arrived to a racially diverse group of 150 less than two years later, now organized permanently "as an Interdenominational, interracial, as well as intercultural Church." He saw that racially diverse groups could worship together harmoniously, and this spirit could carry over into community life: "This is of the profoundest significance both for Democracy and for Christianity."

Through these years, Thurman kept up his correspondence with Mary McLeod Bethune, his lifelong friend and perhaps the person he admired the most outside of his own family. In one letter from 1950, in which he hoped Bethune could arrange for a fund-raising dinner in Washington, DC, for the church, he made known his concern about the seeming distancing from the church by Bethune's friend Eleanor Roosevelt. "When it was in the dream stage, she was very greatly interested and enthusiastic and became one of our first National Members," he wrote to Bethune, but he now found Mrs. Roosevelt's attitude puzzling. What Eleanor Roosevelt stood for in the United Nations was precisely what the church was doing at the grassroots level. Perhaps if she had a greater awareness "of our experience here," he suggested, it would strengthen the former First Lady "as she undertakes the same kind of work project on an international and world-wide scale." This particular entreaty, however, proved unsuccessful.

The same war that provided opportunities also extracted its cost from Thurman. As the war ended and black soldiers returned, seeking education and opportunity, Howard University boomed in enrollment. Thurman had to choose whether to resign his post at Howard permanently or to return. He tried gamely to persuade President Mordecai Wyatt Johnson to understand that he could combine both sets of work. They could in fact work in synergy, he thought, with Fellowship Church operating both for the good of the national church community and for Howard University. Earlier, he had written to Johnson that "when I secured my leave from Howard I did not feel that my work there had been completed." He hoped to continue his ministry to returning war veterans, feeding their desire for deeper religious experience. But Johnson would have none of it. He told Thurman to make his choice.

Pulled between his various plans and desires, his love for Howard University and his desire to do something revolutionary within the world of American Christianity, Thurman in 1946 had to commit his energies fully. Johnson apparently had implied that Thurman's frequent speaking engagements and travels had made him less central to life at the university; he resented the insinuation, pointing proudly to his building up the program at Rankin Chapel over twelve years, his work through innumerable nights and weekends, and the connection of his speaking and work at other churches and universities with fertilizing religious life at Howard (including his fostering of student exchanges, for example). But in April 1946, Johnson wrote to inform Thurman that all leaves of absence would end by June. Thurman would need to return to Howard full time or resign. This was not due to any lack of regard for the work Thurman was conducting with the Fellowship Church, but simply because the demands of educating the postwar students required "the full-time attention of the ablest personnel we can secure."

Johnson's position made perfect sense; the end of the war and the GI Bill created a massive demand for college education, and most black students had a limited selection of universities that would accept them. That was not how Thurman saw it. Angered and frustrated, Thurman sent his letter of resignation on May 13 directly to Johnson, adding that he did so "with emotional lacerations and a deep sense of personal loss." Thurman genuinely loved Howard University; "the students and faculty are a part of the very fiber of my life," he noted, and he regretted that the actions of the trustees had made it impossible for him to split his time between his church in San Francisco and Howard. In a separate letter to the chair of the Department of Religion at Howard, he noted his sense of a "deep urgency and an exhilaration" coming from his decision to sever his ties but regretted that he would not be able to use Howard to cultivate possible ministerial candidates to carry on his work of leading institutions such as the Fellowship Church. In another letter to a friend, he described his decision as the most "crucial" one of his life, "because it means burning bridges behind and sailing forth in the open independence of the sea. There is a deep sense of quiet confidence that has come over me now." This joined the loss of his first wife as Thurman's emotionally crucial turning points as an adult.

Around the same time as his resignation from Howard, in the summer of 1946, came the separation from Alfred Fisk and the end of the experiment of copastoring the congregation in San Francisco. Fisk wrote to Thurman that August, indicating his dissatisfaction with the Fellowship Church as a place for his family, most particularly for its lack of any particular family programs. He criticized the lack of any significant ceremony for joining the church and becoming a Christian. That was a spiritual event that should be marked, he thought, with a ceremony at least as significant as that of becoming a United States citizen. Fisk had criticized "churchianity," but at the same time he had lived his life within the organized church and still felt it could greatly influence and benefit society. He had wanted to stay with the church because of his "earnest commitment to interracial brotherhood," but his commitment to his family came first. Fisk seemed to experience the same "emotional laceration" at the break as Thurman experienced with his resignation from Howard. Later, Thurman spoke warmly about Fisk, but the two had no real personal interaction following Fisk's withdrawal from the church. In any event, it seems likely that Fisk simply recognized that Thurman was the star, and there was not that much of a place for him as copastor.

Starting in 1947, the Church for the Fellowship of All Peoples was Thurman's own. He was the star attraction as preacher, and while the church was not that large in size, its influence was outsized. Sue, meanwhile, pioneered in developing intercultural education in the church educational curriculum, continued assembling an impressive doll collection from around the world, and led a group of church members on an international excursion to participate in one of the first UNESCO meetings in Paris in 1949. Sue also collected materials related to African American history in California, later to become part of her work *Pioneers of Negro Origin in California*, and kept up a steady correspondence and interaction with an international community interested in the church's doings. Sue continued her activism within the National Council of Negro Women and in the *Aframerican Women's Journal*, and in 1947 participated in the *Primero Congreso Interamericano de Mujeres* (First Inter-American Congress of Women) in Guatemala City, where the assembled women organized on behalf of peace, justice, and international women's rights. Sue shared Howard's internationalist vision of the postwar world but developed her own black feminist thinking that went beyond Howard's relatively few public considerations of questions of gender equality.

A 1947 pamphlet produced by the church gave one of the earliest accounts of its conception and development, from both Thurman's and Fisk's perspectives. Thurman's part, subtitled "The Historical Perspective," provides one of his many accounts of the "Khyber Pass Experience" in the winter of 1936, at the end of the journey to India. He had seen then, more clearly than ever before, that there was a "fundamental contradiction that lay like a malignant growth at the heart of the Christian movement as it had expressed itself in our own country," making the church "one of the strongest bulwarks in American life defending and exemplifying racial prejudice and the discrimination resulting therefrom." Christian and Hindu Indian students reminded the two founders forcefully of that fact. At the same time, Thurman became interested in the experiment in interracial congregations led by Marjorie Penney in Philadelphia but ultimately concluded that it "did not seem to meet the situation that was at the heart of the problem."

Upon his return from India, Thurman had engaged in experiments in creative worship at Rankin Chapel at Howard, testing not only new worship patterns but also an idea: the "growing conviction that if the Ideal is big enough and the commitment of implementation sufficiently profound, differences of race or color become superficial and trivial." And, after all,

"What bigger ideal could there be than the deepening of an experience of the living God through intercreedal, interracial and intercultural worship and the practical influence of this experience in the stream of life?"

That set the backdrop for Thurman's response to A. J. Muste and then to Alfred Fisk in 1943, and his move to the city in 1944. Thurman came determined not to fall into certain traps that historically had hampered the work of American churches. The location of the church itself was one; a church committed to desegregation, placed in a normally segregated American neighborhood, would simply replicate the very patterns that it was supposed to eradicate. Moreover, Thurman expressed his contempt for turning the church into a sort of community settlement house, "for this would merely make of the church a kind of 'dumping ground' for uplift and sacrificial helpfulness that often is terribly degrading to the personalities of all the people involved." Thurman's vision also involved being related to a historic Christian denomination but not being a direct church of that denomination. The Presbyterians provided crucial early support, without which the church could not have survived, but Thurman's dream was that a denomination could see the church as the "growing edge of a radical implementation of the Christian ideal in human relations," an ideal not replicable at present within the framework of historic American denominations. And thus the growing edge would serve as "both a challenge and as a leaven within the church itself." But that proved to be impossible, the failure itself showing the "historic dilemma" of race and American Protestantism.

As Thurman conceived it, the church should be *a church*, with a focus on worship, choral singing, and opportunities for encounters with God. The fact that the church was "born essentially in the womb of a social issue" created difficulties in maintaining its spiritual center: "the social issue is so acute that it required tremendous care to vouchsafe the religious genius." Thus, Thurman empowered study groups in the church to focus on "an understanding of mystical religion as the dynamic for such action." Ultimately, the dream was to "combine social awareness, spiritual motivation, and creative fellowship in a single unifying experience." It was not a church of just whites and blacks, or a neighborhood church, but one that sought to achieve "authentic fellowship across denominational, class, cultural, and racial lines," with a local and national membership, associate members, and support from friends "whose concern for the ideal to which we are dedicated is greater than the tendency to separateness and exclusiveness that is the curse of America and so often the disgrace of Christianity."

Toward the end of his term at Fellowship Church, a longtime friend of Thurman's, Dorothy Henderson, expressed her enthusiasm for Thurman's project and her qualms about how much could be accomplished within the world of organized religion. Thurman had written her that "it is important that we keep the frontiers moving lest we be overtaken by normalcy." Henderson responded, "This community idea is a tremendous one, for it is at this point that the church (so-called) has delighted itself with theories and generalities thus avoiding the necessity of even taking very definite stands on anything. We worship very happily in our little cloisters; then feel pretty free to adjust all over the place when we come out into the really big test of community living. This has always been my own big concern—but any effort of a lone individual seems pretty futile in the face of the well-oiled machine of organized religion." She worried too about the "delicate transference" involved when a figure such as Thurman leaves, for "when a movement is built around a personality, it is a difficult time for the movement when power moves from that one to others." Her forecast proved accurate.

In 1951, Harold E. Fey of the *Christian Century* magazine provided one of the most complete summaries of the history of Fellowship Church and snapshots of the present-day organization. Fey trumpeted a grandiose vision for Thurman's dream: "Today Gabriel stands where the Pacific Ocean, no longer a barrier but a bridge between peoples of different races, rolls through the Golden Gate. His trumpet is ready to sound." While raising some reservations and criticisms, Fey championed Thurman's fundamental idea that such an interracial and intercultural fellowship could ultimately "exert an influence out of all proportion to the size and wealth of its membership," precisely what Thurman himself had projected. And it would do so not as a self-conscious vehicle of social justice achieved through politics, but as something that would flow "directly from the power released in the lives of its members through Christian faith." That would take time to catch on, the more so, Fey said, because the church refused to "magnify its most distinctive characteristic into its one reason for existence. Its main quest is for spiritual illumination rather than to crusade against segregation or anything else." The church sought to magnify "that of God in every man."

Fey quoted from the *Growing Edge*, the church's newsletter, to give Thurman's firsthand views of his work. As Thurman reflected on his decision to take up the interracial project in San Francisco, he sought some understanding of why the church had made so little impact on the "tensions and the tragedies of human relations." He wondered why the church was the "chief of sinners in the matter of racial separateness and prejudice"? While in India, he determined that he would eventually have to "leave the relative particularism of an academic atmosphere and move into a situation in an environment not under control where an honest attempt could be made to test the validity of the religious faith of men of good will." When he was contacted about the San Francisco opportunity, he knew this was it, "if I dared to accept it"; it was precisely the "kind of opening for which we had hoped and prayed." And the result was that he "sallied forth without any assurance beyond a dream in my heart and mind and a small group with which to work."

In his own Quaker-like way, Thurman sought "the inner light of personal guidance and power," rather than pressing people directly or overdramatizing the message. Fey commented: "He has reverence for personality, but not much for the mass psychology of the typical American Christian group." He sought to give people a complete Christian experience, with much emphasis on music and the arts. Thurman reflected in everything he did, the article astutely emphasized, "the powerful influences of his Baptist and Quaker heritages, in which quietism continually struggles with a revolutionary urge to direct action." Thurman challenged the church to confront the fact that American Christianity had betrayed the religion of Jesus, with the result that the one place "in which normal free contacts might be most naturally established and in which the relation of the individual to his God should take priority over conditions of class, race, power, status, wealth or the like—this place is one of the chief instruments for guaranteeing barriers."

Thurman and Fisk both were involved in ministry to Japanese Americans and integrated Asians into the congregation. In California during the war, Thurman later wrote in his work *Luminous Darkness*, one saw "billboard caricatures of the Japanese: grotesque faces, huge buck teeth, large dark-rimmed thick-lensed eyeglasses. The point was, in effect, to read the Japanese out of the human race; they were construed as monsters and as such stood in immediate candidacy for destruction. They were so defined as to be placed in a category to which ordinary decent behavior did not apply. . . . It was open season for their potential extermination."

The Fellowship Church took on the project of reintegrating Japanese Americans into San Francisco society. In January 1945, the copastors held a dinner honoring returning Japanese Americans (many returning from internment camps), and the church attracted a few prominent local Japanese Americans to be members. In May 1947, Thurman wrote to James Baker, a Methodist minister and bishop in the state, about acquiring the services of Hiroshi John Yamashita, a second-generation Japanese American who served Methodist congregations in California. "Because of the general climate on the Pacific Coast that in some ways is not congenial to Japanese Americans," he told Baker, "we are particularly anxious to provide an experience of complete integration within our religious fellowship for Japanese Americans on all levels of participation in what we are doing." Thurman sought to place a Japanese American in a position of religious leadership in interracial congregations, after Japanese Americans had sustained "a profound injury both spiritually and psychologically from which it is extraordinarily difficult for them to emerge with some measure of vitality and health as American citizens." He did not succeed in securing Yamashita as a pastor, but the Japanese American Methodist frequently supplied its pulpit during Thurman's absences. That provided an opportunity, Thurman said, for Yamashita to "give wings to his thoughts and his spirit that in the very nature of the case, he cannot experience in a segregated church."

Meanwhile, Thurman observed patterns of discriminatory behavior against African Americans in San Francisco, a city where black workers had been packed into small neighborhoods, without adequate social services. When Thurman became aware of San Francisco public buses passing up black patrons, he complained to the superintendent of transportation in the city, who thanked him for the note and indicated that the crew could be disciplined if the charges bore themselves out. Again, despite his reputation as a mystic floating above social life, Thurman for decades directed his efforts against racist practices at local officials and institutions. He looked to break racial barriers where he could.

During these same years, he had to consider how his daughters Olive and Anne would fare as black women in a racist society, given the unusually welcoming environments in which they had lived. Olive had graduated from Vassar in 1948, and Anne was soon to be the first black graduate from the storied Emma Willard School in Troy, New York, the oldest and most renowned girls' preparatory school in the country; the school housed a number of supporters of the Fellowship School. Later, Thurman wrote a friend of his plans to have Anne spend some weeks in the summer at Fisk University (a historically black college in Nashville, where W. E. B. Du Bois had once taught) in a seminar about black life. Having effectively grown up in the interracial cocoon of the Fellowship Church, Anne would need some grounding in the racial realities of everyday American life, apart from the idealistic congregation they had created in San Francisco. "This land of ours," Thurman explained, "is still a bitter place for a sensitive Negro man or woman," and lacking a training in that would leave her "vulnerable to the poison arrows of a socially sick environment that expresses itself in gross and refined hostilities." The world of the Fellowship Church extended only so far; the world of hatred, violence, and racism lurked just beyond its doors.

Thurman doubtless was also thinking of the experience of his mother. She passed away in his home on May 2, 1950, after having been too frightened to stay at the hospital associated with Stanford University despite being cared for there by Thurman's own personal physician. Alice Thurman Sams had lived the life of the dispossessed, never fully able to escape its psychology that her son had so brilliantly dissected and analyzed.

Thurman had a long history of close and intellectually intense relations with white mentors and advisers, but there was always a veil between them. Thurman did not use the term "double consciousness" exactly as Du Bois had, but he meant much the same when he reflected on some of these experiences. He often referred to one of his final conversations with George Cross, in which the noted theologian and his esteemed professor at Rochester had urged him to "attend to timeless issues of the human spirit," without recognizing the kind of white privilege implicit in such a statement.

But on occasion, Thurman found places of fellowship with whites that transcended race. Perhaps his most important relationship in this regard was with George "Shorty" Collins. A graduate of the University of California in 1915, Collins had served in World War I. After seeing its horrors, he came home a committed pacifist, joined the Fellowship of Reconciliation, and became its southern field secretary in 1923. In that capacity, he traveled to universities in the South to advocate for FOR's position, and when visiting Morehouse College impressed the younger Thurman. The two did not see each other in person often over the years, but they always were friends. Collins had a magnetic personality and an ability to find the right advice or reading suggestion for people. Collins introduced the young nature mystic Thurman to the work of Olive Schreiner, his lifelong muse and influence.

In 1951, Thurman wrote Collins, after having missed seeing him in person in California, to thank him for what he had meant in Thurman's life. He still remembered when Collins had "invaded" the South in the early 1920s and "established little islands of understanding and fellowship in a very stormy and turbulent sea of racial tension." What Thurman especially appreciated was that Collins had done that without resorting to the kinds of paternalism that affected Thurman's relationship with many other white mentors. Collins did so "with a smile and a winsomeness and great directness." Collins acted as if he did not know how far outside of the mainstream of white Americans he was; that is what gave students confidence in him—his manner of "simple naturalness." It laid the groundwork for "many creative expressions of goodwill" in the years to come. When Thurman found whites with whom he felt a sense of affinity and spiritual kinship, he treasured their friendship and spirit. The fact that it happened so infrequently, even with fellow Christians, suggested how much the apostle of sensitiveness still lived behind the veil.

THURMAN, RELIGION, AND POLITICS IN THE POSTWAR ERA

On occasion, albeit not often, Thurman's writings took a political turn, as in his essay "The Fascist Masquerade" from the period just after World War II. A supporter of Henry Wallace-style left-progressive politics, Thurman viewed with alarm the rise of right-wing fascist groups. He deplored in particular their association with the term "Christian." "To be American is to appeal to pride of country, and, what is more important, pride of section that gives to the average individual a certain sense of separateness. . . . To be a Christian American is to be but less than an angel," he wrote of one such organization based in Houston, Texas. What explained the appeal of such groups? One attraction, Thurman posited, was simply the military style of such organizations and the sense of urgency they brought to their tasks; such was the genius of Father Coughlin, the "radio priest" who organized his listeners to act on behalf of his version of a quasi-Catholic fascism. The groups also inspired sacrifice and a "sense of collective destiny." They were also empowered by the fact that large groups of alleged Christians nationally "have stood, and, at present, stand on the side of a theory of inequality among men that causes the Church to practice in its own body some of the most vicious forms of racial prejudice." And so, hate groups had established "squatter's rights in the minds of believers because there has been no adequate teaching on the meaning of the faith in terms of human dignity and human worth." The church had the great responsibility of teaching this great truth. In not doing that, it had tacitly given support to fascist-style pseudo-Christian movements.

The demands of the state, the realities of having to advise people on whether to sign loyalty oaths, and the general atmosphere of America in the late 1940s and early 1950s left Thurman in delicate situations. For example, one church member sought his advice on involving the church with the Civil Rights Congress, a group that had some connections with the Communist Party. Thurman was deeply sympathetic to the goals of the Congress, but not at the expense of filling his church pews with government agents, surveilling the activities of the potential members or activists in the Congress. Neither did he approve of organizations that were not fully forthcoming with their allies and allegiances. "My own theory is that the channels through which I work must be channels in which I have abiding confidence," he wrote to a church member. He felt the same about the California Labor Council—ironically, precisely the kind of group that Albert Cleage had encouraged in the church during his brief internship prior to Thurman's arrival, and the focus of much animosity between him and the cofounder of the church, Alfred Fisk. But for Thurman, direct involvement of the church in potentially controversial groups ill fit the mission he saw for the congregation. Involvement with organizations branded as fronts of communism or directly involved with it, he told the congregation in 1948, would require the church to be allied either with its advocates or with red-baiters on the other side. And in either case, "we find our tongues tied."

Thurman continued preaching for years on the state of the postwar world and maintained periodic contacts with those he had met in India. A member of an international Christian organization wrote to him in 1952, remembering his time there and his talks on improving the relationship between India and America. He requested that Thurman write an article for the group's publication about black-white relationships in America: "I remember you telling us, particularly Mrs. Thurman, that the position was unfortunate. She was telling this with considerable feeling." He hoped the war might have improved matters, but "we are still reading in the papers about lynchings going on here and there in your country though not in the old extensive style. Still the problem seems to remain there."

Like everyone else who had paid careful attention to India, Thurman was devastated by the news of Mahatma Gandhi's murder on January 30, 1948, just six months after India gained its independence. The passing gave Thurman a chance to reflect on the meaning of Gandhi's life. He did so in a sermon/eulogy preached before the Fellowship Church in February 1948 (the eulogy was a form in which Thurman excelled). Thurman told the congregation of his conversation with Gandhi, and in particular his query about why the ideal of nonviolence had failed. Gandhi had replied that *ahimsa* could not function before the masses had been disciplined and trained to understand it profoundly.

But they could not, for two reasons. One, they had more basic physical needs that outstripped any idealistic expression of this philosophical ideal. And so Gandhi had withdrawn from some political activity, hoping to redeem Hinduism. He returned to the spinning wheel, hoping that by taking care of the "elemental physical basis" of life he could provide a base for a new "moral and spiritual vitality."

The second reason, the one that surprised Thurman, was not that the British had broken the self-respect of Indians but rather the brute force of untouchability within Hinduism. Gandhi started by changing their names from outcasts or untouchables to Harijans, a word that meant "child of God."

Gandhi had said, according to Thurman, "if I can make a caste Hindu call an outcast a Child of God, every day, I will create finally the kind of moral problem deep within his spirit that cannot be resolved until he changes his attitude towards him." And so Gandhi had seen, ultimately, that "peace is the byproduct of righteousness, of social and economic justice." If the peace advocate could work for that justice, for a society where men could live without fear, then (and only then) could the concept of peace spread to nation-states and the possibilities of international comity exist. Such a new order of human relations started on one's own street.

For Thurman, this could be the great contribution of Christianity to India, that the spirit of Christianity, the religion of Jesus, could "work towards the release and the redemption of the untouchable." But the "greatest handicap" to the spread of the word of Jesus, Gandhi told Thurman, was simple: "Christianity." Thurman would carry that distinction—the religion of Jesus versus organized Christianity—throughout his life. Thurman concluded by comparing Gandhi with Jesus. Gandhi had told Thurman of his ability to wait, that he was not in a hurry, because "God cannot be defeated in India." Gandhi's expressions of love for all put him among the "great redeemers of the human race," along with Jesus, because Jesus also believed that true liberation from oppressive states came from loving the oppressor. Because he projected that idea to his followers, "there was let loose on this planet, a faith in the possibility of love that provided a psychological and social climate in which Gandhi could do his work." Without Jesus, Gandhi simply would have been slaughtered, "but because of what Jesus had thought and taught, but more important released in the climate of life, men had adjusted themselves to the notion of the possibility of Ahimsa." And so, although Gandhi now was dead and violence had won a battle, he remained confident that "only love will win the war."

In March 1949 Thurman gave four lectures to the YWCA, then meeting in San Francisco, analyzing the America of the Cold War. The challenge posed by Axis totalitarianism had been stark, precisely because the fascists were so clear in their goals and aims—they sought a "new order based upon the doctrine of the inequality of man," and that doctrine empowered their vision of a collective destiny. The democracies had to respond with a unified collective statement, which response was hindered by the difficulties they faced, for example, in disagreements between Roosevelt and Churchill over the Atlantic Charter and the future of colonialism. And now the same fears had been replaced by paranoia about Russian communism, something that arose "in direct proportion to our lack of faith in democracy."

The task of the day was to find a "common faith to guarantee the unity of the race." And to learn a fundamental principle—"the experience of unity is more compelling than the dogmas and prejudices that tend to divide." The experience of unity, of wholeness, was "the very essence of stability, of peace of mind, of security within. God is one—life is one. There are no divisions in the world except those man has instituted. . . . The human creation achieves a wholeness that relaxes tension, that transcends turmoil and that makes for tranquility." As always for Thurman, the apparent contradictions of life, so evident on the surface, masked deeper unities below.

Thurman's years in San Francisco, especially the late 1940s, also coincided with the flourishing of his career as a published author. He had long been interested in publishing his work (his protestations to the contrary notwithstanding) and had queried some publishers before and issued mimeographed and more informally produced copies of his sermons. In the later 1940s, however, his career as a national lecturer took off with the Ingersoll Lectures on Immortality, delivered at Harvard University in April 1947. The publication of those lectures later as *The Negro Spiritual Speaks of Life and Death* gave him a national audience beyond the smaller circle of friends, congregants, and admirers who formerly had followed him. And they clearly fueled Thurman's desire to write. During the next two decades he published more than twenty books, many based on sermon collections or formal lectures delivered for churches or universities. For example, Thurman gave an address titled "The Genius of Democracy" to the Commonwealth Club in San Francisco in June 1947. Earlier he wrote to its executive secretary that his views on democracy were those of an American citizen, not just those of a Negro, and he wished to speak on that subject in general terms (presumably the original request was for a talk on a racial theme).

Thurman took pride in, and at times (uncharacteristically for him) boasted about, his successes in public speaking, often mentioning the standing ovations and letters of commendation he received. After his appearance before the Commonwealth Club, as well, he expressed his pleasure at his reception, noting that "the name Fellowship Church is becoming a part of the vocabulary of San Francisco. This is very much in order because the plans that we have call for a first mortgage on the city." The poor young black boy from Florida was enjoying his bit of national fame from his experiment in San Francisco.

Thurman's sermons during his tenure at the Fellowship Church deepened the themes he had preached on for years at Howard. In "The Tragic Sense of Life," from late November 1948, for example, Thurman explored the gulf between our highest aspirations and our actual struggles. Although not generally a fan of the apostle Paul, Thurman here explored many of the same quandaries expressed in the New Testament: why we do the things we don't want to do and do not pursue the things we most desire for ourselves. This gulf produced in us a "restlessness," Thurman said, a desire to be further along than we were. What did this restlessness mean? "The gulf between what I saw and what I am able to achieve, the gulf that is never quite filled in," Thurman said, had this religious significance: "that man finds that he can never be complete in himself, that life isn't and can never be complete in itself, that the meaning of all of the struggling of life is that life is trying to spell out an ultimate meaning." Thurman concluded with words that in a sense summed up his own life's journey: "Life is trying to learn how to say 'God.'" And because of that, he argued, "all religions, in the last analysis, are trying to say the same thing." Thurman here produced his own twentieth-century version of nineteenth-century Transcendentalism.

Thurman publicized the philosophical quests of the church in its newsletter, which he initiated in 1949, the *Growing Edge*. He had long since taken to that phrase, something he derived from his nature mysticism and his love for the nature writings of Schreiner. He turned the phrase into the title of the church's publication, meant for both a local and a national audience. For him, the phrase signified, as expressed by Thurman scholar Walter Fluker, "a sign of the purposiveness of life, always surmounting problems, always rising to new levels." The "growing edge" of something was the part of the organism "striving to come to its own realization." The growing edge was the unrealized potential that was "symbolic of life, a creative manifestation of life. Life seems, at its heart, to be irritation, some form of agitation that is trying to reveal a hidden something not disclosed."

For Thurman, the meaning was both biological and social; as was often the case in his writings, he drew from life science metaphors (even if, sometimes, from outdated biological concepts). He saw in those ideas a means to reflect on how to overcome deep social evils. Beyond the hatred and sin and violence of everyday life, there was something there, the growing edge, the potentiality of overcoming social systems of hatred. For Thurman, the fascinating paradox of life was that "it is working always for fulfillment, transcending the status quo, transcending that which is, in anticipation of that which is not. So it becomes symbolic of growth, and the destiny of the growing edge is finally to 'get there.'" But once "there," "it shoots past the goal to the next thing. So the paradox is that the growing edge is always working to be finished, to stop being a growing edge, to settle down and be; and yet the very nature of the growing edge makes that state forever impossible. . . . Nature is always finally against that which has arrived, that which is ripe, that which has completed itself."

Here Thurman reflected philosophically on his own life, a constant set of explorations, never quite finished. As well, the passage touches on his love for the mystical derived from metaphors of nature. "I must always be working toward completing something that I never complete; for if I complete it, life is through with me," he concluded.

The same held true for his vision of Fellowship Church, perfectly represented in the title of its newsletter. Thurman hoped it could be a place where interracial and intercultural religious experience would simply be accepted as "rational and normal," and proven so because in living together as a congregation "we can demonstrate it and feed our faith with the facts of our experience." If they could do this, then God's presence would "keep our minds always churning with ideas that have not been tried, with dreams that have not been fulfilled, with hopes that stagger us, but yet will not let us alone."

In "Love Your Enemy," another sermon from this era, Thurman thought deeply about how to overcome "the necessity" of hatred. "God expects men to be like him," he began. This is incredible, because "the creative mind and spirit of God *dares* to assume that it is within the range of possibility for human life that man shall become and shall behave and perform like God." This gave a particularly "radical interpretation" to the "meaning of dignity and human worth." People were of infinite worth, and thus worthy of re-spect, even if they were enemies. "I have in myself a basic confidence that there is in me that which is holy and divine and beautiful," which is easy to extend to friends. But how was it possible to do so with an enemy who had stepped outside our sense of "oneness and understanding," and thus outside our compass of "any sense of moral obligation or moral responsibility or moral relationship to him." Thurman here reflected back on his concep-tion of whites as a boy, as people who simply existed, entirely outside of his moral universe.

Jesus did so by putting enemies under the umbrella of their own worth, an action that could lead them to understand their own deeds and complicity in oppression. That was the lesson of Jesus and the tax collector. But could that be applied to an entire system of oppression; could an early Christian love Rome, the "great impersonal enemy," for example? The same principle applied, Thurman argued. Jesus allowed a person to see how to come out from under "Roman necessity" and become just a person: "This centurion thus became one with all of the mass of human beings who have experienced great affection and tremendous frustration in fulfillment of it. And when that happened, Jesus saw no longer just a Roman centurion, no longer even a Roman at all, but a human spirit emancipated by selfless love." And so Jesus taught us the more general lesson about how it was possible to love one's en-emy: "Somehow I must work at the job of making my enemy come out from under the type of necessity that makes him my enemy. And I must come out from under the necessity that makes me his enemy. Then, together, we can see ourselves as children of God."

Thurman sought to apply the more ethereal experiences of encountering truth to the harsh realities of injustice, violence, and hatred. In "Judgment and Hope in the Christian Message," he asked, "Is it reasonable to assume that the universe is grounded in a limitless vitality that can sustain the revo-lutionary demands of the Christian ethic?" For Thurman, the "guarantee of the ethical demand is to be found in the underlying vitality of the universe as expressed in the aliveness of life, which in turn is sustained by the God of life." But it was never far, as he saw it, from the grandest visions of this kind of mysticism to the realities of race in America. "If it be true that the normal relationship between men is activated kinship, grounded in a common dynamic origin," he explained, "then attitudes of mistrust, of fear, of prejudice, whatever may be the extenuating justification for them, are a repudiation of the ethical meaning of life." Those who sought brotherhood, therefore, could depend on God to sustain them even in the moments of deepest frustration, and most especially in "discovering techniques of implementation that will make so great a commitment a common part of the daily round of experience. Our hope is in a devotion to life in this dimension and our judgment is in the barrenness which we sustain in not living this religion."

Thurman was sometimes attacked for being an idealist, drawn to a mysticism that could not ultimately deal with the realities of life. His response came in numerous works, written and oral. One of the most memorable was a sermon in 1948 in which he repeated his common point that humans found it easy to show courage in areas not necessarily involving their own security, but in matters of their own security, the tendency to self-protection took over. And the same applied to the world situation. People resisted having "theoretical idealists" take over the control of institutions, but Thurman asked, "The world has been run by practical, hard-headed people who know what the score is. And what has happened? Two world wars in twenty-five years, hunger everywhere, madness everywhere, fear everywhere. It is the practical man who has created that kind of impasse. It may be a fairly decent idea to give another sort of man a try at it; he can't do anything worse than have another world war, nor make more mistakes than have been made." Similarly, in an Easter sermon that year, Thurman explained to his congregation how the meaning of life came to one in a flash of intuition, that moment when "it seems that at last all the meaning of life has broken open in our mind. And without knowing, you understand, and without trying, you *are*. . . . It is the God in life that does that. The vision of the great creative ideal, the simple methods and techniques by which that ideal may be implemented and become a part of the warp and woof of human experience . . . a power, limitless in resource, and infinite energy, available to all who reach out, or reach in."

Thurman's sermons also reflected on the grace of God, which he compared to the "grace note" of a musical performance, the part not written on the staff that gave a special quality to human relations. The extra note, the "something more," he thought, "becomes an expression finally, in religion, of a movement from God into the life of man that has as its purpose the development and maintenance of a creative and harmonious relationship between the individual and God." God's grace gave us the best part of ourselves, and the part that we had in common with every other living thing. It had to do with "inner qualities," the "qualities of mind and qualities of personality," the "extra something" in a person that makes us love him or her—like a grace note in music "over and above what appears on the lines and the spaces" that gives the music its "glow." And so, finally, grace was "a movement from God into the life of man that has as its purpose the development of and the maintenance of a creative and harmonious relationship between the individual and God." Grace was always a movement of God toward man, but it is also a recognition that "God is already in you and moving back towards himself. And that's how it bridges the gap between the finite and the infinite." God was moving back toward himself through human personality: "It is the God in you that is moved to respond to God." Because everybody was a recipient of grace, everybody had that something extra, the plus that represented God's movement in the soul of a person.

Thurman saw the development of the statement of commitment of the Fellowship Church as more evidence for the movement of God in the souls of the people. This statement went through various iterations, reaching its final form in 1949. Through three drafts, it moved partly away from being a Christian statement to something referencing Jesus but more universal. The Declaration of the Church called the church a "creative venture in interracial, intercultural, and interdenominational communion. In faith and genius it is Christian. While it derives its inspiration primarily from the source of Hebrew-Christian thought and life, it affirms the validity of spiritual insight wherever found and seeks to recognize, understand, and appreciate every aspect of truth whatever the channel through which it comes. It believes that human dignity is inherent in man as a creature of God, and it interprets the meaning of human life as essentially spiritual." The statement in part reflected Thurman's own move away from the Christianity of his youth and toward a more universal vision of cosmopolitan spirituality, humanitarianism, and what he called "sensitiveness"—what we might call a kind of mindfulness oriented toward social action.

A prominent liberal Unitarian minister, John Haynes Holmes, rejected the initial draft as "disastrously limiting" for focusing on "a vital interpretation of God as revealed in Jesus of Nazareth whose fellowship with God was the foundation of his fellowship with men." For Holmes, religion was "universal—its revelation everywhere, in every great prophet, and in every human heart. I should be faithless to my own spiritual conviction if I attempted to bind [it] in any way to a distinctively 'Christian fellowship.'" Holmes abhorred divisions within Christianity and "the larger divisions of religion itself. . . . There is one God, and all men of every diverse faith are children of that God, and therefore brothers one of another." Thurman resented the "pontifical" tone of the letter. But such sentiments, doubtless aided by those in the congregation who sought a more universalist vision, had their effect, as the final commitment statement retained the reference to Jesus but placed him within the context of the "other great religious spirits."

The final version, which came to be the church's official statement in 1949, was the product of three iterations. Thurman cared deeply about this project and saw it as building a "floor upon which people of . . . radical diversities may stand together." Thurman preached several sermon series, explicating the commitment point by point, particularly emphasizing those points that had not been changed. The final commitment read like this:

> I affirm my need for a growing understanding of all men as sons of God, and I seek after a vital experience of God as revealed in Jesus of Nazareth and other great religious spirits whose fellowship with God was the foundation of their fellowship with man.
>
> I desire to share in the spiritual growth and ethical awareness of men and women of varied national, cultural, racial and creedal heritage united in a religious fellowship.
>
> I desire the strength of corporate worship through membership in this Church for the Fellowship of All Peoples with the imperative of personal dedication to the working out of God's purpose here and in all places.

Thurman emphasized that there were many inequalities in men—in income, abilities, and nearly everything else in social life—but there was one great equality—the infinite worth of the individual. Every person was a "creation whose worth can never be measured in any terms that are quantitative."

That worth would be extended through the act of corporate worship—the worship of God, not of Jesus Christ. It was in the worship of God that congregants had an "immediate awareness of the pushing out of the barriers of self, the moment when we flow together into one." And such an experience was available to all, even to nonbelievers, for God could wipe out all barriers that separated people in worship. Everyone could be caught up in the "all-pervading worship of God; that the ground of life, and the essence of life and of the brooding creative spirit that hovers over all the aspirations and the yearnings and the desires of men, can bring each man into His presence with a new and wonderful transcendence. We *believe* it in this church because we *experience* it." All could have the "vitalizing, purifying, exciting moment of Presence."

Thurman also used the church as a venue for experimentation in worship aesthetics, especially music and dance. With the help of noted musician and arranger Corrine Williams, Thurman developed a music program at the church, later to be led by Raymond Fong. Thurman took pride in the choir as evidence of his ideas about worship as "the highest act of celebration of the human spirit," in which the "worshiper sees himself as being in the presence of God. In His presence, the worshiper is neither male nor female, black nor white, Protestant nor Catholic nor Buddhist nor Hindu, but a human spirit laid bare, stripped to whatever there is that is literal and irreducible." The key to the church was not the mixture of peoples but rather the "duality of the individual's religious experience achieved through worship and the effect of that experience on daily behavior." He saw Sunday morning as a time that "for each person present" was "a moment which becomes *his* moment in the presence of God." This was consistent with Thurman's larger vision of churches as centers of spiritual nourishment, from which people could then be empowered to pursue social transformation.

"As I moved more and more into the center of the process at the church I began feeling the urge to put into written form some of the things that were stirring within me," he later wrote in his account of the church, *Footprints of a Dream*. One of those things stirring was the "weekly meditation written out of the heart of my own spiritual struggle," which appeared in the church calendar. Soon people demanded that these meditations be more widely distributed, and his written words became a "means for a wider participation in the fundamental idea and an ideal upon which we had set our course."

In part through the venue of his church, Thurman was becoming a national celebrity. *Life* magazine featured him in 1953 as one of twelve "great preachers" in the country (at a time when such a list still mattered); he was profiled there with Billy Graham, Norman Vincent Peale, Fulton Sheen, and others. By that time also, he had become known for *Jesus and the Disinherited*, his most powerful and influential published work.

JESUS AND THE DISINHERITED

The book *Jesus and the Disinherited* began as the Mary L. Smith Memorial Lectures at Samuel Huston College in Austin, Texas, in April of 1948. The five lectures in the series constituted a "very fateful moment," Thurman told a friend upon recounting the enthusiastic reception he had received, but he could not possibly have known how fateful they would be for the history of the civil rights movement and liberation theology in the United States. *Jesus and the Disinherited* was, in fact, a foundational text for both.

The publication of the actual text was, by Thurman's autobiographical account, rather fraught, although in his correspondence, now published in his collection of papers, he seems forthright and pragmatic in his responses to some rather heavy editing the book received (including a complete revamp of the introduction). Certainly Thurman was not used to the intrusive hand of editors, picking apart his prose and simply dismissing what had been a lengthy introduction. The editors, moreover, wanted him to amplify the original text, as it was not quite at the length or heft that would fill out a book.

Abingdon Cokesbury Press, associated with the Methodist church of the South, had first rights of refusal on the book, and Thurman assumed the "southern bias" of the press would lessen or eliminate its interest in the manuscript. But, in one of the many ironies surrounding the publication of the text, that was not the case. The editor of the press, Nolan Bailey Harmon, hailed from Meridian, Mississippi. He served for years as a circuit-riding minister, then journal editor, then bishop for southern Methodists. Harmon had a long history of racial paternalism and support for versions of a "Lost Cause" theology extolling the virtues of Stonewall Jackson and Robert E. Lee.

Most notably, Harmon was one of the eight southern "moderate" religious leaders that fell under the withering condemnation of Martin Luther King's 1963 classic "Letter from a Birmingham Jail," a missive that actually condemned southern moderates as a greater enemy to racial progress than the Ku Klux Klan. Harmon had joined in a letter to King urging that civil rights protestors "observe the principles of law and order and common sense." Harmon himself thought racial progress would come only after the "slow, slow, slow processes of time." Thus, he was the perfect exemplar of the attitude King so memorably lacerated in the letter—the idea that, somehow, time would heal the wounds. As King responded, "time" itself was neutral, and would by itself solve nothing.

Jesus and the Disinherited was Thurman's most succinct, and in many ways grittiest, expression of the fundamental idea he pursued throughout his career: that the meaning of Jesus could be found in his status as a poor, disinherited Jew living under an oppressive Roman regime. This idea had appeared in bits and pieces over previous decades, but here it appeared in memorably encapsulated form. In the work, too, Thurman explored how the "hounds of hell" pursued the disinherited, and how the same fear and hate that shaped the rules of the dominant regimes also deformed the psychology of the dispossessed. In one of his most memorable passages, Thurman explained that the very religious iconography of American Christianity, symbolized by images of a white Jesus, had led blacks to disparage themselves. Thurman reasoned that if segregation was considered "normal, it was then correct; if correct, then moral; if moral, then religious." Segregation needed the divine to be white. And so God was "imaged as an elderly, benign white man," Satan as "red with the glow of fire," and "the imps, the messengers of the devil, are black."

For Thurman, the "implications" of this view were "simply fantastic in the intensity of their tragedy. Doomed on earth to a fixed and unremitting status of inferiority, of which segregation is symbolic, and at the same time cut off from the hope that the Creator intended it to be otherwise, those who are thus victimized are stripped of all social protection. . . . Under such circumstances, there is but a step from being despised to despising oneself." A generation later, black theology pushed these insights further. Whereas Thurman's generation would have preferred to de-racialize Christ, to remove his whiteness but not replace it with blackness, the theological generation of the 1960s perceived imparting blackness (whether physically or metaphorically) on the Divine as a necessary instrument of liberation. But both generations understood the devastating effects of the association of the Divine with whiteness, symbolized by the white Jesus that dominated American art from about the 1830s forward, culminating in Thurman's own era with Warner Sallman's image *Head of Christ*, which soon spawned upwards of 500 million reproductions at home and abroad. This particular whitened figure of Christ in effect *became* Jesus for most American Christians, white and black.

Thurman's lifework focused on understanding what the message of Jesus meant to those whose backs were against the wall. At the end, he concluded, the disinherited would have to recognize the hounds of hell pursuing them—fear, deception, and hatred—and "having done this, they must learn how to destroy these or to render themselves immune to their domination. In so great an undertaking, it will become increasingly clear that the contradictions of life are not ultimate. The disinherited will know for themselves, that there is a Spirit at work in life and in the hearts of men which is committed to overcoming the world." That's the spirit his grandmother (in Thurman's recollection and recounting) had; she remained his symbol for the triumph of the disinherited over the hounds of hell.

Thurman was delighted at how his lectures were received, but perhaps nothing gave him more pleasure than his mother's response to the book. She asked, "I wonder where you got so much knowledge from God only Could give It to you I am very thankful to God for permitting me to be your mother." There were the haters as well, including a Baptist pastor from North Carolina who mailed Thurman his responses to the book. "What is your purpose in trying to undermine the faith of God's people in his precious word?" he asked Thurman, and concluded, "I am expecting you to answer my letter and my questions." Thurman replied with a bit of acerbic humor (by his standards), reminding the gentleman of the verse, "Judge not that ye be not judged."

Besides the lectures that became *Jesus and the Disinherited*, Thurman pursued other lines of theological inquiry in sermons for his congregation and many other audiences nationally. In "The Quest for Peace," from 1949, Thurman puzzled over the attractions of war, the way its sheer irrationality offered some a frisson of excitement to the "rational pattern of daily life."

And for that reason, peace advocates needed to seek "aesthetic equivalents" as well as "moral equivalents" to war, "for life has to have some poetry in it. . . . There must be something that tingles—something that gives you a lift." Thurman considered deeply the troubling implications of persuading other people to one's will, even when it was a larger moral good. There was a kind of nonphysical, "creative violence," by which people came to accept an ideal that possessed another person. But when creative violence operated in that way, in the "fulfillment of that commitment—whether it be for peace or for violence— . . . often I am immunized against the simple, normal feelings of warmth and tenderness and kindness and graciousness that possessed me *before* I was laid hold upon by this commitment." And so, even peace advocates using means of persuasion wielded a great power in their hands. Though the ideal of peace could be righteous or even a "supreme ideal," it still was contingent "upon the kind of stamina and courage and body of the human beings who are manipulating it."

Ultimately, the Fellowship Church ran its course. Through it, Thurman moved history. He did so less through his creation of interracial visions and more through his translation of universalist ideas into an American religious idiom. Thurman was a "seeker" before we had such a term, and he paved the way for contemporary ideas of religious pluralism. But in the early 1950s, his mind moved in the direction of extending his philosophical conceptions to larger fields and ministries. The Fellowship Church remained a love of his life, but he could see that it would not, by itself, be the basis for remaking American Christianity. That required a larger stage, and a chance to educate a younger generation in his ideas. That chance soon came from friends and colleagues at Boston University.

Thurman's dreams came to be focused on his work in the chapel at Boston University, and his newfound stardom from addresses he recorded for radio broadcast. But his bigger hopes for his term there were dreams deferred. As he learned again, mystic visions of unity are hard to square within organizational boxes.

"The Scent of the Eternal Unity"
Dreams Deferred in Boston

> *Whenever man has the scent of the Eternal Unity in his spirit, he hunts for it! In his home, in his work, among his friends, in his pleasures, on all levels of his functioning.*
>
> —Howard Thurman, Footprints of a Dream

> *The mystic is seldom an organization man.*
>
> —Walter Muelder, "Apostles of Growth"

By 1953, Howard Thurman sensed that his work in San Francisco could be coming to its natural end. He was fifty-two and planning to retire at sixty-five. As he wrote to the trustees of the Fellowship Church, "If my life is to be spent to the fullest advantage on behalf of what seems to me to be the great hope for mankind, it is important to work on its behalf where there is the maximum possibility of contagion." Thurman hoped the Fellowship Church would be a point of contagion from which similar interracial experiments would flourish. "Whenever man has the scent of the eternal unity in his spirit," Thurman once wrote, "he hunts for it in his home, in his work, among his friends, in his pleasures, and in all the levels of his function." He had settled into something like a conventional pastorate. As had been true at Howard previously, settling into the conventional made him restless. The great adventure in San Francisco, fulfilling though it was, left Thurman with a hunger for more; he kept on the quest for the "scent of the eternal unity." He was ready to consider other possibilities, places where he might expand his religious vision to greater audiences.

That opportunity came, after much wooing, from Boston University (BU). The historically Methodist institution offered to make him its first tenured black professor and dean of the chapel. Thurman had received, in 1952, an initial letter of interest from Dean Walter Muelder; he wrote back indicating that his full commitment was still with Fellowship Church but implicitly leaving the door open for further discussion. Thurman long held a connection to Boston via his friendship with President Harold Case. While Case was a Methodist pastor in Pasadena, California, Thurman enjoyed a number of visits to his congregation. And prior to that time, in 1937, when Thurman had been excluded from a hotel dining room following a talk he gave at a large Methodist conference in St. Louis, Case and his wife offered their apologies and assured Thurman they would take some dramatic action in the future to demonstrate that this was not in keeping "with the true genius of the Methodist Church."

Fifteen years later, discussions with Case, now president at BU, followed, and Thurman warmed to the idea of moving cross-country again. As Thurman explained to Case, he wanted not simply to be a professor and take charge of the chapel at this predominantly white institution, but he wished to be given the task of creating a religious community there. Thurman found it "very stirring to think that any academic institution that is church related would be daring enough to move experimentally in the direction of a religious concept that is capable of floating the demands of the human spirit for a one-world community."

Dean Muelder pressed the case for coming to BU. With Case as president, he told Thurman, "Religion has an opportunity in Higher Education unequalled, I think, anywhere else." Furthermore, the university was creating an African American studies program, with which the School of Theology could be connected in the future. The size and quality of the School of Theology, with over four hundred students from across the United States and fifteen foreign countries, presented a compelling opportunity to shape the very future of Christianity in Thurman's own image.

These arguments spoke to Thurman's heart. Evidence of that comes from Thurman's lengthy explanation to the Fellowship Church's trustees in late January of 1953. There, he reproduced virtually all the arguments Muelder and Case had presented to him. What most attracted him was the opportunity for the "widest possible dissemination" of his ideas and his visions for remaking the very nature of religious experience as it would come to be in the future. He also thought it fully in line with the "vision which first sent me forth from Howard University to live and work in the church here." He spoke with Case and others while on the East Coast. On the train home, he meditated on the decision. By early March 1953, he pretty well had decided, although he asked Case a series of questions about the budget for the chapel, his precise role, and the relationship of the chapel to the School of Theology.

In fact, the issues he was mulling over would bedevil his career in Boston over the next years. For one thing, the School of Theology arose directly from the Methodist church and served it, but Thurman had no desire to put the chapel under its sway. The church community he hoped to form from within the chapel "should not be regarded as a Methodist church," he reminded Case. In addition, he asked a question critical for his own conception of this opportunity: "Am I right in assuming that the pulpit is free, the assumption being that the preacher is thoughtful and committed but that no limitations are placed upon the range of his thinking so long as sensitive courtesies and reverences are maintained." Finally, Thurman hoped that some connection could be maintained between the Fellowship Church and his prospective new work in Boston. Thurman had thrown himself into the work in San Francisco like nothing else in his life. As he put it, "This church is as much of my life as any dream or its projection could possibly be." That March, Thurman requested a "leave of absence" from the church, indicating that he hoped to return to preach or otherwise help out during the summer months. He wrote to his friend Coleman Jennings about the "emotional lacerations" his decision had caused him. Jennings admired Thurman's decision but well understood how church members might feel about it. How would they carry on without the church's guiding genius spirit, and by themselves face the "haunting questions of how your years of work will stand up in your absence"? It turned out that they had good reasons for those fears.

Thurman's decision left some of his faithful church members in San Francisco reeling. They responded as wounded lovers who had been jilted. One of them wrote to him that he would not be so hypocritical as to wish him "God-speed in your new venture," because in fact he was personally devastated by the decision. He concluded: "Perhaps if I had known Howard

Thurman the man better, I wouldn't feel so let down, but you see, Dr. Thurman, I have used you as the very cornerstone of my faith, and now I must clear the debris and start again." Thurman had become, for a select group of followers, the very emblem of a new faith in the coming of a new world. Thurman's charisma was irreplaceable.

Thurman's correspondence upon leaving the church gives some idea of his hopes for its future, as well as the difficulties involved in reaching those aspirations. He left the board of trustees his thoughts on a replacement but considered very few men equipped to become minister of this particular church, which was practically a thing unto itself in the American religious world. A few of the leading black ministers nationally would not be able to come. If they were abundantly qualified for the position, it by definition meant they were already in a prominent position or pulpit and would be hard pressed to accept the salary cut necessary to become the pastor of the modestly sized start-up congregation in San Francisco. Two younger white interns (including the man who eventually did become pastor there, Francis Geddes) could serve in the interim. Thurman's friend Benjamin Mays had suggested a white Presbyterian minister and activist from North Carolina, Charles Jones, who had been involved with early freedom riders on the Journey of Reconciliation in 1947. But, as Thurman saw it, "we are not far enough out of the woods in our society for any considerable number of non-Caucasians to cast their lot with confidence in an enterprise led predominantly by a Caucasian . . . my remark comes out of ten years on the firing line."

As it turned out, Thurman's first two successors at the Fellowship Church, Dryden Phelps and Francis Geddes, were white, and Thurman's influence loomed large well into the future. Later in the 1950s, for example, when he was planning one visit back to the West Coast and to the church, he suggested to the chairman of the board of the church that another venue be found for his preaching service. If held in the church, visitors would clamor to be seated and longtime church faithful would be inadvertently excluded. Geddes had done his best to be gracious about the situation of having a star emeritus minister, Thurman politely said, but "it remains a real hardship on his role as the minister of the Church, when I zoom in like a comet visiting the solar system, and zoom out again," and after he left "a lot of little pieces must be picked up and painfully cemented together."

The problematic relationship of Thurman with his former church continued during his term in Boston. It led to a series of passive-aggressive letters between Thurman and Geddes. Late in 1959, following the fifteenth anniversary of the congregation, Geddes wrote to Thurman with appreciation: "Your mind and spirit have been more influential in my own unfolding than any living person. I shall ever carry an authentic imprint upon my ministry and being because of you." And yet, it was precisely the depth of Thurman's influence that was a problem in the church's growth and development. Geddes felt that Thurman was "crowding" him. Thurman provided the means to access financial support and was a spiritual help, but it had come at the cost of the church's independence. An adolescent sometimes had to make his own decisions outside the control of the parents, and so it was for the church if it was to "find its own destiny."

Thurman responded that he understood Geddes's position. Indeed, Thurman wanted to do what he could to keep the church from being tied up with him as a person. He thus planned to resign from his unofficial position as minister at-large and simply be minister emeritus, meaning he would not "speak on behalf of the Church in any way that is official and will take no responsibility for its leadership at any point." Thurman felt keenly that "so much of our lives have been deposited in the life of the Church; we have paid with irreplaceable energy and heart for the privilege of being God's servant in a hard place at a hard time in the struggle for decency in human relations." As a result, he as a person had become identified, too closely, with the church.

Geddes and Thurman continued their tense correspondence during Thurman's world tour of 1960; even while abroad, Thurman could not escape the drama in San Francisco. "It is I suppose, part of the irony of existence that you and I . . . ministers of reconciliation are estranged," Geddes wrote to him in August 1960. Thurman had been in San Francisco in March but had (as Geddes experienced it) given Geddes a "rebuff." And Geddes was not interested in hearing any excuses about a "pressing schedule," given that Thurman had met and talked with other church members. As Geddes saw it, the longtime church members simply wanted a repeat of the experience they had had with Thurman, not realizing that subsequent ministers would bring their own gifts. The church, he thought, does not have "39 Articles and a close definition of belief and as a consequence the direction it takes will depend a great deal upon the minister who happens to serve the church. Whatever his gifts and capacities are . . . that will reflect in the direction the church takes. . . . My gifts are different from yours and I see different things of importance."

The dialogue continued during Thurman's absence and sabbatical from BU from March until September of 1960, when he hoped to find "restoration of powers, renewal of creative insights, and identification with man's deepest hurts and needs." The trip included travel from San Francisco (where Geddes had his "rebuff") to Honolulu, then Japan, Hong Kong, the Philippines, Thailand, Singapore, Ceylon, Egypt, Lebanon, Greece, Italy, France, and finally to a respite of two months in Edinburgh, Scotland. On the trip he put in an appearance as a preacher at St. Martin-in-the-Fields in London, in July. And the trip even forced Thurman into plane travel, a rarity for the train buff who considered flying on jets an assault on the human spirit.

Thurman wrote Geddes in August, referring to a statement from Geddes that integrated churches were now a proven commodity. Such an assertion could not be sustained, Thurman retorted, "as long as America is prejudice ridden, as long as there is as much sheer religious, class and racial prejudice with basic discrimination, as there is even in our beloved San Francisco." As a result, such a demonstration of interracial fellowship had to be "continuous," had to be a *living tradition.*" That was true even for a well-placed person such as himself, Thurman knew from personal experience. Thurman pointed out that, in his initial inquiries for a place to live in San Francisco following his retirement, he had trouble finding real estate agents that would deal with him, even though he was something of a local celebrity. And thus, "the witness in the community is needed, even the interracial emphasis."

As Thurman saw it, every time he had tried to withdraw himself to give Geddes space, he had done so voluntarily and without being asked to: "you should know me well enough to be assured that *you* could not pressure me into withdrawing from involvement with Fellowship Church, into which a lifetime of dreaming and commitment are deposited. Only my love for the Church and my love for you would make me do it." He wondered what really ate at Geddes's soul: "I wonder what you are really fighting, Francis. What is there that is being so threatened by what I symbolized that you must strike out against it? What is the real enemy or who is the real antagonist of your spirit? To flare out against me is fighting windmills." Thurman felt Geddes was leading the church away from its founding emphases on inter-racial equality, and Thurman later wrote another friend of the "poisonous bits of propaganda" spread by Geddes, that Thurman was somehow waiting in the wings, ready to return.

Thurman concluded this correspondence with a lengthy letter of expla-nation to the chairman and board of directors of the Fellowship Church in 1960, explaining why he had resigned as minister at-large. The church originally housed a sizable at-large community, of affiliate members and supporters from around the country, and after Thurman decided to "convey the Fellowship dream" to BU, he thought it wise to maintain that connection and help funnel minister-interns to the church. They could then take that dream to other parts of the country. In the meantime, however, the church had effectively withdrawn from this kind of national role. Given that, as well as Thurman's own demanding duties at BU, he felt it natural to step down from being a minister at-large.

The afterlife of his relationship with Fellowship Church thus proved fraught and painful. Something similar awaited him toward the end of his years in Boston. Thurman left a huge legacy wherever he worked, but he pursued his calling so independently, and was so resistant to organizational structures and plans laid for him by others, that his connection to the insti-tutions in which he worked frequently was fraught. The apostle of sensi-tiveness left plenty of sensitive, sometimes wounded, people in his wake. As his friend and ally in academic politics at BU, Walter Muelder, later put it, describing Thurman's personality with some whimsical humor, "the mystic is seldom an organization man," because the inability of the mystic to rely on the "securities of mediated grace" necessarily gave "uneasy hours to the ecclesiastical bureaucrat." Those words, given at Thurman's retirement cele-bration, well summarized a good deal of Thurman's experience and struggles in defining the role of Marsh Chapel as both religious fellowship with partic-ular commitments and spiritual community open to all seekers after God.

But Thurman also left lines of disciples and admirers, many of whom would carry his philosophical and theological ideas forward into the future.

THURMAN'S PLANS FOR THE CHAPEL

Prior to Thurman's arrival, Daniel Marsh, president of BU from 1926 to 1951, had been replaced by Harold Case, also a Methodist minister but a president who recognized that BU no longer was a specifically Methodist institution. Indeed, Thurman's appointment was part of a more general push by Case to move the School of Theology beyond its denominational origins, into something more professionally open to diverse traditions and scholarly approaches. Boston also long had been home to an important intellectual and theological school, Personalism. Influenced by the theological thinker Bowden Parker Browne, the so-called Boston Personalists emphasized the spirit of the human person as the fundamental ontological category. Thurman did not identify himself as part of that school. But his intellectual approaches and writings from that era meshed easily with the more general intellectual climate he found at BU. He was a Personalist before that was a thing referred to with the capital *P*, "Personalism."

Thurman's job at BU, as it had been at Howard in 1933, involved reviving the life of the chapel. The leaders at BU gave him free reign, at least at the beginning, to create a "non-creedal, non-sectarian, interracial, interfaith, and intercultural religious fellowship." As Thurman saw it, this gave him the opportunity for the "widest possible dissemination of the ideas in which I believe."

Thurman worried about the inevitable infighting and jealousies and cases of disrespect that would come from achieving such a prominent position in a predominantly white university. Little did he know just how much of that he was about to experience, even from the office of his longtime friend President Case. As he had previously with Mordecai Wyatt Johnson, Thurman experienced a series of intra-administrative problems and struggles with the Case administration at BU. In this case, as with Johnson, a former mentor and supporter ended up as an academic administrator that often gave him fits. And Thurman's restless and sometimes stubborn spirit no doubt gave his academic overseers fits. He was not the easiest faculty member to manage.

He would be in charge of the religious affairs of the university and have a position alongside the other deans of the university, a level of responsibility and respect given to almost no other black academics at a white institution in that era. Thurman recognized the significance of the opportunity—it was something "completely unprecedented" in American education, he told the trustees of the Fellowship Church. Moreover, Thurman had much experience with speaking engagements both at Boston University and at other institutions in the Boston area (including delivering the Ingersoll Lectures at Harvard in 1947). BU boasted a relatively long record of graduating black students, including granting a doctor of divinity degree to J. W. E. Bowen in 1887. And its dean, Walter G. Muelder, advocated for issues of peace, justice, and civil rights. As a result, he was listed as one of "Methodism's Pink Fringe" in a 1950 *Reader's Digest* article that trolled figures from the Protestant mainline. Muelder and others suffered from the investigatory excesses of the McCarthy era. Further, the school's president for twenty-five years prior to Thurman's arrival, Daniel L. Marsh, had grown the campus greatly and finished his term with the completion of Marsh Chapel, a modestly sized but impressive structure built next to the School of Theology in the heart of the BU Campus, just off Commonwealth Avenue. Marsh remained a friend and supporter of Thurman throughout his term there. Just as Thurman took up his post, *Life* magazine hailed him as one of the "great preachers" of America, those bringing "America back to the churches." Others in this cohort (he was the only African American) included Norman Vincent Peale, Fulton J. Sheen, and Billy Graham, who was near the beginning of his epic career that would carry him through the subsequent decades as the unofficial state minister of America. Thurman was also featured in an *Atlantic Monthly* article written by one of his most ardent admirers, Jean Burden, who hailed him as a "prophet" who stood for "justice in an unjust society."

This article channeled Thurman, as indeed did his first biography, written by Elizabeth Yates and published in 1965 under the title *Howard Thurman: Portrait of a Practical Dreamer*. Both the article and the book essentially reproduced Thurman's autobiography before, later in his life, he wrote it himself. But this was one of the earlier introductions to Thurman's life in a national publication. In it he recounted his earliest struggles, his innate desire for religious experience (where he said, "When I was born, God must have put a live coal in my heart, for I was His man and there was no escape"), and his aspirations for deepening religious experience at Boston University: "Whenever man has the scent of the eternal unity in his spirit, he hunts for it in his home, in his work, among his friends, in his pleasures and in all the levels of his function. It is my simple faith that this is the kind of universe that sustains this kind of adventure." He hoped that eventually it would be "the way of life for everybody." Here, Thurman joined those who were creating the rise of "spirituality" as a central American concept. Or, perhaps it could be said that Thurman was both spiritual *and* religious.

Thurman had big plans for Marsh Chapel. In a sense, he wanted to combine what he had done at Rankin Chapel at Howard with his work at the Fellowship Church and create something that did not yet exist. He sought, as the scholar Walter Fluker puts it in volume 4 of the Thurman papers, "an interracial, international, and interreligious fellowship using worship to bridge human division and separateness, a fellowship that was equally at home with the interiority of private religious experience and worship and the public demands of social witness and action." He really saw himself moving his work at Fellowship Church to the East Coast and not leaving anything behind. He believed, in his own words, that he could found a "community church at the university, membership of which would come from the university family and the community of Boston. This would be a non-creedal, non-sectarian, interracial, interfaith, and intercultural religious fellowship."

Thurman soon encountered a basic contradiction in his scheme: he was seeking to develop a religious fellowship, a church, in which the members were bound to one another, but he was doing so at a university chapel in which he would welcome all "to come before God in the high act of celebration." He wanted there to be a collective agreement of covenant for members of the Marsh Chapel community, but he also wanted an open fellowship that would serve the university community. Ultimately, that was a circle that could not be squared.

In his first annual report as dean, Thurman commented that, at present, the chapel represented in effect "Protestant Christianity on the campus," a "sectarian emphasis" that Thurman sought to transcend. But the dean of the chapel should focus, he thought, on the entire religious life of the university and develop a "center for religious worship in the heart of the university to which any and all members of the university may come for spiritual renewal and regeneration." If that was not possible, then the dean "should become the official Protestant mouthpiece," and Thurman's judgment on that outcome was terse: "The present Dean of the Chapel has no interest in that alternative."

Thurman and a committee from the university eventually hammered out an initial statement of commitment for Marsh Chapel. It contained some Christian language, more than Thurman probably wanted, but it concluded ultimately that the "experiences of spiritual unity wherever they occur, are more compelling than the creeds, the ways of life and the ideologies that divide man." The "Statement of Affirmation" was finalized in 1960 but rejected by the board of trustees of BU in 1961.

Part of the decision was practical. Most university faculty worshiped in their own congregations, meaning the chapel would be serving mostly students, and such a transitory population could not be expected to have the kind of permanent bonds of fellowship experienced in a regular church. Another problem, for Thurman, involved those who considered the chapel "the formal representative of Protestant Christianity on the campus." Some in the BU community felt that the chapel should be, in effect, the Protestant center on campus, an equivalent to centers for the Catholic and Jewish groups, whose connections with their traditions were clear and unmistakable. Thurman was not interested; this was contrary to his inclusive vision of a spiritual center for seekers that could draw from any particular religious tradition but not be bound by any one allegiance.

Thurman proved to be as inspiring an orator and minister at Marsh Chapel as he had been at Rankin Chapel at Howard earlier in his career. He soon attracted an audience of students and Boston residents, eventually reaching a steady congregation of three hundred, and sometimes filling the chapel to its maximum capacity of five hundred. This was remarkable for a minister who delivered deeply intellectual and often ethereal homilies. One local resident, a student of Hinduism, wrote him in 1956 that, until that time, he had never heard a Christian minister "who could be put on the same level of spiritual understanding as the great Swamis of India." Thurman's sermons at Marsh Chapel also reached a sizable radio audience, and taped versions of his orations were a hit during an era in which recorded sermons, ranging from those of Billy Graham to those of the black Detroit minister (and father of Aretha) C. J. Franklin, sold well nationally.

The Thurmans soon became central to the social life of Boston University. As a popular minister at Marsh Chapel and an early public radio star, Thurman drew much attention to his renewal of spiritual life. In their residence at 184 Bay Street, moreover, right at the center of BU, the Thurmans hosted a steady calendar of social events and groups, including a monthly social get-together for the chapel choir of sixty-five people. During the Christmas season, the Thurmans (with Howard cooking) fed a variety of international students who were staying there while school was on break. And a sizable portion of his work was taken up with what had become one of his calling cards, personal counseling. He counseled something like an average of eleven people a week, often taking an hour for a session. This was a burden that, as he explained to his academic supervisors, was not sustainable over the long term. As Thurman wrote laconically in his first report about the activities of the chapel, "the demand was greater than time and energy to meet."

Thurman also became something of a local celebrity thanks to his years of appearances on the program *We Believe*, broadcast from WHDH-TV in Boston. At first suspicious that the electronic media would make him disconnected from the spirits to which he was preaching, Thurman soon discovered a larger audience for his meditations, so much so that "Friday after Friday I felt that I was in an encounter with many minds absent and minds present." Thurman preached on *We Believe* for more than seven years, and even prerecorded nearly an entire year of episodes before his sabbatical tour of the world in 1960. He loved reaching new audiences through electronic media, and recordings of his addresses on tape later became the basis of the "listening rooms" that were part of the Howard Thurman Educational Trust. Fortunately, hundreds of these digitized recordings are now freely available online, a product of his work during this era.

Thurman's sermons from this time drew audiences from around the city and furthered his reputation as a preacher of unusual intellectual distinction. As had been the case at Howard, he attracted crowds to hear him not just from the university community but also from the surrounding city. He became a local intellectual celebrity.

Thurman continued his philosophical explorations of the meaning of religion in his sermons from that era. For him, religion was the place for seeking the truth of the infinite God in a world full of pain. The world was the kind of place where "that which cannot be borne must still be borne anyway." And thus the purpose of religions was to teach one how to channel spiritual energies in the pursuit of communion with God. God could not change the tragic facts of the world, but "through prayer, through inner exploration, through the deepening of my inward parts, through medita-tion—all the disciplines—I must learn through them how I can make avail-able in me at the point of my tragic fact the limitless resources of God," such that "what I must bear, because I have no alternative, instead of enduring it, I can float it. Float it." This made religion more than "mere sentimentality," because through it, "I discover that what I know of myself I cannot possibly endure, I will endure."

In his chapel addresses and recordings for public television and radio, Thurman also articulated his ideas of how worship, properly constructed, brought the human soul into relation with God. As he put it, worship was the "highest act of celebration of the human spirit. It is the moment of all moments when the worshipper 'images' himself in the presence of his God, when he has a sense of encounter with the supreme object of his devotion, where he is stripped of everything that is not literal and irreducible in him-self and the ultimate grounds of his self-respect are laid bare to him." During that time, the worshiper was not one of his specific identities, but a "human spirit in vital touch with what he recognizes as the God and Creator of his spirit. It is as if the tidal wave of communal fellowship which he experiences in the congregation casts him up to the surface, and he stands there alone." The sermon would not "interfere with or challenge the unity of the service," but rather sustained that unity: "Ideally the sermon is a lung through which the worship service breathes one breath and the worship service is the lung through which the sermon breathes one breath." And when that happened, the worshiper could perceive that the meaning of service was "uniquely available to each as his private insight."

Thurman's addresses at Marsh Chapel developed further his theme of how to be a person who could challenge, but not be overcome by, evil. The key was not to be overcome by hate, not to develop a hate or bitterness toward those things that sought to destroy you, because then they had given to you the work of destroying one's self. He gave an example from Tolstoy, who, when pinned down by a bear, looked up into the bear's jaws and saw above him the beautiful blue sky, and thought, "What a beautiful blue." And so it was that when fighting against evil or fear, the minute it overwhelmed a person and got inside of him, then it had won. "When I hate as an answer to hatred," he asked, "what happens? Something worse than the evil that I fight against begins to take place inside of me. . . . The disintegration of my own soul so that inside I begin to go to pieces; inside I begin to disintegrate; inside the world and its meaning falls apart and turns to ashes in my hands. . . . And then I become what I fight against and evil has won and my soul has lost." To overcome evil with good, he concluded, was a form of "madness that will redeem the world." These were the kinds of teachings that would settle down deeply in the souls of students and disciples of Thurman in the years to come.

Likewise, Thurman remained a committed modernist, uninterested in defending the literal truth of biblical events as opposed to exploring their metaphorical significance. As he explained to one correspondent querying him on his views on the virgin birth, the story was not "essential," because it added nothing to the life and significance of Jesus. He felt the same about the bodily resurrection; again, the importance was not in the physical event, but rather it demonstrated a "universal insight; namely, that death is something which takes place in life but not to life. The discovery which the disciples made after the crucifixion of Jesus was the fact that his life was not imprisoned by the event of the cross."

In "He Looked for a City," a Thurman staple, from January 1955 in Boston, Thurman developed some of his most concise formulations of the connections between inner transformation and combating social evils. What was necessary, he thought, was not "better schemes, better utopian dreams," but rather that the innermost self be "transformed in the light of an increasing exposure of our innermost selves to the mind of God." And likewise for the United States, he wished not for more arms "by which we may share in the strangulation of the human race," but that the soul of the country be transformed. Anything else would be a delusion. And that kept people of faith working and not despairing, in spite of failures, because in them was the city "whose builder and maker is God."

Thurman received frequent requests to speak on themes that we would now refer to as "civil religion." The topic was in its ascendancy in the 1950s, the era in which the motto In God We Trust went on the currency and "under God" was added to the Pledge of Allegiance. Thurman used his sermons and addresses to point American civil religion toward remedying the greatest evils still present in the country. In "Freedom under God," from 1955, for example, he proclaimed that "Whatever works against life, works against God." The point of the ideal of the United States was to be "involved in the far-flung purpose of God to establish a world community of friendly men living beneath a friendly sky." Thurman addressed (as the only black speaker) an annual convocation at Washington University in St. Louis on "the blessings of liberty." A good deal of his address might have been delivered by other participants. Yet within it he referred to the building of a world community. And he took a jab at St. Louis, the historically segregated city where Thurman had suffered a wounding humiliation in 1937. Anything that restricted the "blessings of liberty to a particular class, group, or type of human being" was a violation of the Constitution, but also something that "contributes directly to moral and spiritual delinquency." Thurman thus injected his critique of American racism into what was otherwise a fairly conventional set of paeans to American liberty.

Thurman also spoke frequently to professional groups, particularly to nurses, with whom he felt a bond as a sort of fellow worker in tending to human needs and suffering. (Indeed, Thurman's ministry to people in hospitals and to those in the later stages of passing away is one of the more overlooked parts of his career, because the evidence for this kind of private consolation doesn't survive in his papers in comparison to his more public work; but the evidence survives in the heartfelt tributes to Thurman that came later from those who worked in the healing professions.) To the National League of Nursing in 1957, he indicated how important it was to nurture their professional sense precisely by cultivating their personal journeys. He knew all too well "how easy it is to become the prisoner of your own profession, to develop a sense of exclusiveness and a false kind of pride." The answer was to cultivate one's own internal resources: "the professional must be an authentic human being," one able to "draw for the renewal of your own inward parts in times of barrenness and desolation." When humans were stripped bare, that is when they turned to religion—not any particular kind, but whatever answered the "hunger in the human spirit that can only be met by drawing upon a resource that is greater and more abiding than the individual life of man." Everyone needed to be sustained by something "not dependent upon the vicissitudes of Fortune or the incidents of Fate," and it was the "insistence of religion that this is the need that God meets in the life of man."

One of Thurman's closest students of that era represents the success Thurman had in fostering an intercultural and interreligious fellowship at Boston University, a larger version of what he had hoped to do in San Francisco in his years at Fellowship Church. Zalman Schachter-Shalomi was a refugee from Nazi Europe who initially studied Jewish orthodoxy with the Lubavitcher Hasidim in Brooklyn but soon was seeking out a broader set of spiritual resources. He came to BU and enrolled in the "Spiritual Disciplines and Resources" course. But Schachter (then his last name) wondered if studying with a Protestant minister at a Methodist university was the right path. As he later remembered it, in a conference with Thurman, he raised his objections, and Thurman responded, "Don't you believe in the Ruach Hakodesh?" Thurman used the Hebrew phrase meaning "holy spirit." Schachter ended up taking the course. Later, he led a Jewish spiritual renewal movement in the 1960s, remaining always a close friend of Thurman and an advocate for his ecumenical ideas of developing spiritual resources.

Thurman's former student and now friend Rabbi Zalman Schachter probably best summed up Thurman's role and life in Marsh Chapel as Thurman prepared to retire permanently in 1965. Schachter wrote him that, in effect, Thurman's new title, minister at-large, simply ratified what he already had been during his time at BU, and that "no matter how wonderful and flexible the institution was, it could not quite contain you. I suppose that is what is meant to be in the image of one's Maker, whom the heavens can't contain."

Thurman also became a teacher of considerable renown, in part by taking over rather musty courses (such as homiletics) and converting them into enriching experiences beyond just developing academic techniques of analysis. His goal in much of his teaching was to distill his lifetime of spiritual experience and show to others a kind of wisdom that "could be caught," even if he thought it "could not be taught." Each year at BU until 1962, he taught a two-semester sequence called "Spiritual Disciplines and Resources." In it, Thurman led students in a study of thinkers from various traditions, ranging from Quaker mystics (such as those who had deeply influenced him when he was younger) to Catholic intellectuals to the Zen Buddhism of D. T. Suzuki, the latter also a major influence on the Beats (particularly Gary Snyder) of that era. The follow-up semester compelled students to engage in a search of their own soul in order to find their own way to God.

In 1963, Thurman published *Disciplines of the Spirit*, a work that in effect distilled some of the principal teaching of this course into a volume usable for a larger audience. Thurman's goal always was to "clear away whatever may block our awareness of that which is God in us." One of Thurman's favored techniques was to combine a reading of biblical passages, particularly a psalm (Psalm 139 was his favorite), with an extended period of personal meditation on the psalm accompanied by classical musical selections from Bach or other composers that could help students musically find their way into encountering the deepest meaning of the passages. The Thurmans were music lovers. Mozart's bright melodies remained Sue's favorites, but for Howard (who late in his life took up clarinet playing to go along with his favorite avocation of painting portraits of penguins), the late quartets of Beethoven were the ultimate expression of spiritual struggle in music. "If I could share the mystery of the lonely giant Beethoven I would have the clue to my own solitariness," he wrote in his autobiography.

Just a few years into his term, Thurman gathered a group interested in pursuing a broader religious community of the chapel. It would be substantially different from the religious groups already existing on campus. In his aspirations for "creative experimentation" in the chapel, he hoped to open a "worship center in the university open to everybody, cutting across all lines of race, creed, etc.," a place for "shared experience of religious friends to the exposure of the scrutiny of God." There was no need to duplicate the efforts of the Jewish organization Hillel, the Newman Center for Catholics, and like groups. Rather, the focus would be on meditation and prayer and an openness to all religious experience. The idea would be to achieve what already was stated as the chapel's purpose in its weekly bulletin: "The Sunday morning service addresses itself to the deepest needs and aspirations of the human spirit. In so doing it does not seek to undermine whatever may be the religious context which gives meaning and richness to our particular life, but rather to deepen the authentic lines along which our quest for spiritual reality has led you." It was part of the university's intent to "recognize religion as fundamental to the human enterprise."

At the very same time, though, the first of Thurman's frequent conflicts and misunderstandings with Harold Case had arisen. Thurman's correspondence is (by his standards) furious. He always reacted sensitively when his prerogatives were (he felt) violated, most especially by outside authorities or university administrators who were not giving him his deserved autonomy in his work. In this instance, Case had sent a letter to Thurman's secretary outlining particular rules of chapel policy especially for the summer. The items covered were minor, basically notes to regulate the functioning of the chapel during the times between semesters. Feeling preempted and slighted by the letter, Thurman wrote back indignantly. In responding to these relatively minor matters, he indicated also his frustrations in pursuing the kind of chapel program he desired. When he had arrived at BU, he told Case, "I found a situation completely demoralized with all kinds of hostilities and conflicts." Since then he had worked to build a "spirit of fellowship and understanding within the Chapel itself," but one letter directed to a secretary threatened to destroy all that in an instant.

Ultimately, Thurman's hopes and visions for Marsh Chapel came to naught, as the university moved toward establishing it as a specifically Protestant ministry, with the dean of the chapel to serve not only as the "principal administrative officer for the religious life of the campus" but also as "chairman of the Council for the Protestant ministry." This was in no way what Thurman ever had in mind. For him it violated the implicit agreement he made with BU. He resigned from being dean of the chapel and become a university minister at-large, a sort of self-created ad hoc position that allowed him some connection with the university community but also a wider opportunity than would have been available to him simply as a part of the university chapel. In particular, Thurman worried that continued involvement with the chapel would give him little time to spend working with the black community in Boston, something he feared had been lacking in his work there to date.

THURMAN, MARTIN LUTHER KING, AND BLACK POLITICS

Thurman attracted an audience of future notables to his chapel addresses, just as he had at Howard. One was Barbara Jordan, then a law student at BU, later the noted congresswoman from Texas, who found Thurman's messages "moving and meaningful." Martin Luther King Jr. was another admiring listener. Thurman long had had a relationship with King's family; he and King's father were close to the same age, and Thurman was teaching at Morehouse when King Jr. was born in 1929. Sue Bailey Thurman was a roommate of Alberta Williams, King's mother, in 1920–1921, at Spelman Seminary. Of more consequence, Thurman and King shared a social gospel outlook deeply informed by, but also suspicious of the rigidities of, their own black Baptist tradition. It's little wonder that King responded with such enthusiasm to Thurman's *Jesus and the Disinherited*. It expressed King's vision of a liberatory gospel as much as it did Thurman's. Thurman never had King in a class, but they interacted socially (once enjoying together a World Series broadcast of a game featuring Jackie Robinson playing for the Dodgers against the Yankees) and later carried on a respectful correspondence and had at least the fateful conversation in 1958 recounted in the introduction to this book.

But in the years before then, the younger King, far from being a national icon, was a man in his early twenties, still fairly early in his intellectual formation. At one point, in fact, the president at Dillard University inquired of Thurman who might make a good dean of the chapel at this historically black college in New Orleans. He had heard some good things about Martin Luther King Jr. Thurman responded somewhat hesitantly, as he did not know King well, that "I understand that he is a good preacher," perhaps with little experience directly with students but "a man has to start some time." But Thurman had another person in mind—Major Jones, just then finishing up a PhD in religious education and previously for several years the pastor of a Methodist church in Atlanta. (Jones later became a well-published author in black theology and the president of Gammon University in Atlanta.)

Thurman later reflected, with ironic humor, on his relationship with King during that short time when their paths intersected in Boston: "I suppose I am one of the few members of the faculty of the Graduate School of Theology at Boston University that while he was there had no influence on his life." That was a self-deprecating exaggeration, given Thurman's long relationship with King's family and the influence *Jesus and the Disinherited* exercised on King, who was developing his social consciousness as a theology student. The two corresponded periodically during and after the Montgomery bus boycott, leading up to their meeting in the hospital after King's stabbing in 1958. In writing to King, Thurman, as was his custom and his strength, sought private conferences, where he could exercise his mentoring and counseling skills. Writing back to Thurman in March 1956, King mentioned how he had been encouraged to interact more with Thurman by figures such as the southern white author Lillian Smith and Homer Jack, a pacifist Unitarian.

King was one of many young African American theology and ministerial students who came under Thurman's sway. James Earl Massey, who went on to a long career as a professor and dean of the School of Theology at Anderson University (a Holiness Wesleyan school), was one of them. From his first preaching post in Detroit, he wrote Thurman an appreciative letter about all Thurman had meant to him at BU, and his devotion to studying Thurman's writings. Earlier he had heard Thurman preach in Detroit in 1949 and was deeply "moved" by the sermon, Massey later wrote in his own autobiography,

> partly because it all validated my own spiritual quest and findings in a way that no other preacher's words or pulpit approach had ever done, and partly because of the realization of divine presence I experienced in connection with his witness. . . . There was no stormy struggle in his manner, no loud blaring of his words; his was rather a soft-spoken, assured and assuring witness, a statement that seemed to me more like an "inside word" about some treasured truth and not an outside attempt to break into the truth. His style seemed so uniquely at one with his subject. Thurman helped me to experience spoken truth more vividly than any preacher I had ever heard before.

Massey's description fits well with the memory and testimony of many others from that era. Later, in the early 1970s, Massey prepared a biography manuscript of Thurman. Upon reviewing it (and noting that Sue also had done so), Thurman advised Massey that it was more an "anthology" of selected quotations from his writings than an "interpretation of their significance as the material passes through your creative mind and spirit." As always, Thurman wanted his disciples to reflect more on their own inward journey than on repeating the words of others, even of the spiritual master. The manuscript was left unpublished; Massey later went on to publish extensively on preaching and spiritual disciplines.

Shortly before his world tour in 1960, Thurman, sponsored by the United Negro College Fund (UNCF), spent January visiting black colleges, including Hampton Institute, Bennett College, and Tuskegee Institute. He visited informally with students and faculty without delivering public addresses, as he usually did on his travels. Thurman wrote to the director of the UNCF that he was "completely exhausted but profoundly exhilarated" by the trip. And little wonder, because a few weeks later students from North Carolina A&T College, joined by students at Bennett College, started the sit-in movement at the Woolworth's in downtown Greensboro, initiating a new era of the civil rights movement that would incorporate students centrally into the effort to compel Americans to confront the realities of racial segregation.

The young political science professor Charles V. Hamilton, teaching then at Tuskegee, wrote Thurman a note of appreciation for the "impetus and stimulation" that he provided when visiting his class. The results included civil rights rallies, student activism, and significant involvement in the Tuskegee Civic Association, a group that later submitted a voting rights proposal to Congress. "They are learning more political science than I could possibly convey in lectures," he concluded. At the same time, the internal tensions involved became evident when, later that year, Hamilton was dismissed from Tuskegee, a result of his opposition to gradualism and legalism as a civil rights strategy. Hamilton encouraged student activism, as did Thurman.

Thurman remained politically involved during these years in movements and organizations for peace, civil rights, and global conciliation, including the National Committee for a Sane Nuclear Policy (SANE) and the World Federalist Society. Thurman had resigned from Fellowship of

Reconciliation, a group that long had drawn his support and volunteer labor, because of his other responsibilities. But he still spoke on its behalf and used its material. He signed a statement authored by A. J. Muste titled "A Christian Approach to Nuclear War" that called for disarmament of the major world powers and a rejection by the United States of cooperation with "imperialist and reactionary regimes" abroad. Authored by the Church Peace Mission, an organization for various Christian pacifist groups, Thurman signed the statement and wrote to Muste, "You must know what a real source of inspiration your continual witness is to all of the rest of us." Most of all, Thurman was a committed internationalist, a true globalist, who continued to pursue his vision of "friendly men under a friendly sky." For Thurman, the initial ideas of the United Nations remained a source of inspiration, and he remained committed to his vision of a one-world community.

Thurman selected his times and opportunities to speak directly about problems faced by African Americans and about the ongoing civil rights struggle. He connected it with some of the predominant philosophies taught in theological programs at BU, particularly Personalism. For Thurman, segregation was an attack fundamentally on the basic human person of the black American and a violation of the "sacredness of human personality." Further, the emphasis of the "Boston Personalists" on a broadly accommodating theology that put more emphasis on a pluralistic acceptance of human dignity than any specific theological dogma fit well with Thurman's general style. Thurman long had been friends with the primary exponent of Personalism in Boston, Edgar S. Brightman, who passed away just as Thurman was arriving. And Brightman's work by that time already had exercised a significant influence on the young Martin Luther King, who had read the work of the Personalists during his study at Crozer Theological Seminary near Philadelphia, prior to his own arrival in Boston in 1951.

One of Thurman's longest-abiding concerns was black education. In an address from 1957, published in 1958 in the *Journal of Negro Education*, he reflected on the inherent frustrations built into the American system of segregated higher education, which had become a "practitioner of the cult of inequality." It did not set out specifically to become that but was invariably compromised into being so. As a result, for example, he and his fellows at Morehouse College in the 1920s already knew to curb their expectations.

There were certain walks of life not open to them. Thurman himself had a natural inclination to philosophy but found no such fully developed program awaiting him at Morehouse; such was not the province of young black men. If students like him were "exposed to the creative process which causes them to raise profound questions about meanings and to seek answers," Thurman commented acidly, "they may go on to raise questions about the structure of the institution which made it possible for them to get their college education." And that would require calling into question the entire structure of segregation in education.

Thurman raised the question: "How can you put at the disposal of the students the full and boundless insight of the Christian ethic and the moral imperative which it carries, and at the same time, not become a handmaiden of the cult of inequality?" White professors at black colleges in an earlier era sought to do exactly this but ended up as strangers in a strange land, alienated from both whites and blacks. Another answer was simply to accept the cult of inequality and to limit one's "ethical awareness" to one's own kind. Here, Thurman retold the story of growing up in Daytona Beach, when it "did not ever cross even the periphery of my awareness that I should recognize any moral responsibility to any of the white people in Daytona, Florida. . . . They were ethically out of bounds." And of course, the same held true for the white boy at the First Baptist Church. And even worse, long after the state had been forced to take positions in defense of democracy defined against fascism—and thus had to deal with the racial fascism at home—the church could not match that in its enactment of an "ethical imperative." And thus, the armed forces were desegregated in 1948, while Sunday morning at eleven o'clock remained the most segregated hour in America. But finally, blacks entered a new era in which the forces of higher education could lead to hope rather than frustration, that blacks too could follow truth "wherever it leads, transcending all barriers and all contexts."

In late 1955, to a sorority awards dinner in Boston, he spoke of the gulf between technological achievement and moral advance, the lack of the latter being evidenced by "the state of Georgia blacklisting Negro teachers for belonging to an organization whose only purpose is to insist that the Constitution of the United States be obeyed," not to mention the notorious murder of Emmett Till in Mississippi and threats to the life of the civil rights pioneer Rev. J. H. Delaine in South Carolina. Some of Thurman's earliest extended thoughts on the early years of the civil rights movement appeared in *Pulpit Digest* in 1957. In the article, he reflected on the amoral nature of the relationship between blacks and whites, a great moral chasm from his childhood that continued to the present day. But now, the opening up of human community was a possibility and could be encouraged by white and black ministers working together.

Here, Thurman expressed a philosophy very much akin to what Martin Luther King preached in those same years. Because of his epic 1963 piece "Letter from a Birmingham Jail," King is remembered now for his excoriation of "moderates" in the South. But for much of the 1950s, King still thought white southern ministers could provide moral leadership. Speaking at Vanderbilt in 1957, he professed his belief that "there is in the white South more open-minded moderates than appears on the surface. These people are silent today because of fear of social, political, and economic reprisals." He urged them to lead the region through its necessary transition to equal treatment for black citizens and reassured all that the aim of the movement was not to "defeat or humiliate the white man, but to win his friendship and understanding."

In effect, Thurman made much the same points in his 1957 piece. He outlined various approaches that ministers could take in response to the demands of the civil rights movement. One was simply to "withdraw from any and all social involvements," a stance Thurman would not even deign to discuss or refute. A second was to ask the question, "What would happen if, in any community, the work of salvation were to include the redemption of the spirits of the believers from all forms of racial prejudice and anti-Negro or anti-white attitudes?" The result, Thurman thought, would be that "*Social* responsibility would be the inevitable result flowing from his experience of *personal* redemption." Such a minister would teach that racial prejudice was simply sin before God and seek to purify lives of that sin. A final method was for ministers to be actively involved in improving the lives of southern communities during this time of change. Finally, the ordinary minister who never saw himself personally as racially prejudiced would wake up to a world changing before him.

In the process this minister would discover that he actually knew nothing of black life and could experience a spiritual crisis that would challenge him fundamentally to redefine his task, which now was "not only one of atonement as the catharsis for his guilt but also a new sense of social responsibility" as a part of his Christian commitment. He may discover within his congregation a member of the White Citizens' Council who needed creative ministering. But he would awaken to his mission of taking a stand for a court decision in line with Christian imperatives. And that minister could establish relationships with the black community, and with sympathetic whites (no matter how few they were). And so this minister's voice could be heard and provide a rallying point for the shaping of a new community. "Whatever others may think or believe," he concluded, "the minister knows that the contradictions of life are never final contradictions, and that the test of life is often found in the amount of pain a man may absorb without destroying his joy."

During this time, as well, Sue Bailey Thurman worked to revitalize the study of African American history among people not specifically in academia. Together with her daughter Anne, she put together *The Historical Cookbook of the American Negro*, and early in the 1950s she began her long work in black history in California with *Pioneers of Negro Origin in California*. Howard took an intense interest in this work, although Sue was clearly the prime mover. He wrote to James Nabrit, then president of Howard University, inquiring about making a space at Howard University for the National Museum of Negro Life and History. He feared that the Association for the Study of Negro Life and History had become a dusty academic forum, without much hope of gaining larger audiences. But it could be an organization "reaching into the heart of Negro life, giving a sense of dignity and appreciation for the past without which the present and the future do not have their rightful significance." It could reach ordinary black communities and students: "I think that one of the needful things, as our young people storm the gates on the Frontiers of Freedom, is some sense of history that will enable them to share responsibly in laying out the new city." Sue's work also led to the creation of what is now called the African American Freedom Trail in Boston, and more generally fostered an interest in African American history. Following that trail today, from the Boston Commons through Beacon Hill, a visitor travels through some of the most significant spots of nineteenth-century black American history. The visitor may see the houses where prominent abolitionists and writers such as David Walker and Marie Stewart lived, and read the attendant commemorative plaques, and end the tour at the African Meeting House, a black Baptist congregation established in 1806 that now serves as an African American history museum. As she had done at Howard University and in San Francisco, Sue Thurman's impressive efforts at historical collection, preservation, and public dissemination of knowledge of African American history were impressive, if still too unknown by scholars and students.

FINAL YEARS IN BOSTON

Thurman's plans for Marsh Chapel never fully came to fruition. Looking back over his work, Thurman addressed the vice president for student affairs in 1961, explaining his history with the chapel, his constant seven-day work-weeks, and his agreement with President Case that his national ministry through the Fellowship Church would only be enhanced with his position in Boston. Thurman added the personal word that the only way he could feel fully in line with this vision and God's plans, and not be exploited by the university for its own benefit, was the reassurance that his gifts would be "available to be shared beyond the boundaries of Marsh Chapel and particularly to be shared with Negroes who live and work and suffer in American society." This was all the more important because "the high hope which I had that it would be possible to develop a religious fellowship that cut across the barriers that separate men from each other in our society, once a climate could be established in Boston University, had to be abandoned."

Thurman's new title starting in 1962, minister emeritus, left him free from any official association as an officer of the university. It meant that he had to give up his office space and his ability to direct affairs within Marsh Chapel, and he had to move out of his university apartment on Bay Street to a residence nearer to downtown, at some remove from the university. The Thurmans came to appreciate the distance, and the chance to live more as ordinary citizens of the city of Boston. "It is the first time in 10 years that we have a sense of being private citizens," he wrote.

But he was furious at the process of replacing him. BU appointed Robert

Hamill dean of Marsh Chapel and publicized the transition in a way that implied that Thurman had retired completely. Hamill's job, it became apparent, was to implement the plan of making Marsh the principal center for Protestant worship on campus, directly contrary to the vision Thurman had been pursuing during his term at BU. Hamill implemented a new order of service, which Thurman characterized as "a traditional orthodox Trinitarian Protestant Christian service of worship." This left the three religious traditions at BU each with its own separate fortress, with the official university chapel officially committed to the Protestant tradition. "In the public worship of God we are back where we were in the 18th century," he bitterly commented.

In Thurman's last semester at BU, he became involved, indirectly but also quite wittingly, in the "Good Friday" experiment with psychedelic drugs, an epic moment in the rise of the American counterculture in the 1960s. The Good Friday experiment was conducted in April 1962 principally under the leadership of Walter Pahnke (with whom Thurman had a long and cordial friendship), and secondarily through the influence of Harvard psychologist Timothy Leary (with whom he had a short and contentious interaction). Then in the process of writing a doctoral dissertation on the possible religious significance of psychedelics, Pahnke had spoken with Thurman about his interests in the 1950s. Thurman evidenced some interest in the possible effects of psychedelics in inducing mystical experiences and opening up new spiritual worlds. Pahnke planned a scientific double-blind experiment on that Good Friday; Leary had no interest in any rational experiment but wanted to pursue opportunities of expanding consciousness. Thurman gave Pahnke permission to use a part of Marsh Chapel in the floor below the main venue, while Thurman's Good Friday service would be broadcast into this space (Robinson Chapel).

With Robinson Chapel locked and guarded, and the participants instructed to retain a reverent silence, the experiment proceeded while upstairs, in Marsh Chapel, Thurman led a lengthy service featuring biblical readings, slow contemplative music, and a reading of Edna St. Vincent Millay's poem "Conscientious Objector." Meanwhile, some of those in the basement ingested small doses of psilocybin. One of those was Huston Smith, soon to be a renowned scholar of religious studies. He remembered it as a central spiritual event in his life. He admired Thurman less for the precise content of his messages than for his spiritual ability to move people deeply and bring them to encounters with God (in this case, with the aid of the psychedelics). At the time, and later in his autobiography, Thurman said nothing of the experiment; his energies, as always, were focused on the contemplative events going on in the chapel. Later, when a magazine reported on the experiment, in an article titled "The Miracle of Marsh Chapel," Thurman let the editor have it; the idea that he had somehow "sponsored" this, much less participated in the procurement of the psilocybin, was false, he insisted. (In truth, Thurman knew much more about it than he let on, primarily through his close relationship with Panhke.) Thurman later said that spiritual explorations could take many paths, most of which were simpler and lacking the need for subterfuge contained in the psychedelic experiments of the 1960s. But he was not fully forthright (certainly not in his autobiography, which skips this incident entirely) about the degree to which he was at least willing to consider the possibility of drug-altered states of consciousness as a path to spiritual truths—the very path that William James famously had followed at Harvard much earlier in the twentieth century. It seems highly unlikely that the generally formal and reserved Thurman would have tried such a path himself (as opposed to, say, meditative silences or reciting sacred poetry); but it was entirely in his character as an inward journeyer to be interested in the paths of those ardently seeking after spiritual enlightenment. But the counterculture that emerged from psychedelics left Thurman cold.

On his trip east that same year, Thurman spoke to the thirty-fourth convocation of the Howard University School of Religion. Here, Thurman continued one of his favorite themes: the apparent contradictions of life were so only on the surface, and a deeper quest would lead the seeker to see the unity. As an example, he gave the desire for peace. There never had been a time of true peace—only periods of armistice between unceasing wars—and yet the human aspiration for peace survived. And so, ironically, there remained the deeper contradictions underneath the more superficial ones, but even they were not of ultimate significance. The world was malleable; it could be shaped. Its contradictions on the surface were not ultimate, because there always was another world in the making, underneath them. And religion at its best was a part of that transformation of chaotic elements into holistic ones. Religion as such always had both personal and social dimensions. On the personal side, religion was "the whisper of God in the human heart," to which the human responded with a feeling that life had a "transcendent security and strength and vitality." This was the religion of personal devotion and piety. But that form of religion necessarily was connected with the second, the relationship of religion to the social world. Religion provided a basis for "*integrated action*," a "touchstone" point, the ground of meaning for all the other action. It provided the demand to surrender something important in a quest for something deeper. Whatever the person was most willing to sacrifice, whatever that may be, was his religion And finally, religion provided a sense of "collective destiny."

In this talk, Thurman was in fact pitting the demands of the state at the height of McCarthyism against the integrity of the individual. One response to the demands of the external powers-that-be was simply to withdraw into one's private religious life: "I can always withdraw from my involvements, and deep within my own self commune with my own spirit and my God, and no one can invade me there." Worldly powers could not kill what was inside. But that was not a sufficient answer to the question of what to do when the powers of the world invaded one's conception of religion in a social sense. Then, the person would have to decide, "How much can I yield without doing violence to my overmastering loyalty? Where is the line beyond which I can't go without destruction?" Those without a "Transcendent Person" could easily sell out to the highest bidder, in this case to the state that might make demands in excess of what could be given by people with deeper commitments. Such was often the fate of intellectuals, who lived in a world of intellectual doubt and uncertainty, and thus left an intellectual vacuum for the "powers of this world" to come in and occupy. Thurman thus had been a part of the civil religion of the 1950s, championing the blessings of American liberty; but he used those very dialogues to advance challenges to the identification of God with the American state.

During the 1960s, while Howard was on sabbatical, the Thurmans traveled around the world, and later Thurman wrote a report on his journeys for the alumni magazine of Boston University. In it, he was beginning also to write what became his autobiography, *With Head and Heart*, and to reflect deeply on spiritual lessons gained from his childhood that he brought into his adult work of ministering. He went back to the oak tree in the yard of his Florida childhood. "How many people the world over have their oak trees? How many people have something, a symbol, from which they gain spiritual strength?" He had to "learn how to honor cultural and theological barriers, without making them roadblocks to communication and understanding." As a boy, he had encountered "many violences," but the one he kept returning to was the violation of his father's soul conducted at his funeral. He could only dimly understand this at the age of seven, but "as I grew older, this trauma became more meaningful." And thus even as a boy, he had to find some "inner resource that could give me enough immunity to the violence of my environment to enable me to have a sense of normalcy and worthwhileness in being a human being," and something that could "meet the devastations of this experience in a creative and sustaining manner." That's what the oak tree provided him; it was his "windbreak against existence." He could also return there and "talk things over. It was the one thing in our yard that did not give when the seasonal hurricanes came." Beyond being his windbreak against existence, it was also a "trysting place where I met and communed with God." For him, the tree that withstood all storms symbolized the strength of God's power; "always it stood," both the tree and God.

Later, as he recounted it, Thurman's trip to India made him aware of one of his central life quests: "What could we do to bring about a better understanding of all people of different races and religion?" His ministry in San Francisco provided one answer; later, his work at Marsh Chapel continued that quest, as he sought "additional answers within the framework of an urban University whose roots go deep into the soil of Protestant Christian traditions" but whose constituency was diverse. Thurman's journey in 1960 had given him further exposure to what he faced in Marsh Chapel: "Any Sunday morning there are present in the congregation men and women from the ends of the earth, often of varied creeds, faiths, and cultures. Here is a service addressed to the deepest needs and aspirations of the human spirit." And thus on the trip, as he gave sermons or lectures in Tokyo, Beirut, or

London, this was "but an extension of the ministry of the Chapel itself, the same challenge, the same cross-section, the same timeless urgencies." He was more aware than ever that sheer physical need was paramount, and there was little he could do about it. And so he advised finding "the way by which we can confirm our own faith in the values which are important, and at the same time, include in the confirmation of those values the redemption of the stomachs of the people."

Meanwhile, whatever leadership America could provide would be affected by the "hatreds evident in American life, the isms that contradict the philosophy of our way of life." This to him had only deepened his "sense of urgency about the mission which I have felt all of my life." It had confirmed his belief that he could never be what he ought to be "as long as there is any single human being anywhere in the world who is being held up because of conditions over which he is unable to exercise any control." As he put it, "I think that my freedom is locked up in his." Thurman returned to one of his quote touchstones from Eugene Debs, which reinforced for him that "I feel that God cannot be what God is destined to be in the world as long as any man is being held back and held down." Because "wherever a man is in prison, God is in prison."

In a letter (ironically) to his successor as dean of Marsh Chapel, Thurman provided one of his most positive perspectives on the meaning of his experience in Boston. After nine years of "impossible effort," he explained, a congregation at Marsh Chapel finally had taken hold. "It is, perhaps, the most dramatic work of the Holy Spirit in my experience," he told Hamill. And yet, it was not a work that fulfilled what he perceived to be the vision of the Holy Spirit for a completely inclusive human and religious community in which all would meet on common ground. Ultimately, he could not achieve that to his own satisfaction; and ultimately it was not achievable.

Yet, to accomplish what he had, as a prominent black mystic and cosmopolitan at an overwhelmingly white and historically Methodist institution, was remarkable. Thurman probably came closer to achieving his vision at BU than he had during his "great adventure" at Fellowship Church. But as he prepared to return to San Francisco, where he would make his home after his retirement from BU in 1965 until his death in 1981, he was still on the search for common ground, the search that would provide the title for his last major book of essays, published in 1971. In returning to San Francisco, he was going home again—this time as a true spiritual wanderer and minister to a world at-large and to a small group of younger disciples who would carry forward his vision.

6

"The Way the Grain in My Wood Moves"
Thurman's Wider Ministry

I have never considered myself any kind of leader. . . . I'm not a movement man. It's not my way. I work at giving witness in the external aspect of my life to my experience of the truth. That's my way—the way the grain in my wood moves.

—Howard Thurman, quoted in Lerone Bennett,
"Howard Thurman: 20th Century Holy Man"

One of the most personally gratifying days of Howard Thurman's life came on May 25, 1963. It was Howard Thurman Day in Daytona Beach, Florida, his hometown. Thurman reflected on the meaning of this event given his difficult early years in a city where he was "introduced to the terror and trauma of being born a Negro." Even to this day, he commented, "scar tissue marks the places where the early blows made their mark and the searing pain invaded body and spirit." A dinner that evening was attended by around 150 people, a crowd about evenly divided between white and black; it was an experience of community that provided a "fleeting glimpse of the potential promise of community realized." The city was still segregated. Yet it recognized the local boy made good. Seeing his primary school teacher there left Thurman deeply moved. The beloved community had not yet been realized in a still-segregated Daytona, one in which leaders of the local civil rights movement soon staged protests against segregation. That division was a familiar one for Thurman. Yet, as always, the unities, not the contradictions, were ultimately the important thing. Through his last years of retirement, what he called his "wider ministry," that's the vision he pursued. His years of stardom had passed, eclipsed by the meteoric careers of younger black men and women. And he delighted in that; he knew the quietly influential role he played in making what he called the "Negro revolution" possible.

Howard Thurman retained his affiliation with Boston University until 1965. But in effect, from the fall semester of 1962 forward, he was a sort of dean emeritus, no longer with a home in the middle of the campus community. Soon thereafter he entered into a period that he later called his "wider ministry." In effect, for the last eighteen years of his life, Thurman was a freelance mentor: overseeing the Howard Thurman Educational Trust, traveling across the world, and continuing to tutor younger African Americans who were coming out of the civil rights struggle and into places of leadership. In some senses, Thurman had the chance to pursue exactly what he was best at. He ministered, counseled, preached, lectured, and mentored on an ad hoc basis, without the institutional and bureaucratic demands that had so long bridled him in the past. His spirit was free to roam, both physically and metaphorically; to the end of his life it moved freely. He listened for that which is God in us and communicated the lessons he learned from that to a younger generation who formed a small but loyal group of disciples. A good number of those younger followers, influenced by black theology and similar movements, disagreed with Thurman on philosophical points of power and nonviolence, but they revered him in spite of those differences, as they recognized Thurman's profound authenticity, the way he embodied and expressed the central ideas of his life, and his long service in the freedom struggle.

During these years, as well, Thurman produced his final books. Shortly before passing, he published his autobiography, *With Head and Heart*, a symbol of the mental and spiritual forces he had tried to combine through his life. Reaction to the book was mixed, and included negative reviews in publications such as the *Nation*. Like many authors, Thurman claimed to pay no attention to reviews of his works; but like many authors, he in fact did. The irony was that the autobiography of this man who ministered personally to so many left some readers frustrated that Thurman did not reveal himself fully.

For that reason, although the book is moving and important, it is not a classic in the line of African American memoirs. The autobiography leaves one at some remove. Thurman uses his personal experiences and his intellectual reflections to impart lessons to readers, but Thurman the man remains a mystery. Perhaps in part for this reason, some years after his death, a hospice worker who had known Thurman well (and Thurman had a close relationship with those in healing ministries) commented to a friend and colleague of Thurman's about a conference on Thurman's life and thought: "I did feel at times though that some of the academics missed the point." People remembered Thurman saying that those researching him from an academic perspective could not know the part of him "that was whimsical and rich and deep": the preacher who painted penguins in his office and took up the clarinet in his later years; the dean of the chapel who delighted in playing chef for students who came and enjoyed his culinary concoctions and his extended conversations about their studies and their personal struggles; the train aficionado who immersed himself in detective novels; the pacifist who loathed violence and (at least when younger) loved prizefights and thrilled to Joe Louis; and the earnest minister who rode on a fire truck as an adult and blew the siren "with a child's glee." And perhaps most of all, the mystic and saint and seeker "intoxicated by God" who could reflect about himself as follows: "I have always felt that a word was being spoken through me, and three-fourths of the time I didn't get it right. I am, simply, a man who is earnestly engaged in an effort, an exercise, a *commitment*, to become a religious man."

Readers sent him letters, many of praise, some of frustration that they were left "wanting to get *inside* the experiences you only sketched briefly on the *outside*." This reader recalled a talk with Thurman when "you told me you were stymied (my word, not yours) by the problem of writing truthfully about the dissolution of your two major jobs (Boy, was I trying hard to read between the lines of Howard University and Boston University)." Was there also, he wondered, a "strain" in the Fellowship Church? Thurman's old friend Ed Kaplan, a professor of literature at Wellesley College, wrote to ask him, "What is the clue to your sadness and the way in which you transmute it into a deep confidence tinged with a tragic sense of your fragility? What is that melancholy with which I identified?" He continued: "You have left an indispensable historical record and I have been inspired by it. But perhaps you have left too much feeling aside. Your special genius, in your personal relationship to me, has been to understand and to articulate in the most concrete and subtle terms, the nuances of feeling and of interpersonal rela-tionships. The autobiography is *not* a pious one, but it seems to me more of a document than an expression of personal need."

But Thurman's colleagues, friends, former teachers, and in some cases complete strangers sent in their letters of appreciation, and surely Thurman treasured those as he approached his last days. A letter from his beloved teacher from Florida Baptist Academy in Jacksonville, Ethel Simons Meeds, expressed the hope that Thurman was "paying no attention to any dispar-aging criticisms of your magnificent book." She was impressed with the "weaving of your philosophy throughout the telling of the story showing so clearly that long entrenched custom can be uprooted, long deferred, greatly needed changes in this our life can be made without self aggrandizement or violent assault." Reading the autobiography provoked a former student of his at BU to remember Thurman's quality "to concentrate all your attention and love on one human being at a time and make that person feel it. Never have I met someone who possessed that gift to the extent you do." For a younger African American woman from Indianapolis who had been brought up in the church, the autobiography helped her reconcile "the hypocrisy of Chris-tianity as we have been taught. It was difficult for me to understand a Christ of fear, pain, and revenge. At times I felt that there was something missing." But after reading about his time India, she realized that she could follow the true teaching of Christ "and not the teaching of Jesus Christ as it has been promulgated in the Western world. I realized that something seemingly so basic had escaped me in my learning." A Methodist reader in Pittsburgh had learned from Thurman that "the center of everything is within." He had to leave the organized church "because I could not work for statistics only with no seeming regard for a person's spiritual well being." For him, Thurman was ahead of his time in his writing and his work. "Only now are more and more people beginning to speak about meditations and the spiritual life."

Other responses included a Jewish haberdasher in Rochester who bought and read Thurman's autobiography because Thurman had ordered suits from his store for many years following his time in seminary; a student who wrote to testify on his behalf for conscientious objection; a son of an old ministerial friend of Thurman's who worried about Thurman seeming, at least by insinuation, to embrace psychedelic drugs as a possible path to the divine; and a budding young scholar who sought Thurman's counsel and advice and wondered how much he charged for autographed books. As always, Thurman drew friends, admirers, and total strangers who felt they could talk to him and be heard. His "wider ministry" existed in people with whom he interacted, in his discipling of younger ministers and scholars, and in the republic of letters. After his passing, the letters continued, as seekers sought advice from Sue on what Howard might have said about this or that subject of great concern to them. One correspondent from Dallas wrote to Sue in 1984, recounting her career trying to make her way as a black woman in the ministry but finding that "the community around me is so denominationally embedded" that she felt stifled. The correspondent knew that Howard would appreciate her struggle, after having heard him when he visited a black educational institution in Dallas.

During the early 1960s, Thurman may have entered a period of wider ministry, but he had not yet given up on Boston University, nor on his quest to make Marsh Chapel the kind of place he had long envisioned. Thurman's replacement, Robert H. Hamill, moved into Thurman's spot and changed the chapel's order of service into a more recognizably Protestant one, what Thurman called a "traditional orthodox trinitarian Protestant Christian service of worship." Thurman pointed out to President Case that "a large group of our people within our kind of heterogeneous university can get no help, or inspiration from that service and I include myself among them." Case responded that a new dean of chapel would make the changes he deemed appropriate, just as Thurman himself had done when he arrived. Thurman continued leading some services at Marsh, particularly during the more informal summer months. But he was dismayed that his vision for Marsh Chapel never came to fruition. It was one of the more significant professional disappointments of his life.

Thurman continued to produce annual reports on his ministry, including one from 1962 to 1963 that he titled "The Wider Ministry," expressing his notion of how he was to spend his later years. During this time, Thurman visited a meeting of the Federation of Saskatchewan Indians and later traveled to Winnipeg, Manitoba. Thurman discovered among the Saskatchewan Indians the struggles under oppressive regimes, the dehumanizing misery but at the same time humanizing resistance, that he recognized from the African American experience. As he explained it, "The rest of the story is as old as human misery. It is what the Indians speak of in their recommendations to the Canadian government. It is a story of the native people of South Africa and those who would give them courage and hope; the story of Mississippi, and the tragedy of the ghetto of Warsaw."

During the same trip, he met with a former student from his "Spiritual Disciplines and Resources" course, Rabbi Schachter, who had encouraged his Hillel students to attend Thurman's addresses titled "Quests of the Human Spirit." Together, the two attended the rituals at a Trappist monastery. As Thurman described it, "Somewhere in the march of the moments, the Conservative Jewish Rabbi, the gentile preacher, and the Trappist monks became children of Life, finding their way into their father's house." Thurman particularly appreciated the concluding service in a darkened chapel, when a statue of Mary was raised above an altar and "flooded with light. There were more prayers and chants and then the lights were extinguished. In the silence, every heart found its own rest and peace—a tranquility beyond forms, contexts, and altars." Thurman and Rabbi Schacter later sat quietly in a car, saying nothing, contemplating the "surrounding landscape with a milk-white glow." Thurman was in his element; the nature mystic and the spiritual seeker were at one in that moment.

Thurman had one major journey left in him—to Africa. He knew he needed to go, and Sue urged him. But first he reveled in participating in the March for Jobs and Justice in Washington, DC, where Martin Luther King gave his most famous address. Thurman was exultant that late August day in 1963; he was, he said, "part of the vast throng who heard and felt the unearthly upheaval of triumphant anguish: 'Free at last! Free at last!'" He wrote of it later:

> Nothing like this has ever happened in the history of our country. I was one of 200,000 people sharing a moment that contained all time and all experience, when everything was moving and everything was standing still, a moment that had in it the stillness of absolute motion. From where I sat I could look at the face of Abraham Lincoln deep within the shadow of the Memorial but with his countenance illumined by a floodlight. . . . America was present in Washington on the 28th: white and black, young and old, Protestant, Catholic, Jewish, free-wheeler, male and female, con-

servative, middle-of-the-roader, labor leaders and workers, the schooled and the unschooled, the halt, the lame, the hale and the seeing—it was the guts of America spilling out along Constitution Avenue.

For one day, at least, Thurman's vision of human unity seemed achievable.

In October, Thurman embarked on a six-month expedition around the world that involved, principally, a stay of two months in Nigeria, where he was a visiting professor at the University of Ibadan. Thurman felt, at the beginning, "as if I had come to the end of a period of a phase of my life never to be entered into again." He had finished his official time as dean of Marsh Chapel, with some bitterness on what had not been accomplished but with a feeling of excitement about moving into his "wider ministry."

Thurman's attitudes toward Africa were complex. Earlier in his life he had felt a call to India, and he had traveled extensively since, but, as he put it, "for a long time I had no ripe desire to go to Africa. It is hard to analyze it—only that it is true. Sue kept before me the necessity of the Pilgrimage. She insisted that I needed it for my own fulfillment and rounding out. I did not see this nor feel it." But after Thurman met K. Onwuka Dike, a Nigerian academic official, at a commencement ceremony in Boston, the two corresponded, and Thurman arranged his residency in Ibadan.

For one of the few times in his life, Thurman kept a rather lengthy personal journal of a trip. Thus, during this particular venture and during his time in Africa, we get a better sense of the inner Thurman, working through his own reactions and attitudes and problems, outside of the measured and carefully wrought prose that characterizes his public offerings. Perhaps for this reason, or perhaps because Thurman genuinely felt more adrift and more of an outsider on this journey than was usual for him, he comes across as slightly unsure of himself. At the same time, Thurman remained connected to the people of Ibadan and the university, serving as an adviser to its religious studies program in future years. During his time there, President John F. Kennedy was assassinated, a shocking event that brought forth an idealistic eulogy of a political figure he clearly admired.

Thurman's journal through this period is unusually introspective and conversational. "For the first time since I can remember," he begins, "I was completely overwhelmed by a new kind of sadness. . . . It seemed as if I was not merely saying farewell to my homeland and separating from my family and close friends but that I was saying goodbye to a whole way of life—as if I had come to the end of a period or a phase of my life never to be entered into again." Some of this came from the particular circumstances of this trip—traveling without Sue, and not yet knowing for certain about his visa to enter the country (he would acquire that once he was in London). And yet, he felt a kind of "fire burning" inside that he couldn't comprehend, a feeling of being "alive in my mind and spirit. It is as if I am being readied for a fuller life than I have ever known—maybe it is a mere prelude to my earth leave-taking." Thurman as a spiritual seeker always sought avenues of spiritual awareness and exploration, connections with worlds unseen that could be sending messages. He listened for them and sought them out.

The quiet time on ship—Thurman commented that he smiled and nodded to passengers but made little effort to engage in conversation—gave him time also to reflect on significant people in his life. For one of the few times in his reflections and writings, he spoke of his two daughters. And of the two, clearly he felt the most connected with Anne, his daughter with Sue: "I shall die at ease that the essence of Sue's and my life will be preserved and blossom in ways that neither of us can imagine." Thurman saw the reflection of Sue in Anne, with her "clear unmuddled mind that functions like a sharp tool in the hands of an expert—when she wants to. Then she becomes alive, eyes face whole countenance vibrates with a kind of hidden . . . energy." Of Olive, his firstborn daughter from his brief marriage with Katie before her death, Thurman felt a keen pain. He was never free to be a "father as I was with Anne," and her care in some of her younger years was entrusted to others while he made his voyages, including the one to India. Thurman felt a "sense of failure or guilt or remorse that for many years clung to me like a kind of sickness. I suppose that what I mean is that I was always trying to redeem something in my relation with her." Yet most of his references to his daughters are about the joy they brought him. Both were involved in helping disseminate his work after his death.

Thurman also expressed his insecurities about being monolingual in a multilingual environment, and over the fact that people responded to him as a scholar of religion from within their own sectarian frameworks, simply because that's how religion inevitably was identified. He saw too that

Southern Baptists and Methodists had considerable sway in making converts around Ibadan. If he were asked to speak at the chapel, he would have another crisis moment, given the demand to speak evangelical language. Thurman wondered too about his own motive for his trip. Was it simply to say that, as an American Negro, he now knew Africa? Was it to "escape from the pressure of the revolution that is going on at home"?

In Ibadan, Thurman remained acutely conscious of his outsider status. "There is a manifest friendliness and then all of a sudden you are not there," he commented of his interactions. He heard an Oxford-trained lawyer praise Billy Graham, wanting Thurman to share that enthusiasm, which Thurman could not. Thurman found himself doing "the kind of hard listening that I have never done before," trying to understand how to communicate best with those around him: "I am listening to the strange world of experience which in its sociology is completely foreign to me." In the university at Ibadan, he had trouble finding his own bearings: "I do not seem to be in touch with any center or core of the place." This was so partly because of tribal tensions between various university leaders.

Thurman gave addresses as part of his visiting professorship and encountered many of the same objections—and some new ones—that he had grown accustomed to since his time in India nearly thirty years previously. In a historical talk on the Negro revolution in America—"making a speech of this kind is not one of my talents," he admitted—he was challenged for skipping over African independence (a slight he immediately admitted) and for omitting reference to the black Muslims in America. Thurman agreed that the black Muslims had made a vital contribution by "giving *heart* to many of the people who felt that they did not count." Still, he could not abide their emphasis on "separateness either within America or as a colonization scheme somewhere else." Thurman saw himself as a "birth-right American. A part of the subtle propaganda is to make the Negro feel that he is an alien in the land of his birth and in which his sweat and blood have laid the foundation upon which the country is built." That pretty well summarized his skeptical attitude toward "black power" in the later 1960s as well; he appreciated the anger that generated it, but he could never abide philosophies that emphasized human separation over ultimate unity. His last major book of theo-philosophical explorations, *In Search of Common Ground*, explored precisely this theme.

Toward the end of his African journey, word came of Kennedy's assassination. The American ambassador, Joseph Palmer, sent word to Thurman, then in Oyo, that he wanted him to deliver a eulogy in Lagos, the capital. Thurman had just hours to prepare an address to about nine hundred people assembled at the ambassador's residence. Thurman briefly wondered about the audience, but as he started writing, as he described it, the words simply flowed. He expressed his personal reaction to Kennedy. When he became president, Thurman felt, "the youth of the land and the young in spirit were caught up on the sweep of his confidence, his sense of purpose and his direction. There was an [aura] of destiny in his assurance." Thurman saw his establishment of the Peace Corps, for example, as an example of Thurman's own "apostles of sensitiveness," those who put their "talents at the disposal of human need everywhere without benefit of anything other than the opportunity to give."

But for Thurman, Kennedy's activism in civil rights stood out; Thurman gave far more credit to Kennedy in this arena than did many of his contemporaries in the movement, or historians now do, for that matter. But to Thurman, despite the "impatience" some showed about "the speed with which his leadership affirmed itself, there was never any doubt that he was acting out of the center of an informed heart and conviction as to the true spirit and meaning of democracy and the American dream." And that was a dream, Thurman said, that he had extended to "all the nations of the earth."

Thurman's stay in Africa led him to reflect deeply on the meaning of old slave-trading stations that he saw. He returned to some of his familiar themes of human strength and survival through situations of utter desolation:

> From my cabin window I look out on the full moon and the ghosts of my forefathers rise and fall with the undulating waves. Across the same waters, how many years ago they came! What were the inchoate mutterings locked tight within the circle of their ears? In the deep, heavy darkness of the foul smelling hold of the ship, where they could not see the sky nor hear the night noises nor feel the warm compassion of the Tribe, they held their breath against the agony. How does the human spirit accommodate itself to desolation? How did they? What tools of the spirit were in their

hands with which to cut a path through the wilderness of their despair? . . .
Nothing anywhere in all the myths, in all the stories, in all of the ancient
memory of the race, had given hint of this torturous convulsion. There
were no gods to hear.

The impact of seeing the slave-trading coast firsthand was nearly overwhelming, producing this unusually intense personal reflection, without
the theology of hope that he usually stressed even in writing of dire situations from the past.

Upon his return, he faced again new challenges in Boston. He was a freelance minister with a national audience but without any particular institutional home. He continued to write and speak in Boston and around the
country, ranging widely in his topics and passions. Some highlights include
addresses on religion and science, on mysticism, and on nonviolence.

Thurman loved science, particularly the life sciences that put one in
touch with the natural world that provided so many lessons for the human
world. And Thurman saw science and religion as complementary. Religion
"must accept the challenge to give empirical validation for its claim," while
also recognizing "that the integrity, the nitty-gritty, of the experience does
not ultimately rest upon any empirical validation. In the last analysis the
integrity of the religious experience is the experience itself." For Thurman,
the purposiveness of life was the key, and man's discovery of his own purpose was the role of religion. As Thurman expressed it: "A man wants to
know what it is after all that he ultimately amounts to. It is here that man
seeks personal assurance and confirmation; it is here that he experiences the
satisfaction of being totally dealt with in a manner that is private, personal,
and at the same time social and universal. It is this second level that his
experience has in it the elements that make it religious." The central quality of a truly religious experience, an encounter with God, is "that which
transpires totally in a man's personality when he feels himself to be in direct
touch with the kind of reality that gathers into a single focus all of the values
and meanings which the individual at other times has thought, sensed, or
felt." As a "time-binder" by nature, an observer could be aware that "events,
experiences in which he may be involved do not ever quite contain all that he
is at any particular moment in time." People could stand outside their own

experiences and watch themselves experiencing, but still there remained something mysteriously internal and unknowable.

Religious experiences fostered "communication between the individual and a consciousness that is an infinite expansion of his own consciousness. . . . The thing that makes any experience a religious experience is the door which the experience opens that makes possible an awareness of encounter between the essential self and a greater expansive living consciousness." And that encounter would then produce purpose. Religious experience as a means to unify life could bring the individual to become "a part of all that is when the narrow walls of his own conscious life seem to become enlarged. It is as if his little life becomes the door through which he enters into a larger and fuller dimension of what he has known himself to be all along. The purpose of all spiritual exercise is to aid and abet this development. This is the meaning of worship whenever it is found."

Thurman's best examples came from Quaker services. He reflected deeply on one experience in particular. Asked to speak once in a Quaker meeting, Thurman prepared nothing but simply tried to "experience the depths of dynamic silence." He felt, at first, a panic, but then gradually, as he experienced it, the barriers between him and the congregation melted. His mind fixated on a series of words that formed part of the Sermon on the Mount, and they took shape in his head as he extemporized the address in his own mind. And then, just as he was ready to speak, another congregant rose and began to speak from the same verse, as did others. And for him, it "seemed that all in that room were sharing deeply in the same kind of transcending experience which greatly confirmed and sustained us all but was at the same time much, much more than any one of us, in and of himself."

During this time, at the height of the nonviolent civil rights movement, Thurman continued his philosophical explorations into the ideas he had been so important in fostering and spreading. In 1963, he published *Disciplines of the Spirit*, parts of which explored the history and purpose of nonviolence. Like others, he insisted that "non-violence is not a negative attitude— it is a positive act of resistance. It is not passive; it is positive and creative." It once was considered weak and cowardly but was no longer considered so after the life of Gandhi and the dramatic developments within the United States during the civil rights years.

Nonviolence, Thurman insisted, was not "merely a mood or a climate, or even an attitude," but a "particular kind of art or technique." It was not simply the choice of the only available tool. If it were, it would participate in the very order it was struggling against; in this case, it would have "the same moral basis as violence and cannot be separated from it in essence." But nonviolence could be one of the "great vehicles of reconciliation because it tends always to create and to maintain a climate in which the need to be understood and cared for can be honored." Those practicing nonviolence could be full of rage, of an internal will to violence, but nonviolence was a rejection of both the physical and the psychological tools of violence. The tools of nonviolence were those aimed not merely at changing a situation but requiring "a man to face *himself* in his action—to see how he looks to himself in the violent act itself without regard to what he hopes the violent act will accomplish." The tools of nonviolence placed upon men "the demand to absorb violence rather than to counteract it in kind," something that profoundly challenged people to face naked fear: "There is rioting in the streets of the spirit, and the price of tranquility comes terribly high. Order and reconciliation must be restored within—it is here that the major conquest must be achieved." As with Martin Luther King, Thurman saw nonviolence as a fundamental philosophical principle, not just a stratagem.

Thurman related a story from the civil rights movement about a woman who had been pinned to the ground by a policeman but at that moment felt a sense of peace within herself. For him, it was an example of how "nonviolence is the tapping and the releasing of the resources of vitality and energy in the human spirit that make it possible to relax and overcome the spirit of retaliation." That spirit had become apparent in recent years, and was evident in Supreme Court acts, in the quiet tramping of feet on the streets, and in every place where people sought justice where "injustice abounds, to make peace where chaos is rampant, and to make the voice heard on behalf of the helpless and the weak. It is the voice of God and the voice of man; it is the meaning of all the strivings of the whole human race toward a world of friendly men underneath a friendly sky." The way had been opened through the "dramatic loss of fear on the part of the masses of Negroes," because violence always fed on fear as its "magic source of energy," and "as long as men react to it in and with fear, their lives can be controlled by those in whose hands the instruments of violence rest." This had come for many reasons, but most importantly "due to the sense of direct, conscious, and collective participation in a joint destiny." For Thurman, the goal of the beloved community remained the ideal, the ultimate aim of what he called the "Negro revolution." He had been envisioning and forecasting it from his younger years at Howard University to his pastoral tenure in San Francisco.

THURMAN AND THE MOVEMENT

Some contemporaries of Thurman, and nearly all scholars since, have pondered the paradox that Thurman was a mentor of the movement but was not a movement man. That is, he educated a generation in precepts of nonviolence and a kind of internal transformation that would lead to a societal revolution, but he himself stayed in the background. As he told the *Christian Century* in 1973, "I didn't have to wait for the revolution. I have never been in search for identity, and I think that [all] I've ever felt and worked on and believed in was founded in a kind of private, almost unconscious autonomy that did not seek vindication in my environment because it was in me." Thurman's vision of the church emanated from that. As Thurman saw it, individuals in the thick of the struggle should have a place to "be able to find renewal and fresh courage in the spiritual resources of the church. . . . The true genius of the church was revealed by what it symbolized as a beachhead in society in terms of community, and as an inspiration to the solitary individual to put his weight on the side of a society in which no person need be afraid."

His works influenced King, but King drew from many sources. His teaching inspired James Farmer and many others from Howard, and Thurman was on committees, boards of directors, and advisory groups—but rarely if ever on the front lines. At the beginning of his trip to Africa, in the momentous autumn of 1963, Thurman himself wondered if he was leaving the country in part to escape the pressures of the revolution happening at home. And later in the 1960s, activists from the left and proponents of black power actively challenged Thurman and his ideas. For them, power differentials in society overcame any imaginary spiritual "unity" between souls. By that time, Thurman was well into his sixties and attached to the same demeanor and personal habits as always. He was a formally dressed, quiet, and introspective man in a particularly tumultuous era. He listened to Beethoven rather than the blues or bebop to animate his spiritual reflections and speak to his soul. He understood, but fundamentally dissented from, the precepts of black nationalism gaining currency in the late 1960s. In one letter to an old friend, he gently mocked the argot of the era: "I got thoughts, man!" he told him. More than anything else, Thurman preferred the one-on-one conversation, or the classroom, or the formal sermon, to encounters on the street or public demonstrations. He distrusted "proclamations" of all sorts and preferred deeply felt statements that arose from one's soul.

And perhaps he also carried with him the Gandhian emphasis on the cultivation of a small group of spiritual elites who could carry forward the message of nonviolence. As Sue later expressed it, "We had a feeling that those who were leading in the civil rights movement had to have some place to rest their hearts at night. They had to fight all day, all day long. And then at night, they had to go somewhere and find their rest, or find their peace that the next morning would bring renewed energy. So he pastored to civil rights people." As she remembered, "They did call him in the dead of night and he did take hours on end, either writing them or speaking to them by phone or having a touch with them as they came up to Boston, just to see him for a few hours and go straight back." Thurman was thus more interested in the personal touch than the public proclamation.

And yet, Thurman was friends with and a mentor to many who espoused ideas with which he fundamentally disagreed, even when he understood where those ideas came from. Political figures and movement activists such as Whitney Young and Jesse Jackson, black historians such as Lerone Bennett and Nathan Huggins, and early critical legal theorists such as Derrick Bell—all spoke reverentially of Thurman even as they challenged some of the central ideas that motivated his life and ministry. They understood his long history in the movement, what he had done in years past that had prepared the way for the 1960s. The Thurmans were particularly important for the historians, scholars, and activists Nathan Huggins and Vincent Harding. When Huggins was a boy, he and his sister had been effectively abandoned by their father, and Huggins was partly raised by the Thurmans in San Francisco as their adopted child. Huggins went on to a distinguished academic career, and he dedicated his landmark work *Harlem Renaissance* to Sue. Harding's work of African American history, *There Is a River*, directly reflects Thurman's thought on black history, even though the Harding of that era, influenced by the black power movement, had come to rather different conclusions about the place of African Americans in the United States. But as Harding later wrote, "I have a feeling that Howard Thurman's greatest contribution is going to be to the future of black religious thinking. . . . [He said to us] that it is possible to take all of the struggles and the sufferings of the black experience and recreate them in such a way that they can be used to open up a whole new arena of human encounter and human relationships." Otis Moss, a minister and organizer in the movement, said Thurman was not in the marches, but he "participated on the level that shaped the philosophy or creates the march—without that, people don't know what to do before the march, while they march, or after they march." Or, as Thurman described himself, "It's the way the grain in my wood moves." The grain in the wood defined and gave a texture to a piece of furniture, without anyone specifically taking note that it was there.

Thurman played his part in sending letters of protest, in making sizable financial contributions to the Southern Christian Leadership Conference, and perhaps most of all in interpreting the movement in speeches, lectures, sermons, and writings for a national audience. In *The Luminous Darkness: A Personal Interpretation of the Anatomy of Segregation and the Ground of Hope*, published in 1965, he gave an extended set of reflections on the psychology and theology of segregation. "For generations fear has been the monitor, the angel with the flaming sword standing guard to make the pattern of segregation effective," he explained. That fear was "spawned and kept alive by the perpetual threat of violence everywhere, on all sides," but it was a one-sided violence, a "violence that is devoid of contest." Whites could easily accept such a pattern and be secure (whether intentionally or indifferently) in feelings of superiority. But a white person who even passively accepted the system thus became a "party to a monstrous evil executed in his name and maintained in his behalf. The responsibility for the social decay and defiling of the spirit is inescapable, acknowledged or unacknowledged. For segregation is a sickness and no one who lives in its reach can claim or expect immunity."

For Thurman, the civil rights movement pointed a way out of this psychology of fear and hatred, toward wholeness and community: "It makes a path to Walden Pond and ignites the flame of nonviolence in the mind of a Thoreau and burns through his liquid words from the Atlantic to the Pacific; it broods over the demonstrators for justice and brings comfort to the desolate and forgotten who have no memory of what it is to feel the rhythm of belonging to the race of men." For Thurman, the alternative presented in the 1960s of black power had the virtue of courage but the weakness of depending on the "way of retribution and vengeance. It is one more turn of the same wheel that moves round and round but does not gain an inch. . . . It says the contradictions of life are not only final but ultimate." Thurman always held the spirit of beloved community over the psychology of separation. "When the battles are over," he said, blacks and whites would have to live together and "to forget this is the great betrayal of the future."

One of Thurman's other most extended and deepest discussions of segregation and civil rights, written during this time but published many years after his death, came at the request of the political scientist Samuel DuBois Cook, in what was originally to be an honorary volume for Benjamin Mays. Thurman titled it "Desegregation, Integration, and the Beloved Community." He wrote it in 1966, as the movement entered a new phase and riots had just decimated parts of Watts in Los Angeles.

As Thurman saw it, there were two meanings to integration. One was the more limited sense of "free and open access to association with each other." Before the deeper meaning of integration could be found, it was first necessary to struggle for this guaranteed right within the American political contract. But beyond that was a deeper meaning having to do with the "quality of human relations," and with the "private, personal experience of individuals and groups of varied backgrounds as they discover that there is a unity among peoples that can contain and support diversity as an expression of its self." This form of integration could not be mandated by law, because it was founded on a sense of "dynamic integration" that has to do with the "individual's total experience in the society." Thurman recounted that, in the Fellowship Church, the presence of people of diverse backgrounds did not mean the church was integrated in this deeper sense, because that sense required that people have forms of "natural communal association."

As Thurman put it, "Meaningful experiences of integration between peoples are more compelling than the fears, the inhibitions, the dogmas or the prejudices that divide. If such unifying experiences can be multiplied over an extended time interval, they will be able to restructure the entire fabric of the social context." Here, Thurman expressed again his lifelong dream of a unity that overcame all apparent contradictions.

This kind of "beloved community" came precisely because of the "quality of the human relations experienced by the people who live within it." The beloved community was not something achievable by "fiat," but rather was an "achievement of the human spirit as men seek to fulfill their high destiny as children of God. As a dream of the race it has moved in and out on the horizon of human strivings like some fleeting ghost. And yet it always remains to haunt and to inspire men in all ages and all conditions."

Those pursuing it would see the actions of the civil rights movement as a means rather than an end, and would "refuse to separate the means open to revolution from the ends to be achieved by revolution." Some would say that such a community could not be achieved in our "diseased, prejudice-ridden society," but Thurman, as always, insisted that the contradictions of life are not ultimate, and that the "presence of the beloved community is always manifesting itself in the lives of people in the very midst of the social decay by which they are surrounded. It begins in the human spirit and moves out into the open independence of the society."

Thurman rejected any sense that people gave to a beloved community of something soft and sentimental, something that simply conjured up images of "tranquility, peace and the utter absence of struggle and of all things that irritate and disturb." A beloved community was not a conflict-free one, but rather one in which there were no "artificial barriers separating man from man or groups from one another—where the precious ingredient in each personality, unique unto itself, may be so honored by his fellows that it will enrich the common life even as it creates its own light in which to stand." There would be no "hard or critical lines of conformity yielding a glow of sameness over the private or collective landscape." There would be conflicts, and human differences not expressed in destructive social patterns but ones "real and germane to the vast undertaking of man's becoming at home in his world and under the eaves of his brother's house."

Thurman continued his correspondence with Martin Luther King through the 1960s. They frequently sent preaching invitations to one another or simply tried to find time to connect. As it turned out, those plans never came to fruition. In their last correspondence, in September of 1966, King thanked Thurman for his latest donation and expressed his regret for them not getting together over the years. "I do hope that the day will come soon when we can sit down together several hours and discuss many of the concerns close to our hearts. More and more I feel the need for retreating. My life is given so much to endless activity that I often fail to get the kind of spiritual refueling necessary to carry on." Given King's nearly manic travel during this period, and the constant internal chaos that threatened to overwhelm his movement, these words read now with a particularly stinging pain. And King was repeating, in effect, the counsel Thurman had given him in 1958. King still carried that kernel of Thurman's advice with him. King concluded by noting that "I do manage to find a few minutes occasionally to communicate with you through your books," finding in them "my most abiding means of meditation." Surely he did during this particularly tumultuous time for proponents of the philosophy of nonviolence.

Tragically, shortly thereafter, while in San Francisco, Thurman led a memorial service for King at the Fellowship Church, on April 7, 1968, three days after the assassination. Not unlike his rapidly composed response to the Kennedy assassination, Thurman had about two hours to collect his thoughts before being interviewed by radio station KPFK in San Francisco; media outlets later widely distributed his statement. Thurman saw King as someone who was "able to put at the center of his own personal religious experience a searching, ethical awareness." For him segregation and discrimination were not just un-American and undemocratic, but in fact sins against God.

Thurman reflected on his relationship with King, relatively distant as it was, at Boston University. Thurman's primary concern was the state of King's spiritual life. What was most profound about King was that he saw that nonviolence "could not become for him a technique merely for social change." It was possible to embrace the techniques of nonviolence as a manipulative force, to remain personally uninvolved. King saw that, but "insisted that always coupled with nonviolence there must be the other words:

direct action. There must be confrontation; there must be always the test, the checking out so that nonviolence would not degenerate either into a philosophy merely or into a metaphysic or even into a manipulating ethic." And now, in the face of King's assassination, it was "easy to forget that what you experienced in the light is no longer true because you are in the darkness. What you experienced in the light remains true and you must hold this until the light breaks again. And if you do that, you will discover . . . that it is the intent of life that we shall all be one people."

Thurman reflected on the experience of memorializing King with John A. "Jack" Taylor, a former student of Thurman's at BU who had served an internship at the Fellowship Church in 1955 and was set to take its pulpit in 1968. In this letter, about two weeks after King's death, Thurman expressed his best hopes for what the church could represent. Nowhere else in the United States, he thought, "could there be found 500 or more people assembled who had such a deep sense of original community. Despite the monumental disaster of the assassination, Negro and white people were together as one family with no self-consciousness or sensitivity due to the vicissitude of the current mood. This . . . was the harvest from the planting of other years in the Fellowship Church." Thurman hoped Taylor could continue in the quest for "deepening our sense of religious experience." About a month later, though, Thurman wrote to Taylor about his state of despondency about the congregation, with practically all its leadership being white: "This is a critical moment in the human relations in our country and it will take great wisdom on your part to affirm the inclusive genius of the church while recognizing the mood of the present moment."

Thurman's seemingly contradictory letters expressed his conflicted sense of the past and future of the church he had helped to found. Ideally, it remained a beacon of interracialism, but in its everyday functioning it seemed unlikely to fulfill its original potential. Two years later, a memo from Thurman to the congregation explained in detail his disappointment. With a financial mess on their hands, and splits between church members, people had suggested selling the property at 2041 Larkin in San Francisco, a move Thurman opposed because it didn't address the deeper and more fundamental issues, nor did it signal a unanimous congregational commitment. More important than anything, the church had to regain its collective spiritual commitment, for "if we are unable to find in our church community what is needful for our primary nourishment and sustenance, we will have nothing to offer to the world, the alienated, the angry, the frightened, and the suffering." These responses of optimism and a sense of foreboding or despair fundamentally shaped Thurman's vision during the last decade of his life.

Thurman was a master of the eulogy form; it led to some of his most moving short sermons reflecting on the spiritual meaning of individual lives. In his eulogy for Whitney Young (director of the National Urban League in the 1960s and a good friend of Thurman's) in New York, March 1971, at the Riverside Church, he noted that only someone like Young could "bring together the very rich and the poor, the black separatist and the white segregationist." Thurman spoke directly to how "American life is largely controlled and dominated by white society. . . . Ours is an affluent society in the midst of which are to be found vast numbers who may be designated as among the Wretched of the earth." The message of *Jesus and the Disinherited* still rang true, despite the undeniable revolution of the civil rights years. On that point, Thurman stayed a man of the black religious Left, where he always had been.

Early in 1970 the Thurmans took a two-month cruise through the South Pacific. Thurman intended it to be a period of rest, a time to be with Sue, with few obligations. He continued the journal he had kept while in Africa, again offering unusually personal, tentative, and at times acute reflections on the influence of American goods, ideas, and products in particular islands he visited. "At last I am beginning to feel a bit rested," he wrote to a friend. "It is the first complete rest that I have had in nearly 40 years. I had no idea what boundless fatigue I had accumulated." He felt the healing power of the sea again, as he had as a boy: "The sea is so healing and slowly something way down deep inside of me is stirring—so much of life comes back into a wonderful luminous perspective." Sometimes that sense of serenity was broken by what he saw on the islands. In Tahiti, he noted that the ostensible carefreeness of the people was a pretension, "more a cliché than a reality." He wondered about his own role as a tourist, while he and Sue were the only black couple onboard. "It is strange how I could not resist the feeling of guilt to be one among the tourists. . . . This has come over me and many times in my travels—a sense of shame to be classified with American white society and regarded in the same way. Sometimes I have wanted to shout, I am with them by necessity but I am not one of them." And his thoughts remained on the racial revolution at home, something he could move away from physically but not mentally.

Thinking over the meaning of his own life against the backdrop of the events of the past decade, he pondered, "A vast change has come over our total landscape. Where are we headed? We are deeply troubled. The glow is going from our faces. It seems as if we have been overtaken by a vast tidal wave of anger and our joy is dying. The mood is sullen and tight. When I see this I shudder because it says to me that we stand on the threshold of a deep inner collapse. What I feel is we are internalizing the hostility and the hate by which we have been surrounded for so many years."

Thurman pondered also the meaning and purposes and attractions of violence, perhaps giving vent to his own anger that he had occasion to feel through his decades of experiencing the violations of race in everyday life in American society. "What I mean," he wrote, almost as if to contemplate the possibility of what he was about to explain, "is that if I can hold over another human being the threat of violence, to that extent I can sustain the mood and the energizing effect of the power of veto & certification over other lives and make them the instruments of my will and control."

Through the 1970s, Thurman continued his ministry of discipling younger black men and women, while maintaining his posture of remaining in the background. In a 1973 letter to Jesse Jackson, after Jackson sought Thurman's active participation in an Operation PUSH event, Thurman supported Jackson's efforts and remained a friend and mentor to him but declined to be a headliner at this event. "All of my life I have shunned publicity and the limelight; it is not my way of working," he told Jackson. For him, working any other than the way he chose was to "stretch myself out of shape and thereby cut myself off from my own resources." Jackson later eulogized Thurman as a "teacher of teachers, a leader of leaders, a preacher of preachers." Thurman spent many of his later years leading small groups of younger people in sessions of spiritual searching, a part of preparing them for accepting positions of leadership and activism in the African American world in the decades to come.

In "What Can We Believe In," from 1973, Thurman reflected back on surviving the psychic wounds of segregation and the struggle to create an "authentic self-image" within such a system. He used the experience of his daughters as an example. When they were children, he had taken them to his home area in Florida to show them where he grew up. They went to a playground, and the girls asked to use the swings. Thurman had to tell them they could not, and once they reached home he explained why:

> It takes the state legislature of Florida, the laws of the state, all the judges, all the policemen, the majority of the churches and their ministers, the majority of the teachers in all the schools, plus the majority of all the people in the state of Florida to keep two little girls from swinging in those swings. That is how significant you are. . . . So I want you to remember that you are so important and so powerful as two little black girls that it takes all of that power to keep you out of two small swings in a playground in downtown Daytona Beach.

As Thurman saw it, "the estimate that a person has of you is measured by the kind of weapon he feels he must use in order to destroy you or control you. This becomes an important clue to the grounds of your own self-estimate." And he repeated that the "contradictions of life are never quite final, certainly not ultimate." The individual easily could come to believe in a kind of dualism, that the contradictions were final and ultimate, in order to evade his "sense of final responsibility for his own actions." Thurman concluded with his contention that a strong belief in one's own self, and an affirmation of that in other people, could build relationships of "mutual sharing of worth." Thurman upheld the validity of religious experience, derived not from observations of nature or participation in ceremonies but rather "found in my awareness of total well-being held in place by a sure sense of Presence. To me this is the very essence of creative spiritual encounter. This is the very heart of prayer." By "prayer" he meant that "highest moment of reality of which I am capable . . . when, in the supreme act of worshipful celebration, I feel myself to be in the presence of God, stripped to the literal substance of my being. Here the deepest thing in me seems to be responding actively to the deepest thing in existence."

In his later years, while not connected in any way with the Fellowship Church, he preached anniversary sermons there, reflecting on the meaning of the origins and history of the church within the context of organized American religion. At the thirty-third anniversary celebration, he warned against any feeling of purity, that we live in a vacuum unaffected by prejudice in the outside world: "no institution in the society can escape reflected as a mirror the environment in which that institution lives." The responsibility of those in a place like the Fellowship Church was "just to work at it," to witness to the truth in spite of everything working against it. Members would have their commitments, but "everything else got a head start," so the test remained "the degree to which it is willing to witness to the truth to which it says it is dedicated with the confidence that if we are true to our truth then the whole universe reinforces, gives energy to us in the way that the whole universe gives energy to an acorn as long as it is acorning." If we remain true to our commitment "in despair and in discouragement, in disillusionment, in paradoxes, contradictions, the pull of the vitality and the energy of the aliveness of life works to keep the leaves green and the fruit ripening on the tree."

In what probably was his last public sermon, given to the Fellowship Church late in 1980 (about five months before his death), Thurman reflected on the meaning of what he and the congregants had tried to accomplish in the 1940s, in the midst of a war where people had been trained to hate and at the height of the Cold War afterward. That was a most inopportune time to found a church that drew no lines of race or color, demonstrating that human beings could "come together . . . to worship as the experience of celebration of the communal life they had lived during the week." The miracle was that "a remnant of the church has survived." And Thurman concluded with some rather dark reflections on the meaning of this entire experience: "whether it is possible to develop a caring, sensitive, loving community in a world organized on violence and brutality and hate, and until religion learns how to deal with the dynamism . . . generating in the hearts of men and women that make for survival that is created by the idiom of hate and bitterness." Hate gave a person a ground to stand on, even while it destroyed that same ground, but "he goes down to the grave with a shout, and religion has to learn how to deal with that at the level that makes for survival on this planet for man. . . . The burden of proof is on our weary shoulders."

Thurman concluded ominously, quoting a favorite anonymous poet, that man was "God-like in image," and "if you don't believe it just pray to die before nightfall." In his surprisingly dark valedictory sermon, Thurman thought hard on the lessons of his long witness for peace, nonviolence, and human community in a world organized on principles of hate, violence, and human separation. The answer, he implied, was not yet evident; and the answer is not evident today.

Mentor of the Movement
Thurman's Influence and Afterlives

The cruel vicissitudes of the social situation in which I have been forced to live in American society have made it vital for me to seek resources, or a resource, to which I could have access as I have sought means for sustaining the personal enterprise of my life beyond all the ravages inflicted upon it by the brutalities of the social order.

—Howard Thurman, quoted in Luther E. Smith,
Howard Thurman: The Mystic as Prophet

He had a great zest for food, flowers, fragrances and scents, and his days were filled with music and laughter. . . . [Thurman] spoke with uncommon force and clarity to the peculiar needs of this century. He spoke at an in-depth level to racism in the church. He spoke to our fragmentation and spiritual hunger and lack of connectedness and relatedness. He spoke to our busyness, our internal noise, and our need to center down . . . standing in the midst of his idiom and reaching out to all other idioms—Christian and Jewish, Hindu and Buddhist, African, Asian, Indian, and European—[he] spoke to this crisis by calling us the task of spiritual reconstruction.

—Lerone Bennett, thirty-fifth anniversery of Thurman's
deanship (1988), typewritten speech

Howard Thurman passed away in San Francisco on April 10, 1981. He had experienced, but survived, some serious illnesses during the mid-1970s but remained active (and busy with personal correspondence as well) until late 1980, when his health rapidly declined. Sue Bailey Thurman lived until 1996, when she passed away at the Zen Buddhist Hospice Center in San Francisco. Sue's daughter Anne lived only five years longer, dying at age sixty-seven in 2001, after spending the later years of her life working with her mother and with early Thurman scholars in publishing some of her father's most significant work. Olive Thurman (Wong) had a varied and extensive career, including a cameo (fictitious) appearance in a novel by Jack Kerouac and a marriage for some years to the Chinese American actor Victor Wong, best known later in life for an appearance in the film *The Last Emperor*. Olive finished her days in New York City, passing in 2012.

In the early years after Howard's death, Sue remained in charge of (and very vigilant about) maintaining Howard's legacy through the Howard Thurman Educational Trust; she was the keeper of the Thurman flame. And Sue's sensibilities as a self-trained historian were vital to her caretaking of the Thurman papers (which now include some bits of her own correspondence as well), which, after some time in other libraries and archives, were finally consolidated at the Gotlieb Research Center at Boston University. The scholar Walter Fluker, who had known Howard and been his disciple, and also knew Sue well, took charge of the Howard Thurman Papers Project, of which five splendidly edited and annotated volumes have so far been published (the first one dating from 2009, the fifth from 2019). Current plans call for a three-volume set of his sermons and writings to published in the future.

After his death, Thurman was eulogized through conferences, symposia, and fora. These occurred mostly in the 1980s, when memory of him was still fresh. Most important, his closest friend and colleague from his Boston years, George Makechnie, put together in 1988 what was effectively a biography, memoir, and collected set of reflections and eulogies titled *Howard Thurman: His Enduring Dream*. What is remarkable there is the compilation of memories, tributes, and reflections of people from so many parts of Thurman's life; included are contributions from people in academia, business, journalism (notably including Lerone Bennett, by then the dean of black American journalism), religion, medicine (particularly hospice workers and nurses, with whom he had a long and fruitful relationship), music, and former students and colleagues. Many of their memories, in fact, impart a sense of Thurman the person in a way that Thurman's own writings rarely communicated about himself: his personal joys, customs, habits, and just his manner of being with other people. Thurman's writings and sermons are serious and even solemn, and Thurman could be given to bouts of depression, anger, and a simple desire to escape brutal human realities. But Thurman as a person also radiated life, joy, and humor; one sees it in spurts in his sometimes jocular personal correspondence, but more than that in the reflections provided by those close to him, including the one by his friend and admirer Lerone Bennett (an important figure in African American publishing) that begins this epilogue. And Thurman's tendency to retreat into his shell was counteracted by Sue Thurman's natural vivacity and extroversion. She knew Howard's strengths and weaknesses best. She pushed him in important directions he might otherwise have resisted, and brought a natural love of family from her happy upbringing that did not come so easily to Howard.

But by the 1990s, as the Thurman Educational Trust gradually wrapped up its affairs, Sue passed away, and Thurman's friends and students moved on, his star faded. Certainly he was not forgotten, and the papers project made sure he was not neglected, but it took some time to take a full measure of the meaning of the man and his life. And we are still taking it.

And so only recently has Howard Thurman's significance and influence in twentieth-century American religious philosophy come to be understood and celebrated. Of the many varied strands of Thurman's life and thought, perhaps the most important is the way he put his background in African American religion in a global and cosmopolitan context. Thurman took the nineteenth-century tradition (dating from Ralph Waldo Emerson, Henry David Thoreau, Theodore Parker, Margaret Fuller, and others) of universalist religious explorations, added to them his deep background in the African American experience and in Quaker-influenced mysticism, and brought to both his personal understanding of all the "ravages" and "brutalities of the social order" inflicted on black people in American society. The result was a synthesis of religious truths that drew from many sources but ultimately was uniquely Thurman's own. Those who perceived the "void in the busy nothingness of the modern world," as Lerone Bennett (the publisher of *Eb*-

ony and an important figure in black public life) put it, had discovered in Thurman "inner resources for the spirit in a homegrown product nurtured and honed to a fine edge not by a mystic from the East but by a grandson of slaves," one who "came out of the Black religious tradition with a message of hope and optimism for all men and women."

Thurman is thus at once a very familiar figure in the history of American religious liberalism and cosmopolitanism and yet unusual in that history when his life and thought are considered as a whole. In *Restless Souls*, the historian Leigh Schmidt has explained how "the convergence of political progressivism, socioeconomic justice, and mystical interiority was central to the rise of a spiritual left in American culture." Thurman's life, career, sermons, recordings, mentoring, counseling, and writings are at the heart of that rise. He came from a storied tradition of American ethical mystics dating from the nineteenth century, but he carried on that tradition in ways that spoke to twentieth-century concerns and conditions.

We may begin with his recovery of the meaning of the spirituals—one of Thurman's most original scholarly contributions, and something for which he is underappreciated. He was not first, or alone, in this, but he brought to the task a particular understanding of their meaning. Only W. E. B. Du Bois wrote about them with greater eloquence. Thurman's writings on the spirituals, produced in books such as *Deep River*, demonstrate a profound understanding of the various meanings and levels of what he saw as songs of survival, of inner endurance of an oppressed class. Of the spirituals, he wrote, "There is no attempt to cast a false glow over the stark ruggedness of the journey. The facts of experience are seen for what they are—difficult, often even unyielding."

Others from Thurman's era struggled to fit the spirituals into a social protest framework and therefore could not hear their poetry. Thurman could. What other people saw as otherworldly or escapist, he saw as precisely the point. Much writing from that era cast the spirituals as a sort of protest music and overread specific directives into them. The so-called escapism, or otherworldliness, of the songs was in reality a "precious bane," he said, because "it taught people how to ride high to life, to look squarely in the face [of] those facts that argue most dramatically against all hope and to use those facts as raw material out of which they fashioned a hope that the environment, with all of its cruelty, could not crush. With untutored hands—with a sure artistry and genius created out of a vast vitality, a concept of God was wrenched from the Sacred Book, the Bible, the chronicle of a people who had learned through great necessity the secret meaning of suffering." This total experience enabled them to reject annihilation and "affirm a terrible right to live." This was an extraordinary accomplishment, he suggested, because they brought out of sheer desperation an "infinite energy." The slave authors "made a worthless life, the life of chattel property, a mere thing, a body, *worth living!*" They discovered God within themselves. The songs were a "monument to one of the most striking instances on record in which a people forged a weapon of offense and defense out of a psychological shackle. By some amazing but vastly creative spiritual insight the slave understood the redemption of a religion that the master had profaned in his midst."

Thurman's writing on the spirituals contrasts but also pairs with his reflections on mysticism. For Thurman, the root of human spirituality lay in a personal connection with God achieved through mystical experience; but for Thurman, such experiences made believers more, not less, connected to the everyday realities of the world. Thurman always attempted to balance his mysticism with activism, his reveries toward God with an emphasis on what should happen in this world because of that connection to God. As well, he emphasized the importance of the "moral essence of vital religious experience" in preparing "those most engaged in sustaining democracy." Love of God would strengthen us to understand others.

Thurman's vision of the church emanated from that. Thurman saw the church as a key resource for those engaged in the creation of a just and loving society. For his critics, Thurman's church was like a lemonade stand, where people would pause to refresh themselves while otherwise living their lives normally. For Thurman, those people would not get to that "somewhere else"—nor would society at large—without those moments of spiritual nourishment, those cool drinks on a hot day. His quiet counsel to many provided that.

Yet he also remained a fierce critic of Christianity as actually practiced. "I belong to a generation that finds very little that is meaningful or intelligent in the teachings of the Church concerning Jesus Christ," he said. For him, the "desperate opposition to Christianity rests in the fact it seems, in the last analysis, to be a betrayal of the Negro into the hands of his enemies by focusing his attention upon heaven, forgiveness, love, and the like. . . . For years it has been a part of my own quest so to understand the religion of Jesus that interest in his way of life could be developed and sustained by the intelligent men and women who were at the same time deeply victimized by the Christian Church's betrayal of his faith." Thurman often retold the story of the slave minister who preached to a congregation that included his grandmother: "'You—you are not niggers. You—you are not slaves. You are God's children.' This established for them the ground of personal dignity, so that a profound sense of personal worth could absorb the fear reaction. This alone is not enough, but without it, nothing else is of value."

Thurman's background as a black southern Christian formed the fundamental root of his philosophy, even when he had left behind that background. "A profound piece of surgery has to take place in the very psyche of the disinherited before the great claim of the religion of Jesus can be presented," he wrote. "Tremendous skill and power must be exercised to show to the disinherited the awful results of the role of negative deception into which their lives have been cast. How to do this is perhaps the greatest challenge that the religion of Jesus faces in modern life." Those in power attempt to keep the disinherited in fear for their lives and livelihood, because if they are able to get a greater vision, that of true liberty, then the "aim of *not being killed* is swallowed up by a larger and more transcendent goal." That is why it was so important to make the dispossessed feel like aliens, without any place in the social order.

Thurman's work profoundly explored the psychology of relations between the powerful and the powerless, but also the very fragility of the power held by authorities. It came, he suggested, with just a thin veneer covering it:

> The experience of power has no meaning aside from the other-than-self-reference which sustains it. If the position of ascendance is not acknowledged tacitly and actively by those over whom the ascendance is exercised, then it falls flat. Hypocrisy on the part of the disinherited in dealing with the dominant group is a tribute yielded by those who are weak. But if this attitude is lacking, or is supplanted by a simple sincerity and genuineness, then it follows that advantage due to the accident of birth or position

is reduced to zero. Instead of relation between the weak and the strong there is merely a relationship between human beings. A man is a man, no more, no less. The awareness of this fact marks the supreme moment of human dignity.

Thurman applied his theology directly to the effects of segregation. For him, any structure that prevented the free flow of human beings with other human beings stifled the love ethic. And thus segregation or other means of separating humans were a "disease of the human spirit and the body politic," for the very existence of that separation "precludes the possibility of the experience of love as a part of the necessity of man's life." And love took work, because love for humanity as such did not exist: "There is no such thing as humanity. What we call humanity has a name, was born, lives on a street, gets hungry, needs all the particular things we need. As an abstract, it has no reality whatsoever." And that meant loving whole people, good and bad, including enemies. The key was to meet people where they were, but to then treat them as if they were already at the point they could reach. "Love demands that we expose ourselves at our most vulnerable point by keeping the heart open. Why? Because this is our own deepest need." We want to be treated not as the product of a single deed or mistake but as an integrated person, to be understood fully: "This is to have the experience of freedom, to be one's self, and to be rid of the awful burden of pretensions."

This may be seen in his influence on what became the civil rights movement. He was, in many senses, the mentor of the movement. He spread the Gandhian gospel and planted the seeds of what would become the ethic of nonviolent resistance to white supremacy in America. Martin Luther King frequently turned back to Thurman's classic *Jesus and the Disinherited*. In December 1955, at the beginning of the Montgomery bus boycott, King said the protests should be shaped by "the teachings of Jesus" and that protesters must love their enemies, and concluded: "We, the disinherited of this land, we who have been oppressed so long, are tired of going through the long night of captivity. And now we are reaching out for the daybreak of freedom and justice and equality."

Here, King channeled Thurman, who spent much of his working life answering the question of what religion might mean for the dispossessed. "The masses of men live with their backs constantly against the wall. They are the poor, the disinherited, the dispossessed." And what did religion say to them? The answer to that question "is perhaps the most important religious quest of modern life." He answered it most fully in *Jesus and the Dispossessed*, his classic from 1949, and his single most important written work. The most fundamental fact of Christianity, he argued, was that it was "born in the mind of this Jewish teacher and thinker" and immediately appeared as a "technique of survival for the oppressed. That it became, through the intervening years, a religion of the powerful and the dominant, used sometimes as an instrument of oppression, must not tempt us into believing that it was thus in the mind and life of Jesus. . . . Wherever his spirit appears, the oppressed gather fresh courage; for he announced the good news that fear, hypocrisy, and hatred, the three hounds of hell that track the trail of the disinherited, need have no dominion over them." Those hounds of hell had pursued Thurman through much of his life, most especially in his younger years, but they had no dominion over him; rather, his spirit had mastered them.

Beyond his influence on particular sociopolitical movements, Thurman also influenced the course of American theology, particularly in the area of mysticism. Drawing from Rufus Jones, himself a descendant of the nineteenth-century Transcendentalists and inventors of "spirituality" as opposed to "religion" as an ideal, Thurman made a distinction between passive and active mystics. He identified with the latter. Thurman the mystic always upheld the power of dreaming, of seeing visions of something different, beyond what was "realistic": "It is part of the pretensions of modern life to traffic in what is generally called 'realism,'" he once said. "There is much insistence upon being practical, down to earth. Such things as dreams are wont to be regarded as romantic or as a badge of immaturity, or as escape hatches for the human spirit." But, he added, "men cannot continue long to live if the dream in the heart has perished. It is then that they stop hoping, stop looking, and the last embers of their anticipations fade away. . . . Where there is no dream, the life becomes a swamp, a dreary dead place and, deep within, a man's heart begins to rot." The dream would not have to be "some great and overwhelming plan," but rather could be the "quiet persistence of the heart that enables a man to ride out the storms of his churching experiences. . . . It is the touch of significance which highlights the ordinary experience, the common event." Thurman understood the presence of evil, but his emphasis was always on what was in the spirit of God in the world to overcome evil. The seeker would not be afraid of life, he said, because "he seeks at every point the emergence of the will and the mind of God from within himself and within the stuff of life itself. What is revealed in life is one with that which transcends life."

Thurman carried on a tradition of those who found God in nature; in this way he drew from Henry David Thoreau and many others. At the same time, Thurman resisted being called a pantheist. Although it was true that God could be seen in nature, God could never be imprisoned in his own creation. Our bodies, he said, function as a whole; we do not become identified with a little finger or any other part. "The body is quite literally a dwelling place of the Most High God, Creator of the Universe." Human relations seem chaotic, often "more diabolical than benevolent," and yet amid the long history of human destruction, there always remained a will to create alternatives; there were always voices for peace amidst war. And there were figures such as Gandhi, coming outside the Christian faith into an empire "whose roots were nurtured by that faith," and he became the embodiment of the intent to create other worlds, alternatives to human chaos and violence. "The moving finger of God in human history points ever in the same direction. There must be community."

The hunger for community can take many forms and can be distorted and twisted, and yet it never disappears, and "prayer is the experience of the individual as he seeks to make the hunger dominant and controlling in his life. It has to move more and more to the central place until the hunger becomes the core of the individual's consciousness." As well, he emphasized the importance of the "moral essence of vital religious experience" in preparing "those most engaged in sustaining democracy." Love of God, silence, and meditative prayer would strengthen congregants to understand others; they would become "apostles of sensitiveness."

In a symposium after Thurman's death, the black theologian James Cone reflected on Thurman's life and influence: "Howard Thurman emphasized the universal dimension of the human search for freedom which he discovered in the particularity of the black religious experience. In all of his writing and speaking about the human spirit, he never forgot his own religious roots in the black community. Even when he was talking and writing explicitly about the universality of religion, as was true most of the time, the black religious experience was there, stimulating his imagination and guiding the cogency of his analysis." As Cone saw it, "the ability to be free in the midst of slavery—that was the heart of Thurman's theology. . . . Freedom was an inner reality, the individual's knowledge that he or she will fulfill the intent of the Creator. To *be* is to be *free*, that is, to be in search of that inner reality which lets us know that we were made for God and for others." Cone particularly was influenced by *Jesus and the Disinherited*, *Deep River*, and *The Negro Spiritual Speaks of Life and Death*, all of which showed that "the contradictions of life are not final or ultimate." Hope was fundamental to his theology, as he showed that "God is insistent that the divine intention for humanity ultimately will not be defeated" and that "God has a purpose for humanity that no particular human being can keep from being realized. . . . Suffering is real and deeply painful, but it is not the last word."

For Thurman, God was the last word, the end of all our strivings. And humans best cultivated that relationship through meditation and prayer, through an extended inward journey employing multiple spiritual resources. "The human spirit has to be explored gently and with unhurried tenderness," he said, and what we learn in those explorations, "in the discipline of silence, in meditation and prayer, bears rich, ripe fruit in preparing the way for love." Howard Thurman translated his particular experiences and training into a universalist cosmopolitan idiom fully grounded in the painful and scarring experiences of African American life and history. His was an American spirituality full of wisdom drawn from sources as varied as his grandmother and early teachers, the trees and waterways where he grew up, his deep reading in religious texts, his training with Quaker mystics and social justice activists, and his experience in teaching students and preaching to congregants through decades of social justice struggles and experimental projects in interracial fellowship. The paradoxes of his own life made him only more aware that the larger contradictions of life were transitory, not ultimate. In the process, he prepared the way for a better world he hoped could come.

BIBLIOGRAPHIC ESSAY

Thurman's autobiography, published late in his life as *With Head and Heart: The Autobiography of Howard Thurman* (New York: Harcourt Brace Jovanovich, 1979), is an indispensable starting point for learning of Thurman's life and thought. So is the 55-minute biographical documentary film *Backs against the Wall: The Howard Thurman Story* (Journey Films, 2019), available on DVD; a lengthy and thoughtful review of the documentary and of the meaning of Thurman within the larger story of Protestant liberalism may be found in Gene Zubovich, "Revisiting the Legacy of Howard Thurman, the Mystic of the Civil Rights Movement," *Religion and Politics*, February 12, 2019, https://religionandpolitics.org/2019/02/12/revisiting-the-legacy-of-howard-thurman-the-mystic-of-the-civil-rights-movement/. Thurman's twenty-one books, of course, also are indispensable; a complete bibliography of those is included at the end of this essay.

Most important of all, scholars have been blessed with an expertly and splendidly produced five-volume set of Thurman's papers, including his handwritten sermons, his notes, his personal journal and diary entries, a good deal of personal correspondence, and numerous unpublished handwritten sermons and addresses stretching over a period of decades. All scholars and readers are indebted to the team of scholars, headed by Walter Fluker and assisted over the years by Luther Smith, Peter Eisenstadt, Kai Jackson Issa, Silvia Glick, Quinton Dixie, Catherine Tumber, Alton B. Pollard, and others, for a work that will be the most basic foundation of all serious study of Thurman in the future. The five volumes, all published by the University of South Carolina Press, encompassing all of Thurman's life, are now available under the following titles: *The Papers of Howard Washington Thurman*, vol. 1, *My People Need Me, June 1918–March 1936* (2009); vol. 2,

Christian, Who Calls Me Christian? April 1936–August 1943 (2012); vol. 3, *The Bold Adventure, September 1943–May 1949* (2015); vol. 4, *The Soundless Passion of a Single Mind, June 1949–December 1962* (2017); and vol. 5, *The Wider Ministry, January 1963–April 1981* (2019). The great majority of the quotations in this text from Thurman's writings, private and public, come from these published volumes. In a few cases, I have used unpublished letters and documents found in the Thurman papers at the Gotlieb Research Center at Boston University. The archive there also contains a great many documents, letters, and papers from Sue Bailey Thurman, and is an indispensable repository for those working on her life. Other Bailey-Thurman family papers, primarily letters within the Bailey family and a large collection of photographs, may be found in the Special Collections at the Emory University Library in Atlanta.

Beyond the autobiography and his collected personal writings, the two indispensable anthologies of much of his best published work can be found in *For the Inward Journey: The Writings of Howard Thurman*, selected by Anne Spencer Thurman (Richmond, IN: Friends United Meeting, 1984), and *A Strange Freedom: The Best of Howard Thurman on Religious Experience and Public Life*, ed. Walter Earl Fluker and Catherine Tumber (Boston: Beacon, 1998).

The scholars Walter Fluker and Luther E. Smith pioneered the field of Thurman scholarship in the 1970s and 1980s. Luther Smith's doctoral dissertation, "An American Prophet: A Critical Study of the Thought of Howard Thurman" (PhD diss., St. Louis University, 1981), eventually came to be published as Luther E. Smith, *Howard Thurman: The Mystic as Prophet* (1981; reprint, Richmond, IN: Friends University Press, 1992, 2007); and Walter Fluker's earlier major work was *They Looked for a City: A Comparative Analysis of the Ideal of Community in the Thought of Howard Thurman and Martin Luther King Jr.* (Lanham, MD: University Press of America, 1989). Recent, invaluable studies include Quinton Dixie and Peter Eisenstadt, *Visions of a Better World: Howard Thurman's Pilgrimage to India and the Origins of African American Nonviolence* (Boston: Beacon, 2011), and Gary Dorrien, *Breaking White Supremacy: Martin Luther King and the Black Social Gospel* (New Haven: Yale University Press, 2017). Another important work that discusses Thurman rather briefly but sets him perfectly in the much longer context of the cosmopolitan "seeker" culture of American culture is Leigh Eric Schmidt, *Restless Souls: The Making of American Spirituality* (Berkeley: University of California Press, 2005; 2nd ed., 2012).

The five volumes of the Howard Thurman papers come from materials collected in their original form at Expanding Common Ground: The Howard Thurman and Sue Bailey Thurman Collections at the Gotlieb Research Center at Boston University. An introduction to the vast Thurman archives there, and a guide for researchers, may be found at http://archives.bu.edu/web/howard-thurman/home. Thurman's self-conception as someone who was primarily a preacher and an orator, an artist with his voice, happily has been carried forward with the hundreds of digitized recordings available at the Thurman archives online; these are digitized forms of reel-to-reel tapes and cassette tapes and radio recordings that Thurman left or had made (including from his years in Boston and both parts of his life in San Francisco) from 1950 to 1980. This oral and aural record of Thurman's sermons and talks is indispensable for understanding the man, because for Thurman his voice was his instrument of foremost importance. The recordings are searchable and playable online at http://archives.bu.edu/web/howard-thurman/virtual-listening-room. Researchers interested in more on Sue Bailey Thurman (1903–1996) will want to consult the Sue Bailey Thurman Papers, with topics within them searchable at http://archives.bu.edu/web/howard-thurman/sue-bailey-thurman-collection.

The definitive biography of Thurman, produced by a scholar deeply involved for many years with the Thurman Papers Project, is Peter Eisenstadt, *Against the Hounds of Hell: A Life of Howard Thurman* (forthcoming from University of Virginia Press in 2021). When I started this shorter biography, I was not aware of Eisenstadt's project but became aware of it when asked to read a draft manuscript of it. Eisenstadt's magnificent, richly detailed biography assisted me immeasurably in filling in many parts of Thurman's life, and since then Professor Eisenstadt has been supportive. I hope anyone who dips their toes into the Thurman waters in this shorter work will also read Eisenstadt's magisterial and definitive work.

While Eisenstadt's is the definitive work, two older biographies are worthy of attention as well. One comes from Thurman's longtime colleague at Boston University, George Makechnie, *Howard Thurman: His Endur-*

ing Dream (Boston: Howard Thurman Center, 1989), a book that includes a final chapter of tributes to Thurman from a wide variety of people, including many from medical professionals that Thurman worked with over the years (a relatively little-known part of his work and ministry). A second is Elizabeth Yates, *Howard Thurman: Practical Dreamer* (New York: Harper & Row, 1964), a work that reads more or less like a transcription of Thurman's oral history of himself (and a biography that even Thurman admitted was not quite up to the task), but is still useful as the first effort by anybody to write his biography. Finally, a collection of essays produced in 1992 provides a valuable early look at Thurman's life from a collection of scholars who knew him personally: Mozella G. Mitchell, ed., *The Human Search: Howard Thurman and the Quest for Freedom, Proceedings of the Second Annual Thurman Convocation* (New York: Lang, 1992).

Another important scholarly piece, to be published later by the University of North Carolina Press but currently in the form of a PhD dissertation, is Anthony Siracusa, "A More Durable Weapon: Religion and Nonviolence in the Black Freedom Movement, 1918–1960" (PhD diss., Vanderbilt University, 2017). Siracusa focuses particularly on Thurman's influence over students at Howard in the 1930s and early 1940s, most notably James Farmer. Another important, recent, shorter piece is Gary Dorrien, "True Religion, Mystical Unity, and the Disinherited: Howard Thurman and the Black Social Gospel," *American Journal of Theology & Philosophy* 39 (January 2018): 74–99. Another important source on some of this same material is Dennis C. Dickerson, "African American Religious Intellectuals and the Theological Foundations of the Civil Rights Movement, 1930–55," *Church History* 74, no. 2 (June 2005): 217–35. See also Walter Fluker, "Dangerous Memories and Redemptive Possibilities: Reflections on the Life and World of Howard Thurman," in *Black Leaders and Ideologies in the South: Resistance and Non-Violence* (New York: Routledge, 2005), 147–76.

Besides the work of Dixie and Eisenstadt noted above, a number of works cover the subject of the black American relationship with India and provide indispensable background for this biography. These include Sudarshan Kapur, *Raising Up a Prophet: The African-American Encounter with Gandhi* (Boston: Beacon, 1992); Gerald Horne, *The End of Empires: African Americans and India* (Philadelphia: Temple University Press, 2008); Sean Chabot,

Transnational Roots of the Civil Rights Movement: African American Explorations of the Gandhian Repertoire (Lanham, MD: Lexington Books, 2012); Dennis C. Dickerson, "Gandhi's India and Beyond: Black Women's Religious and Secular Internationalism, 1935–1952," *Journal of African American History*, Winter 2019, 59–83; and Leilah C. Danielson, "'In My Extremity I Turned to Gandhi': American Pacifists, Christianity, and Gandhian Nonviolence, 1915–1941," *Church History* 72 (June 2003): 361–88. Danielson's biography of A. J. Muste, a major influence on Gandhi and on the entire movement of nonviolence, is also extremely useful: Leilah Danielson, *American Gandhi: A. J. Muste and the History of Radicalism in the Twentieth Century* (Philadelphia: University of Pennsylvania Press, 2014).

A variety of short pieces published online surveys major episodes of Thurman's career. See, for example, the story of Thurman's meeting with Martin Luther King in 1958 in Paul Harvey, "Meet the Theologian Who Helped MLK See the Value of Nonviolence," *Conversation*, January 11, 2018, https://theconversation.com/meet-the-theologian-who-helped-mlk-see-the-value-of-nonviolence-89938. For his trip to India, see Quinton Dixie and Peter Eisenstadt, "When Howard Thurman Met Mahatma Gandhi: Nonviolence and the Civil Rights Movement," *Beacon Broadside Online*, October 2, 2014, http://www.beaconbroadside.com/broadside/2014/10/when-howard-thurman-met-mahatma-gandhi-nonviolence-and-the-civil-rights-movement.html. For more on Thurman generally, see Rich Barlow, "Who Was Howard Thurman? Remembering Marsh Chapel's Path-Breaking Black Dean," *BU Today*, January 7, 2020, https://www.bu.edu/today/2011/who-was-howard-thurman/, and "The Legacy of Howard Thurman: Mystic and Theologian," *Religion and Ethics Newsweekly*, January 18, 2002, http://www.pbs.org/wnet/religionandethics/2002/01/18/january-18-2002-the-legacy-of-howard-thurman-mystic-and-theologian/7895/?xid=PS_smithsonian. An online article exploring Thurman's experience with the Church of the Fellowship of All Peoples is Paul Harvey, "Howard Thurman and the Arc of History in San Francisco," *Boom California*, August 22, 2018, https://boomcalifornia.com/2018/08/22/howard-thurman-and-the-arc-of-history-in-san-francisco/.

Another indispensable source for getting to know Thurman is the two-hour documentary interview conducted by Landrum Bolling, produced originally for the BBC but now freely available on YouTube at "Conversations with Howard Thurman," part 1, at https://www.youtube.com/watch?v=KvJVxsezAwc&t=2710s; part 2, at https://www.youtube.com/watch?v=NPsZBS-2oeU.

Shorter portrayals in magazines and newspapers include Lerone Bennett Jr., "Howard Thurman: 20th Century Holy Man," *Ebony*, February 1978, 84; Benita Eisler, "Keeping the Faith," *Nation*, January 5, 1980, 24; "Racial Roots and Religion: An Interview with Howard Thurman," *Christian Century* 90 (May 9, 1973): 533–35; and "Great Preachers," *Life*, April 6, 1953, 128, available freely through Google Books.

Thurman's most important earlier work, and really the "signature" book of his career, is *Jesus and the Disinherited* (Nashville: Abingdon, 1949). Thurman's two most important later books are *The Luminous Darkness* (New York: Harper & Row, 1965) and *The Search for Common Ground* (New York: Harper & Row, 1971). A fuller list of Thurman's books is provided here. A full bibliography of Thurman's books and published articles and sermons is available in *God and Human Freedom: A Festschrift in Honor of Howard Thurman* (Richmond, IN: Friends United Press, 1983), 196–207. Nearly all the shorter pieces listed there are now published either in the five volumes of *The Papers of Howard Washington Thurman* or in the two collected volumes of his writings, *A Strange Freedom* and *For the Inward Journey*. A full bibliography including Thurman's shorter pieces, some interviews, and his book reviews is included in the bibliography of Luther Smith, *Howard Thurman: The Mystic as Prophet*.

BIBLIOGRAPHY OF HOWARD THURMAN'S BOOKS

Apostles of Sensitiveness. Boston: American Unitarian Association, 1956.

The Centering Moment. New York: Harper & Row, 1969; Richmond, IN: Friends United Press, 1980.

The Creative Encounter: An Interpretation of Religion and the Social Witness. New York: Harper & Row, 1954; Richmond, IN: Friends United Press, 1978.

Deep Is the Hunger. New York: Harper & Row, 1951; Richmond, IN: Friends United Press, 1978.

Deep River and *The Negro Spiritual Speaks of Life and Death*. Richmond, IN: Friends United Press, 1975. These were published together as one volume and later also published as separate volumes.

Disciplines of the Spirit. New York: Harper & Row, 1963; Richmond, IN: Friends United Press, 1973.

Footprints of a Dream: The Story of the Church for the Fellowship of All Peoples. New York: Harper & Row, 1959.

For the Inward Journey: The Writings of Howard Thurman. Selections by Anne Spencer Thurman. New York: Harcourt Brace Jovanovich, 1984; Richmond, IN: Friends United Press, 1991.

The Greatest of These. Mills College, CA: Eucalyptus, 1944.

The Growing Edge. New York: Harper & Row, 1956; Richmond, IN: Friends United Press, 1974.

The Inward Journey. New York: Harper & Row, 1961; Richmond, IN: Friends United Press, 1971.

Jesus and the Disinherited. Nashville: Abingdon, 1949; Richmond, IN: Friends United Press, 1981.

The Luminous Darkness: A Personal Interpretation of the Anatomy of Segregation and the Ground of Hope. New York: Harper & Row, 1965.

Meditations for the Apostles of Sensitiveness. Mills College, CA: Eucalyptus, 1947.

Meditations of the Heart. New York: Harper & Row, 1953; Richmond, IN: Friends United Press, 1976.

The Mood of Christmas. New York: Harper & Row, 1973.

Mysticism and the Experience of Love. Wallingford, PA: Pendle Hill, 1961.

The Negro Spiritual Speaks of Life and Death. New York: Harper & Row, 1947.

The Search for Common Ground: An Inquiry into the Basis of Man's Experience of Community. New York: Harper & Row, 1971.

A Strange Freedom: The Best of Howard Thurman on Religious Experience and Public Life. Edited by Walter Earl Fluker and Catherine Tumber. Boston: Beacon, 1998.

Temptations of Jesus: Five Sermons. San Francisco: Lawton Kennedy, 1962.

With Head and Heart: An Autobiography. New York: Harcourt Brace Jovanovich, 1979.

INDEX

Ingersoll Lectures, 151, 171

institutions/institutional, 155, 169, 196, 205; activist church, 136; church, 12; educational, 7, 15, 22, 84, 90-91, 185, 199; Indian, 80; racist, 145; religious, 8, 38, 40, 71; segregated, 88, 101; social, 27; structure of Christianity, 81, 126; white, 26, 164, 171

Intercollegiate Missionary Conference, 57

International Fellowship of Reconciliation, 101. *See also* Fellowship of Reconciliation

International Institute of San Francisco, 132

internationalism/internationalist, 27, 54, 74, 82, 118, 141, 184

internment camps, 124, 145

interracialism, 57, 72, 130, 214

Jackson, Jesse, 8, 209, 216

Jackson, Joseph H., 115

James, Arthur L., 27

Japanese Americans, 124, 144-45

Jenness, Mary, 63

Jennings, Coleman, 165

Jesus Christ, 8, 29, 30, 63-64, 65, 93, 110, 134, 176; and Christianity as incompatible, 79-81, 144, 225; and church organizations, 28, 38, 39; and de-racialization, 160-61; as member of despised minority group, 46; as emblem of the disinherited, 5, 58-59, 72, 94, 103, 226; as inclusive symbol of God, 105; and India, 68, 72, 73-74, 77, 150; and mysticism, 111; and nonviolence, 84, 89; as Palestinian Jew, 46, 58, 94, 160; and philosophy of human personality, 35; as political insurgent, 92; the religion of, 53, 60, 95, 97-100, 114, 154, 198; and Roman Empire, 58, 94; and salvation narrative, 13; and segregation, 160-61, 227-28; and spirituals, 40-41; statement of commitment and, 156-57; and symbolics of sacrifice, 96

Jim Crow, 8, 14, 28, 89, 91, 119

Johnson, James Weldon, 40

Johnson, Mordecai Wyatt, 36-38, 43, 60-62, 78, 120, 137-39; as early influence, 17-21, 26; as president of Howard University, 51, 54

Jones, Charles, 166

Jones, Major, 181-82

Jones, Rufus, 44-45, 72, 104, 107, 119, 228

Jones, Stanley, 67, 69, 72

Jordan, Barbara, 181

Julie Derricotte Foundation, 83

Kaplan, Ed, 197

Kelly, Frank, 60

Kennedy, John F., 201, 204, 213

Kester, Howard "Buck," 56, 57, 101-2

King, Herbert, 46, 53, 56, 126

King, Martin Luther, Jr., 16, 115, 160, 186, 213, 227; and *Jesus and the Disinherited*, 180-82; and March for Jobs and Justice, 200; and nonviolence, 207; and Personalism, 184-85

Ku Klux Klan, 14, 27, 34, 160

Leary, Timothy, 189

Lester, Muriel, 56, 63, 129

liberalism, 20, 25, 27, 111, 130, 224. *See also* social gospel movement

Life (magazine), 74, 159, 171

Lincoln, Abraham, 71, 200

literalism/literalist, 19, 55, 176

Locke, Alain, 52

Logan, Rayford, 91

Long, Jacob A., 138

Luce, Henry R., 74

Luce, Henry W., 74-75

lynching. *See* violence

Madras Christian College Union, 69

March for Jobs and Justice, 200

Marsh, Daniel L., 170-71

Marsh Chapel, 4, 169, 171-74, 176-78, 180, 188-93, 199, 201

Titles published in the

LIBRARY OF RELIGIOUS BIOGRAPHY SERIES

The First American Evangelical: A Short Life of **Cotton Mather**
by Rick Kennedy

Aimee Semple McPherson: *Everybody's Sister*
by Edith L. Blumhofer

Damning Words: The Life and Religious Times of **H. L. Mencken**
by D. G. Hart

Thomas Merton *and the Monastic Vision*
by Lawrence S. Cunningham

God's Strange Work: **William Miller** *and the End of the World*
by David L. Rowe

Blaise Pascal: *Reasons of the Heart*
by Marvin R. O'Connell

Occupy Until I Come: **A. T. Pierson** *and the Evangelization of the World*
by Dana L. Robert

The Kingdom Is Always but Coming: A Life of **Walter Rauschenbusch**
by Christopher H. Evans

A Christian and a Democrat: A Religious Life of **Franklin D. Roosevelt**
by John F. Woolverton with James D. Bratt

Francis Schaeffer *and the Shaping of Evangelical America*
by Barry Hankins

Harriet Beecher Stowe: *A Spiritual Life*
by Nancy Koester

Billy Sunday *and the Redemption of Urban America*
by Lyle W. Dorsett

Howard Thurman *and the Disinherited: A Religious Biography*
by Paul Harvey

Assist Me to Proclaim: The Life and Hymns of **Charles Wesley**
by John R. Tyson

Prophetess of Health: A Study of **Ellen G. White**
by Ronald L. Numbers

George Whitefield: *Evangelist for God and Empire*
by Peter Y. Choi

The Divine Dramatist: **George Whitefield** *and the Rise
of Modern Evangelicalism* by Harry S. Stout

Liberty of Conscience: **Roger Williams** *in America*
by Edwin S. Gaustad